THE GOSPEL OF LUKE

THE CHRISTIAN COMMENTARY ON THE BIBLE

A DEVOTIONAL, THEOLOGICAL, AND PRACTICAL COMMENTARY ON THE BIBLE

Part 1 – Chapters 1-13

Dr. Robert Bohler, Jr.

OTHER BOOKS BY DR. ROBERT BOHLER, JR.

Pass Your Faith To Your Children
Through the Simple Practice of Teaching Your Child to Pray
(A Practical Plan for Helping Your Child Develop Their Own Authentic Life
of Faith)

Discovering Jesus
Who Was He? What Did He Do? And Why Is He Important?
An Exploration of the life, ministry, death, and resurrection
Of Jesus of Nazareth

Learn the Vocabulary of the Christian Faith
A Mini-Course in Christian Belief

Herod the Great
The Life and Times, The Brilliance and Madness, of Herod the Great, King
of Judea

The Christian Catechism For Families And Disciples
A Teaching Tool For Church And Family

Conversations With Josh
About Sex, Dating, and Marriage

Commentary on the Gospel of Luke
Part 2 – Chapters 14-24

WITH JAMIE SCOTT

Black and White – Two Different Perspectives
An Honest Conversation About Race In America Today
By Bob Bohler and Jamie Scott

Published by Spread The Story, Inc.

Cover picture by Didgeman from Pixabay

ISBN: 979-8-9865223-6-4

DEDICATION

To all those who have taught the Bible to me through classes, books, and commentaries; to those with whom I have studied the Bible in classes, groups, and seminars; to those I have had the opportunity to lead, teach, and pastor; thank you for the opportunity to study, learn, and teach the Holy Scriptures. How fortunate we are to have such access to the scriptures today, and what a privilege to be called to teach them to others.

ABOUT THE AUTHOR

Dr. Robert Bohler, Jr. is a Presbyterian pastor in the ECO denomination. He grew up in Decatur, Georgia and graduated from Georgia Tech with a degree in Industrial Engineering. After working for several years in engineering, he responded to a call to ministry. He has served churches in Lakeland, Florida; Charlotte, North Carolina; and Athens, Georgia. He and his wife, Kim, have two boys. One recently graduated from the University of Georgia in Mechanical Engineering and is working as an engineer. Their youngest son recently graduated from nursing school, having also graduated from the University of Georgia. Dr. Bohler has served the church for over thirty years as a pastor. In his spare time, he reads theology, travels, and takes his wife to dinner.

CONTENTS

Introduction

"How can I understand unless someone explains it to me." Acts 8:31

There is a story in the book of Acts, chapter 8, about Philip and an Ethiopian eunuch (Acts 8:28-40). As Philip was traveling the road from Jerusalem to Gaza, the Holy Spirit prompted him to join a chariot traveling that same route. Inside was an Ethiopian official who had come to Jerusalem to worship. As Philip drew near, he heard the man reading aloud from the prophet Isaiah. Philip asked whether he understood what he was reading, and the eunuch replied, "How can I, unless someone explains it to me?" He then invited Philip to join him in the carriage. Beginning with that passage in Isaiah, Philip shared with him the good news about Jesus. God graciously opened the eunuch's heart to believe, and Philip baptized him. This moment is significant in the book of Acts, as it marks – so far as we know – the first recorded Christian conversion on the continent of Africa.

The Bible is a mystery to many people, but it is not impossible to understand. Most people simply need someone to explain it to them. In fact, with a little guidance and instruction, the Bible opens up. It comes alive with meaning, and God speaks to his people through it. The Protestant reformers believed that the Bible was "perspicuous." By that, they meant it was clear and understandable, particularly in its essential message, especially regarding salvation. They believed that ordinary believers, guided by the Holy Spirit and with a little instruction could understand the Bible and profit from the regular reading of it. The Bible is not just for clergy to understand but everyone. The Bible is accessible to us in our own language. It is every person's sacred privilege and responsibility to study it so they can comprehend the faith and be guided by the Bible's instructions. It is toward that end that this commentary is written.

There are four gospels in the New Testament. Each is slightly different, with the gospel of John being the most unique. Matthew, Mark, and Luke are called Synoptic gospels because they tell the account of the life of Jesus in similar ways. Luke differs from Matthew and Mark in that it is written by a Gentile and for a Gentile audience. It also has its unique perspectives and emphases. For that reason, a study of the gospel of Luke is a valuable exercise.

This commentary differs from others by focusing on entire sections rather than individual verses. For that reason, the scripture passages and commentary are not divided by individual verses. The commentary intends to have a devotional emphasis as well as a theological and practical one. It hopes to work well as daily devotional reading as well as helping the reader understand particular sections in the gospel. It has a theological element that is highlighted by theological insights at the end of each section of commentary. It also has a practical application at the end of each section that draws out a useful lesson from some part of the reading. For those reasons, this commentary is subtitled, "A devotional, theological, and practical commentary on the Bible." Rather than beginning the commentary with a discussion of the gospel's themes, I have chosen to place that discussion at the end. You will find the concluding section on "Themes in Luke" useful in drawing together the various ideas explored throughout the gospel. Because of the length of the commentary, it is available in two parts. The first contains chapter one through thirteen. The second contains chapters fourteen through twenty-four, including the summary section on "Themes in Luke."

The author of the gospel of Luke is generally considered to be the physician, Luke, who was a companion of the apostle Paul (Colossians 4:14). He is also the author of the book of Acts. There are several reasons for this belief: both Luke and Acts are addressed to the same person; there are language, stylistic, and thematic similarities; and Acts references a previous work (Acts 1:1). Luke admits that he learned the gospel from others. He was not one of the original twelve apostles, nor was he a member of the early church community in Jerusalem. In this sense, he is in the second generation of believers. As a Gentile, he would have converted to the faith as part of the evangelistic effort to the Gentiles.

His relationship with the apostle Paul seems to have been close. The "we" passages in the book of Acts indicate this in that Luke appears to have been a traveling companion of Paul during several missionary journeys (Acts 16:10-17; 20:5-15; 21:1-18; 27:1-28:16). It is his close acquaintance with Paul that gave his gospel apostolic authority in the eyes of the early church.

Scholars have discussed and debated the dates around which all the New Testament documents were written. The best general date for the New Testament documents, although not all scholars agree, is before 70 A.D. The destruction of Jerusalem and the temple by the Roman army in that year was a cataclysmic event for the Jewish people. Had any of the New Testament documents been penned after that event, it would certainly have been a major theme of the book. That it is only hinted at in the New Testament is evidence that it was the subject of prophetic insight but an event that had not yet taken place. The gospel of Luke was most likely written between 58 and 64 A.D.

The translation used in this commentary is my own, including the text of Luke and any verses quotes from other places in the Bible. The original language of the New Testament is Greek. For that reason, all English versions are translations. Modern translations are copyrighted, and I have chosen not to use one of them. The translation used is a revision of a version in the public domain, the World English Bible, which is a revision of the American Standard Version of 1901, also in the public domain. I have updated and revised the World English Bible to make it smoother at certain points for modern readers without changing the meaning of the biblical text. I have consulted the Greek original where necessary when making changes.

The Christian faith becomes more beautiful, compelling, and convincing with study. There is no place where Christianity falls apart, withers under scrutiny, or succumbs to the criticisms of skeptics. This is nowhere truer than in the study of the Gospel of Luke. Every word Jesus spoke has meaning. Every action had a purpose. A study of the person and work of Jesus uncovers treasures of wisdom within every part of his story. His parables offer fresh insights even to those who have studied them for many years. The more we study Jesus' earthly ministry, the more astonishing his life, ministry, and ultimate sacrifice become. The purpose of this commentary is to help you come to know the grace and truth of Jesus Christ. Luke promises to give us an orderly and accurate account of the events of Jesus' life (Luke 1:1-4). There is much to learn from Luke's gospel. May the Holy Spirit open the eyes of your understanding and the affections of your heart as you explore the account of the life of Jesus as told by Luke, the physician and companion of Paul.

Dr. Robert Bohler, Jr.

The Gospel of Luke

Luke 1

Prologue – Luke 1:1-4

SINCE MANY HAVE UNDERTAKEN to write an orderly account of the things that have been fulfilled among us, just as they were delivered to us from the beginning by those who were eyewitnesses and servants of the word, it seemed good to me also, having traced the course of all things accurately from the first, to write a well-ordered narrative to you, most excellent Theophilus; that you might know the certainty of the things in which you were instructed.

Every book has a beginning. Writers strive to create a good opening section and especially an intriguing first sentence. J.M. Barrie's novel about childhood, *Peter Pan*, begins with, "All children, except one, grow up." J.R.R. Tolkien's *The Hobbit* began, "In a hole in the ground there lived a hobbit." Charles Dickens began *David Copperfield*, with "Whether I shall turn out to be the hero of my own life, or whether that station will be held by anybody else, these pages must show." Douglas Adam's science fiction classic, *The Hitchhiker's Guide To The Galaxy*, starts with this sentence: "Far out in the uncharted backwaters of the unfashionable end of the western spiral arm of the Galaxy lies a small unregarded yellow sun." The first Harry Potter book began by introducing the Dursleys: "Mr. and Mrs. Dursley of number four, Privet Drive, were proud to say that they were perfectly normal, thank you very much." Ayn Rand's classic, *Atlas Shrugged*, began by posing the question, "Who is John Gault?"

How would one introduce an account of the life of the most important person ever to live? Luke, whom the apostle Paul calls, "the beloved physician" (Colossians 4:14), begins by telling the reason for his writing and naming the person for whom his book was written. In actuality, the Gospel of Luke is not a book in the sense that we think of books. It is a letter. It is correspondence written from one friend to another. The reason for the letter, which would turn out to be a long one, was to give an accurate account of the life of Jesus. Many had apparently attempted to do so in the years since the death and resurrection of Jesus. Perhaps Luke thought those accounts inadequate or lacking in some way. He decided to try his hand at recounting the life, death, and resurrection of Jesus. His spirit was stirred by the desire to write down an orderly account of who Jesus was and what he did.

What made Luke qualified to write an account of the life of Jesus? There seemed, in his mind, to be several considerations. One was that Luke felt that he understood the life of Jesus accurately enough to write it down. This came, no doubt, from his deep involvement in the life of the early church, where the life and teachings of Jesus were a topic of constant conversation. Though Luke was not an eyewitness to the life of Jesus, he affirms that he had learned from those who were and who were appointed to tell his story to others. It also helped that Luke, at one point, became a traveling companion of the apostle Paul. This would have brought him into contact not only with Paul, but also with central figures in the life of the early church, including other apostles and prophets. They and those around them, many of whom were eyewitnesses, would have been a wealth of knowledge about the life of Jesus.

It is also certain that the stories of the life of Jesus were told over and over in the years after Jesus' ascension. It is one reason the stories took on generally accepted forms, as evidenced by the similar ways in which the gospels tell them. Luke would have heard those stories often, so much so that he was able to retell them almost word for word. It would be those stories, and there were many of them, that Luke would include in his gospel account.

One reason Luke seems compelled to write his gospel is for the instruction and encouragement of his friend Theophilus. The name "Theophilus" literally means "Friend of God." We do not have any knowledge about who this friend might have been, except that his Greek name makes it likely that he was a Gentile, not a Jew. He may have been a person of high position, even a Roman official. Luke addresses him as, "most excellent Theophilus." Several people in the book of Acts, also written by Luke, use the term "Most Excellent" when addressing Roman governors (Acts 23:26, 24:3, 26:25). It is possible Theophilus was a person in a Roman position of influence whom Luke had befriended and wished to encourage. He was a Christian since Luke affirms that he had already been taught about Jesus. Whoever he was, Luke went to great lengths and a lot of effort to relate the life of Jesus to him. We are grateful that he did so because we have gotten, from his effort, not only the Gospel of Luke but the Book of Acts.

Luke noted, in his introduction, that many people were interested in writing the account of the life of Jesus, and many had attempted to do so. We have hardly any of those numerous attempts. Instead, we have the four gospel accounts. What happened to the others? The answer is that they did not gain sufficient support from the Christian community to be copied and preserved. Since the printing press would not be invented for another 1,400 plus years, only the most important books were copied. In the end, only four gospels were considered important enough to receive such effort. That Luke's gospel was one of them attests to the church's affirmation of its accuracy and inspiration. While we have a few other documents from the early centuries of the church, some writings were considered useful but not scripture. Others were clearly heretical in the eyes of the church. We have only fragments of most of these or references to them in other writings as they were not copied and recopied by early Christians. Some of these documents also come from later, typically the second and third, not the first century.

The word "gospel" means a proclamation of the good news. Luke's gospel is an accounting of the good news of the coming of Jesus Christ, the long-awaited Savior of the nation of Israel. As a Gentile, Luke understood that the good news extended beyond Israel. It was meant for the entire world, Jews and Gentiles alike. For that reason, Luke wanted his Gentile friend, Theophilus, to understand the gospel clearly and accurately. Luke's account, according to his assessment, would enable him to know who Jesus was and what he did with certainty. In that sense, Luke was not creating or developing a story. He was only recording one and trying to do so accurately.

The consensus of the Christian church is that he succeeded. His gospel has been considered inspired in such a way as to be worthy of being included in Holy Scripture. This is high praise and indicates the unique nature of this writing. Along with what is only three other gospel accounts, God inspired Luke's gospel to be a reliable and authoritative record of the life of Jesus. The church has believed that the Gospel of Luke gives us a true account of the life of Jesus. If it had not, those in the early church who were eyewitnesses and friends of Jesus would not have read, affirmed, and copied it. The church, from its early days, has believed that this gospel account, along with three others, accurately tells the story of the life of Jesus Christ. Christianity believes that he was and is the Son of God who came in human form to become the Savior of the world. If that is true, the story of his life is of supreme importance. If Jesus was and is who Luke says he was and is, then the account of his life is the greatest and most important story ever told. This is the story that Luke intends to tell.

Theological insights
- God stirs our spirits from time to time to do good. Luke's spirit was stirred to write to his friend about the life of Jesus. When our spirits are stirred, we should take those promptings seriously. They may, in fact, be promptings of the Spirit.
- We do not know whether Luke wrote the letter quickly or over a period of time. We know little about his exact process. Did he revise sections after the first draft? Did he labor over sections or write quickly? Did he have a sense that he was writing holy scripture? What we know is that God inspired Luke's writing to give us a trustworthy record of the life of Jesus. This is extraordinarily valuable.
- The written nature of the Bible gives it permanence and extension. That the Bible is written enables people such as ourselves, over 2,000 years later, to know the details of the life of Jesus. It also enables people around the world to learn about him. Jesus lived in a small area during a certain period in world history. The Bible has taken his message throughout the world since that time.

Practical application
    As you approach this study of the Gospel of Luke, realize what a privilege it is to learn about the life of Jesus from the Bible. At times in history, the Bible was not accessible to everyone. Until the printing press, manuscripts were rare and expensive. A person might be fortunate to have just one copy of a single book of the Bible. At times the Bible was not in a language that people could understand. Only scholars could read it.
    We should take advantage of having the Bible so available. As Paul says, "All scripture is inspired by God and is profitable for teaching, for reproof, for correction, and for training in righteousness, that each person

who belongs to God may be thoroughly equipped for every good work" (II Timothy 3:16, 17). It is profitable to know the Bible because it equips us for wise, faithful, and fruitful living. The riches of the Bible can never be exhausted. The more time we spend with it, the more riches it yields.

The Angel Gabriel Visits Zechariah – Luke 1:5-25

THERE WAS IN THE DAYS of Herod, the king of Judea, a certain priest named Zechariah, of the priestly division of Abijah. He had a wife of the daughters of Aaron, and her name was Elizabeth. They were both righteous before God, walking blamelessly in all the commandments and ordinances of the Lord. But they had no child, because Elizabeth was barren, and they were both well advanced in years.

Now while he was serving as a priest before God in the order of his division according to custom, he was chosen by lot to enter into the temple of the Lord and burn incense. The whole multitude of the people were praying outside at the hour of incense. An angel of the Lord appeared to him, standing on the right side of the altar of incense. Zechariah was troubled when he saw him, and fear fell upon him. But the angel said to him, "Do not be afraid, Zechariah; your prayer has been heard. Your wife, Elizabeth, will bear you a son, and you shall call his name John. You will have joy and gladness, and many will rejoice at his birth, for he will be great in the sight of the Lord. And he must not drink wine or strong drink. He will be filled with the Holy Spirit, even from his mother's womb. He will turn many of the children of Israel to the Lord their God. He will go before him in the spirit and power of Elijah, to turn the hearts of the fathers to the children, and the disobedient to the wisdom of the just, to make ready a people prepared for the Lord."

Zechariah said to the angel, "How can I be sure of this, for I am an old man, and my wife is well advanced in years?" The angel answered him, "I am Gabriel. I stand in the presence of God and was sent to speak to you and to bring you this good news. And behold, you will be silent and unable to speak until the day that these things take place, because you did not believe my words, which will be fulfilled in their proper time."

The people were waiting for Zechariah, and they marveled that he delayed in the temple. When he came out, he could not speak to them, and they perceived that he had seen a vision in the temple. He kept making signs to them and remained mute. When the days of his service were fulfilled, he departed to his house.

After those days his wife Elizabeth conceived, and she hid herself for five months, saying, "Thus has the Lord done to me in the days in which he looked on me, to take away my reproach among people."

Families have stories. My mother was one of eleven children, eight boys, and three girls. I remember sitting at the dinner table when I was young listening to my mother tell stories about growing up. With eleven children in the family, there was always something going on, some interesting game they played, some mischief they got into, or some crisis. My mother was a good storyteller, and we sat entertained at the dinner table as she recounted her family's adventures and misadventures.

The Gospel of Luke begins with a family story. It is a story from the life of Mary, the mother of Jesus, and her family. We might wonder how Luke learned this rather intimate family story. There are several possibilities. It might have been common knowledge in the life of the early church and retold, along with the many other stories from the life of Jesus. It is certainly likely that Luke came in contact with people who knew Mary herself and who could tell such stories. Since Mary was probably a teen when she gave birth to Jesus, it is also possible that Luke may have encountered her during his lifetime. We can imagine Luke as someone who might have made a point to sit with Mary and listen to the stories she told about the life of Jesus. If that happened, it would explain, not only how Luke knew the story of Zechariah and Elizabeth, but also the appearance of the angel to Mary herself.

The account of the life of Jesus begins with a family story about a relative of Mary's, Elizabeth, and her husband Zechariah. Zechariah was a priest. In the nation of Israel, this was a position of honor, although not generally of wealth. One could not choose to become a priest; one had to be born into the priestly line, which was the line of Aaron, Moses's brother. The tribe of Levi was designated for the service of the temple, but within the family of Levi, there was a more select group, the priests. They were not only descendants of Levi but also of Aaron. Only they could serve within the temple itself, and it was considered a great privilege and honor to do so. Both Zechariah and his wife Elizabeth were born into this special and chosen family line.

The account of Zechariah and Elizabeth begins with Zechariah being chosen to serve in the temple and replenish the incense on a particular day. There was an altar that burned incense within the temple. This stood alongside a golden candlestick and a table on which loaves of bread were laid each week. Zechariah, since he was not the high priest, could not enter the most sacred part of the temple, the Holy of Holies. This was reserved for the high priest and was only entered once a year. Zechariah could, however, enter the first section of the temple, and a priest did so morning and evening. Their job was to place fresh incense on the altar and make sure its fire was burning. The incense burned before God day and night. It symbolized the prayers of the people, which were, across the nation, offered to God continually. Morning and evening, a priest was charged with refreshing the incense and offering a prayer to God on behalf of the people.

Luke reports that Zechariah was chosen by lot to enter the temple and offer the incense on a particular day. This was a great honor, and Zechariah was no doubt excited. Luke reports that as he did so, the people prayed outside the temple, waiting for him to complete his task, return to them, and dismiss them with prayer. Zechariah certainly would have expected his service in the temple to be meaningful. Perhaps he would feel especially close to God. Perhaps it would be a memorable spiritual moment that he could later share with his wife and friends. He may have wondered if he might have some sort of spiritual encounter. We can imagine that he would have gone into the temple on that day with a sense of expectation.

Luke gives us a picture of the character of Zechariah and his wife Elizabeth. He says that they were "both righteous before God, walking blamelessly in all the commandments and statutes of the Lord" (Luke 1:6). They were both good people, devout in their faith, and careful to observe all God's commandments. We might remark that this will be in contrast to the lives of the high priests and much of the Jewish leadership at the time of Jesus' ministry. But here was a person of integrity, authenticity, and honesty. He was a credit to his calling as a priest and a worthy representative of it.

That was not to say that Zechariah's life was perfect. It was not. There was a wound in Zechariah's life, and it was deep. He and his wife, Elizabeth, had no children. Luke simply says that Elizabeth was barren. Medical science today would have a more technical diagnosis of their problem. For whatever reason, however, she had not been able to get pregnant. The tragedy was that, at the time of this incident, it was, for all intents and purposes, too late. They were too old. The window of opportunity had passed. We might wonder if there was a small root of bitterness in Zechariah's heart against God, who had not answered their many prayers.

If Zechariah had hoped for a spiritual experience in the temple, he got more than he expected. Luke says that as he was fulfilling his duties in the sanctuary, an angel of the Lord appeared to him at the right side of the altar of incense. Luke says that, as is often the case when an angel appears to someone in the Bible, Zechariah was troubled and afraid. The angel, however, spoke comforting words. He and his wife would have a son. They were to name him John. He would be great in the sight of the Lord, be filled with the Holy Spirit from the womb, and turn many people back to God. He would go before the Lord in the spirit and power of Elijah to make people ready for God's coming. This must have been a remarkable set of words for Zechariah to hear.

The angel declared that Zechariah's prayer had been heard. To what prayer was he referring, the one he had been praying in the temple? We cannot imagine that Zechariah, at that moment of service to the nation, was still asking God for a child. Luke seems to indicate that they had given up. Zechariah was probably praying about other things. The angel, however, is referencing the prayer that Zechariah had prayed, along with his wife, many years previous. Though it had taken a long time to answer, God had chosen to answer their prayer for a child.

The reaction of Zechariah is perhaps not surprising. We might expect his heart to leap with joy at the words of the angel but that was not his immediate reaction. The words caught him off guard. Perhaps they seemed out of context at that holy moment. His first reaction was skepticism. He knew how the biology worked. His wife was too old. It would be a miracle for that kind of thing to happen. So he did something people had occasionally done in the Bible, he asked God for a sign. "How shall I know this? For I am an old man, and my wife is advanced in years" (Luke 1:18).

The reaction he got from the angel must have surprised him. If he thought he would get that reaction, he would never have spoken. The demeanor of the angel suddenly changed. He became less friendly. Did Zechariah not realize, he said, that he was no ordinary angel? He was Gabriel himself! He stood in the presence of God and had been sent to bring

Zechariah wonderful good news. Since, however, Zechariah had asked for a sign, the angel would give him one. He would not be able to speak until the angel's words came to pass, which they would in due time. The angel had indeed given him a sign. The nature of the sign, however, was because Zechariah had "not believed his words." Zechariah has spoken carelessly. He would have a long time to think about his next words.

If God wanted to make the announcement of the birth of the Messiah's forerunner memorable, this fit the bill. When Zechariah exited the temple, he could not give the benediction to dismiss the people because he was unable to speak. It must have been an embarrassing moment. Luke says that the people perceived that he had seen a vision in the temple since he kept motioning to them with his hands. No doubt another priest filled in and dismissed the people.

Luke says, simply, that when Zechariah went home after his duties, Elizabeth conceived. As mothers sometimes do, particularly at an older age, she kept things secret for a while, five months, but rejoiced in her spirit at what God had done for her. No doubt, when the village realized what had happened, there was great excitement. "Old Elizabeth is with child!" Many would have praised God for his goodness. Little did they know how much God was at work in the coming of this child.

Theological insights
- It should not go unnoticed that Zechariah and Elizabeth were good, righteous, and faithful people. While faithful service is not always glamorous, God knows those who serve him and has ways to reward them.
- We should trust God with our prayers. Just because we do not get immediate answers does not mean God has not heard. God may indeed answer our prayers in ways and at a time that will suit his purposes.
- God sometimes meets us in the course of our ordinary duties. We should not be surprised when this happens. If we were more open to God's presence, we might see him at work more often in our everyday responsibilities.
- Just as God needed priests in Old Testament times, God needs people to serve him today. As God designated Zechariah for his service, he would also call his son, John, for special duty. While

everyone can serve God in daily life, God needs people who will especially devote themselves to his work.

Practical application

The account of Zechariah and Elizabeth is wonderful and poignant on many levels. We are excited for the old couple who are finally going to have a child. Zechariah, the priest, has a moving religious experience. He will certainly feel the sting of the angel's rebuke but will benefit from it in the end. For nine months, he will find himself on a "retreat of silence." It will, no doubt, be a time of reflection, prayer, and spiritual growth. We can imagine that it did him and his faith a great deal of good.

Most of us do not have remarkable things happen to us regularly, but sometimes God breaks into our lives in surprising ways. We should pray to be more open to God's presence every day. We should ask God to make himself known to us more often. Perhaps if we served God more regularly, we would have more occasions to see him at work. God is never far from us. There are many good things in the world, but none so meaningful as being a part of something God is doing.

The Annunciation – Luke 1:26-38

NOW IN THE SIXTH MONTH, the angel Gabriel was sent from God to a city of Galilee named Nazareth, to a virgin engaged to be married to a man whose name was Joseph, of the house of David. The virgin's name was Mary. The angel appeared to her and said, "Greetings, you who are highly favored! The Lord is with you."

When she saw him, she was greatly troubled at the saying and wondered what kind of greeting this might be. The angel said to her, "Do not be afraid, Mary, for you have found favor with God. Behold, you will conceive in your womb and give birth to a son, and shall name him 'Jesus.' He will be great and will be called the Son of the Most High. The Lord God will give him the throne of his father David, and he will reign over the house of Jacob forever. There will be no end to his kingdom."

Mary said to the angel, "How will this be since I am a virgin?" The angel answered her, "The Holy Spirit will come upon you, and the power of the Most High will overshadow you. Therefore the child to be born will be holy and be called the Son of God. And behold, Elizabeth your relative has also conceived a son in her old age, and this is the sixth month with her who was called barren. For nothing will be impossible with God."

Mary said, "Behold, I am the servant of the Lord. Let it be done to me according to your word." Then the angel departed from her.

One of the exciting events in life is a wedding, especially if it is *your* wedding. Particularly for young girls, the day of their wedding brings thoughts of romance, family, and excitement. How many girls have imagined that day as one of the most perfect of their lives?

The next part of Luke's story of the life of Jesus begins with a young girl who was preparing to be married. Mary was a young girl betrothed to a man named Joseph. When the visit from the angel occurred, it seems to have been during the one-year waiting period that typically followed a first-century Jewish betrothal. If Mary was like many young girls, she could probably think of little else but her upcoming wedding. What is remarkable about Mary is that she responded to an unexpected visit from an angel with grace beyond her years.

How old was Mary? Scholars have debated. Chances are she was younger than most girls who get married today. If she were in her mid-teens, she would have been well within the range of when girls got married in first-century Israel. Her young age makes her spiritual maturity even more striking.

Luke reports that the angel Gabriel appeared to Mary "in the sixth month." This was the sixth month of Elizabeth's pregnancy. This will make John the Baptist six months older than Jesus. Luke specifically reports that it was Gabriel, the same angel who appeared to Zechariah, who appeared to Mary. As we said with Zechariah, an angel's appearance was not the occasion of obvious joy, but rather concern. Luke says that Mary was greatly troubled by his greeting.

As with Zechariah, the angel's initial greeting was full of comfort and encouragement. "Greetings, you who are highly favored! The Lord is with you" (Luke 1:28). There are two important parts of this greeting. One is the angel's announcement that Mary was favored by God. We might find this an understatement. Mary had been chosen to be the mother of the Messiah. Even over getting married, being the mother of the Messiah was a dream that most young Jewish girls in Mary's day would have considered, especially if they were from the tribe of Judah. We might wonder if Mary had done so and if God had somehow prepared Mary's heart for the announcement of the angel. The other part of the angel's words assured Mary that God was with her. Whatever the angel came to announce, it came with the blessing of God and the promise of his help in bringing it to fruition.

The next words of the angel were extraordinary. He told her that she would give birth to a son, whom she was to name "Jesus." He would be great and called the Son of the Most High. God would give to him the throne of David, his ancestor, and he would reign over the house of Jacob forever.

We might ask if these words would have immediately indicated to Mary that she was to be the mother of the Messiah. On reflection, they certainly seem clear to us. Perhaps Mary was able to take them in quickly. She seems to have done so. From our point of view, they clearly indicate the birth of the Messiah. That God would give to him the throne of David and allow him to reign over the house of Jacob forever was messianic language. No one but the Messiah was to have a kingdom without end. As a special indication that the child would play an important role in God's plan, as the angel did for Zechariah, he designated the child's name. Mary was to call his name "Jesus" which is a name that comes from the root word meaning "Savior" and means "God saves."

What do the words, "He will be great and will be called the Son of the Most High" indicate? Mary certainly could not have developed a mature doctrine of the Trinity from that statement. It is, from our point of view, an indication of the child's divine nature. This was not going to be merely a gifted leader but God's Son himself.

The conversation with the angel shows Mary to be quick on her feet. There were obvious questions to be asked. Will Joseph be the father? Should I continue in my betrothal to him? Is this something that will happen immediately or only after my marriage? Mary's question is phrased in a similar way to Zechariah's. "How will this be, since I am a virgin?"

In contrast to the sharpness with which he responded to Zechariah, the angel explained so Mary would understand. In a wonderfully chaste but clear description of how Mary's pregnancy would come to be, the angel declared that God's Holy Spirit would come upon her and the power of the Most High would overshadow her. There is no hint of anything sexual in the words. The child would be conceived in her womb through the power and presence of the Holy Spirit. For that reason, says the angel, he will be holy and be called the Son of God. Then the angel gave her encouragement for any doubts that might arise. Elizabeth, her relative, was also with child in her old age, for nothing was impossible with God.

Mary's response has been noted through the centuries as a model of humility, faith, and submission. The conversation between Mary and the angel, as recorded in Luke, is short and to the point. If there was more conversation than is recorded, we do not know it. It would not be unexpected, however, if Luke records the exact conversation. In the Bible, angels are creatures of few words and they say exactly what needs to be said, without unnecessary conversation. That Mary was able to process the angel's words and formulate her response so quickly is truly remarkable. Her response shows that God's choice of her had been wise. "Behold, I am the servant of the Lord. Let it be done to me according to your word" (Luke 1:38). As quickly as the angel had come, he departed.

Mary's response indicates a heart fully devoted to God with all other things being second. She might have wondered what Joseph would think. That would, at a later point, be a problem, as Matthew's gospel indicates (Matthew 1:18-25). She might have thought about what to say to her village friends when she began to show. Saying that she was the mother of the Messiah would most likely have been met with mockery, even then. If she ever spent time fretting about these things, we have no record of it. She seems oblivious to any problems her situation might create. What was important was that she had encountered God. God had visited her. Not only so but the time had come for God to visit his people through the promised Messiah. It would certainly be the adventure of a lifetime to be the mother of the Messiah, and Mary was up for the challenge. She had encountered God, and nothing in life holds a candle to that! As the account of the life of Jesus goes along, we will see what joys and problems Mary's role will create for her.

Theological insights
- The timing of the appearance of the Messiah was God's own. For 400 years, since Malachi, the last of the Old Testament prophets, the people had waited. Many must have wondered if God had forgotten his promises. But the time would eventually come, and as is always the case with God, it would be perfect.
- The exact nature and identity of the Messiah was hidden in the Old Testament. Most thought he would be a great king like David. Many

hoped he would help the nation shed the yoke of Rome. The angel's words indicate something even more. The child to be born of Mary would be called the Son of the Most High. Not only would he sit on the throne of David but reign over a kingdom without end. In addition, he would be called the Son of God. Little did anyone realize the magnitude of what God was going to do.

- What is the importance of the virgin birth? Is it what makes Jesus both divine and human? It was certainly possible for the Son of God, the second person of the Trinity, to become human with an ordinary father and mother. As the angel said, nothing is impossible with God. The virgin birth is for our sake. It helps us understand the nature of Christ. That he has no earthly father helps us grasp the concept of God himself coming to earth being both divine and human. Christianity calls this the Incarnation, and it is one of the great mysteries of the faith.

Practical application

Mary is rightly praised as an example of faith. Her willingness to embrace the will of God was remarkable, particularly for one so young. Perhaps her youth helped her. Perhaps she had not yet had time to become jaded and cynical. As an idealistic youth, maybe she still believed that all things were possible and that God was going to do something very good in the world. She was right about those things.

We see in Mary a willingness to embrace God's will without excessive anxiety. The average person might have needed to ask more questions. What will this mean for me? What will his role be? Are there things I should do as his mother? Do I need to have a conversation with Joseph about this? How should I bring this up to my parents? That Mary asks none of these questions means that she understood one thing clearly. When God calls, one must answer. This was the experience of the prophets in the Old Testament. A call from God could not be refused, except at great peril. Mary's duty was to accept. In this instance, God's call meant that he was going to do something wonderful for her and the world.

Mary visits Elizabeth – Luke 1:39-56

MARY AROSE IN THOSE DAYS and went with haste into the hill country, to a city of Judah, and entered the house of Zechariah and greeted Elizabeth. When Elizabeth heard Mary's greeting, the baby leaped in her womb; and Elizabeth was filled with the Holy Spirit. She called out with a loud voice and said, "Blessed are you among women, and blessed is the fruit of your womb! Why am I so favored, that the mother of my Lord should come to me? For behold, when the voice of your greeting came into my ears, the baby leaped in my womb for joy! Blessed is she who believed that there would be a fulfillment of the things which were spoken to her by the Lord!"

Mary said, "My soul magnifies the Lord. My spirit has rejoiced in God my Savior, for he has looked on the humble state of his servant. For behold, from now on, all generations will call me blessed, for he who is mighty has done great things for me. Holy is his name. His mercy is for generations and generations of those who fear him. He has shown strength with his arm. He has scattered the proud in the imagination of their hearts. He has put down princes from their thrones and exalted the lowly. He has filled the hungry with good things. He has sent the rich away empty. He has given help to his servant Israel, in remembrance of his mercy, as he spoke to our fathers, to Abraham and his offspring forever."

Mary stayed with her about three months and then returned to her home.

It is great to have someone with whom to share life's meaningful moments. We can imagine that Mary needed someone like that after the angel visited her. The news of the angel Gabriel was astounding. But whom could she tell? Would her friends believe her? Would her parents, if they were still alive? There was one person who would understand; it was her relative Elizabeth. The angel's announcement that Elizabeth was with child must have seemed an indication to Mary that she ought to visit her. Elizabeth would be someone with whom Mary could share her news and who would understand. So Mary journeyed to visit Elizabeth who lived in the hill country of Judea, in the region that belonged to the tribe of Judah.

Elizabeth was a relative of Mary, but how was that possible? Luke specifically says that Elizabeth was of the tribe of Levi and also of the family of Aaron. But Mary was engaged to be married to a man, Joseph, who was from David's line, the tribe of Judah. Since people tended to marry within their tribe, Mary was, most likely, also from Judah also. So how could they be relatives? The Greek word used for relative is a word used for relatives of any type. They might have been distant relatives, for example, such as third or fourth cousins. Since the family line was traced through the husband, it might have been that Elizabeth's father was a Levite but her mother was from Judah. Or Mary's mother might have been from the family of Levi.

Whatever the case, Gabriel himself identified Elizabeth as a relative of Mary, and it is obvious from the account that they had a strong social relationship, perhaps like niece and aunt. An important element of this family connection is that Jesus and John the Baptist were, therefore, also related. This implies that John probably knew Jesus before Jesus came to be baptized. This is indicated by the fact that John recognized that Jesus ought to baptize him instead of the other way around (Matthew 3:13, 14). This would seem to signal that John knew Jesus from family relations and had heard the stories about his conception and birth from his mother, Elizabeth. John may well have known, or at least strongly suspected, that it was Jesus upon whom the Spirit would descend when he was baptized.

Luke recounts a warm and enthusiastic meeting between Mary and Elizabeth. It seems likely that Luke "telescopes" the encounter for the sake of brevity. Unless Elizabeth knew by a revelation from God that Mary was pregnant with the Messiah, she could not have made the comment she made at their first greeting. It seems likely that she made it after Mary had revealed to her what had happened. It was then that Elizabeth realized that the child had leaped in her womb upon hearing Mary's voice. She blessed Mary and related what her child had done.

Elizabeth recognized the unique role Mary had been chosen to play. She also appears to marvel at her humble acceptance of it. She notes that Mary *believed* that there would be a fulfillment of what God had told her. That was in contrast, of course, to her husband, Zechariah. We might wonder if Zechariah, if he was listening, felt like Elizabeth had "thrown him under the bus" by bringing up his lack of faith. Of course, he could not make any comment in return, so he had to endure his wife's commentary. It would all go into Zechariah making sure that, when he got the chance to speak again, his words were appropriate.

What follows in Luke is Mary's song of praise. It is called the "Magnificat," which is the first word of the song in Latin. Like Elizabeth, Mary was also filled with the Holy Spirit and sang a song, what we would call a poem, to God. In it, she praises God and rejoices in what he has done. She notes how God blesses the lowly, among which she is one. He fills the hungry but sends rich oppressors away empty. She also recognizes that God's work in her is the fulfillment of his promise to show mercy to Israel. Her words are prophetic in that she realizes that future generations will envy her role. "For behold, from now on, all generations will call me blessed" (Luke 1:48). She did not realize just how true that would be. She would certainly have marveled that she would one day be the subject of numerous sermons, be mentioned in the Bible, be depicted in Nativity programs by children, and be hailed throughout history as a woman of great faith.

Theological insights
- Friends are important. We need people with whom we can share, not only the everyday challenges of life but also its personal and challenging moments. We should not underestimate the importance of listening to someone who needs to talk.
- We build the faith of others when we share our faith with them. Just as Mary and Elizabeth strengthened each other's faith, so we do when we talk about our faith, study the Bible together, pray together, and join in worship with God's people. We should not be afraid to authentically share our spiritual joys and struggles. Others are built up when we do.
- This section says that Elizabeth was filled with the Holy Spirit as she recognized how God was at work. Mary was also filled with the Spirit when she sang her song of praise to God. This is a reminder that ordinary people can be filled with God's Spirit. It may not happen all the time, but on occasion, God grants us a special awareness and fullness of his Spirit. These times are signs of God's gracious care, presence, and love.

Practical application
Mary and Elizabeth's excitement over their children was understandable. Every child has potential, and they knew that theirs would

have a special place in God's plan. Mary knew that hers would be *very* special though she could not have known just how true that would be.

Every parent has great hopes for their child. This is how it should be. God makes it so that children, if all is well, are born into the arms of parents who will encourage them, nurture them, think they are the greatest thing in the world, and love them no matter what. The truth is that each of us has more potential than we realize. With God's help we, and our children, can become more than even we imagine. For that reason, we should always have hope. God may yet do something marvelous, wonderful, and important in our lives, in our children's lives, and in the world.

The Birth of John the Baptist —Luke 1:57-76

NOW WHEN THE TIME CAME for Elizabeth to give birth, she gave birth to a son. Her neighbors and her relatives heard that the Lord had shown her great mercy, and they rejoiced with her. On the eighth day, they came to circumcise the child; and they would have called him Zechariah, after his father. His mother answered them, "No; he will be called John."

They said to her, "There is no one among your relatives who is called by that name." They made signs to his father to see what he would have him called. He asked for a writing tablet, and wrote, "His name is John." They all marveled.

His mouth was opened immediately and his tongue set free, and he spoke, praising God. Fear came on all who lived around them, and all these sayings were talked about throughout all the hill country of Judea. All who heard them pondered them in their heart, saying, "What then will this child be?" For the hand of the Lord was with him.

His father Zechariah was filled with the Holy Spirit, and prophesied, saying, "Blessed be the Lord, the God of Israel, for he has visited and redeemed his people; and has raised up a horn of salvation for us in the house of his servant David (as he spoke by the mouth of his holy prophets from of old), salvation from our enemies and from the hand of all who hate us; to show mercy toward our fathers, to remember his holy covenant, the oath which he swore to our father Abraham, to grant that we, being delivered out of the hand of our enemies, should serve him without fear, in holiness and righteousness before him all the days of our life.

"And you, child, will be called a prophet of the Most High; for you will go before the face of the Lord to prepare his ways, to give knowledge of salvation to his people through the forgiveness of their sins, because of the tender mercy of our God, by which the dawn from on high will visit us, to shine on those who sit in darkness and the shadow of death; to guide our feet into the way of peace."

And the child grew and became strong in spirit, and was in the desert until the day of his public appearance to Israel.

Many of us talk too much at times. We love to talk about ourselves if someone will listen. I heard of someone who went to addiction rehab. Because he talked incessantly in the group, it was decided by the group that he could only say one sentence at a time. After that, he had to be quiet and let others have a turn. For a compulsive talker, that must have been difficult to swallow. Most of us do not get such brutally honest feedback, but most of us would do well to talk less and listen more. As the old nursery rhyme goes: "A wise old owl lived in an oak. The more he saw the less he spoke. The less he spoke, the more he heard. Why don't you be like that old bird?"

Zechariah certainly had a lot of time to consider his words. He had asked for a sign and had been given one. It was a sign that gave him plenty of opportunity to consider his words, his attitude, and particularly the words of the angel. We might wonder whether Zechariah's wife might have found the nine months of his silence annoying, refreshing, or simply amusing.

The angel had announced that Zechariah and Elizabeth were going to have a son. That was wonderful news, which was being fulfilled before their eyes. Elizabeth was with child, to her delight and the joy of the village. But in Zechariah's mind, there was much more to ponder. As a priest and man of deep faith, Zechariah must have been thrilled by the words of the angel when he considered them. What was the child to be? He was to be "great." This did not mean great in a worldly sense but in the eyes of God. For a man of deep faith like Zechariah, this must have been a tremendous joy. There were stipulations placed on the child's behavior. He was not to drink wine or strong drink. This was a part of the Nazarite vow that set a person apart for God's special service. The Old Testament judge Samson's life had been guided by such a vow. The child would also be filled with the Holy Spirit from his mother's womb.

What would this child do? He would turn people back to God and go before the Lord in the Spirit and power of Elijah. He would turn the hearts of fathers to the children and the disobedient to the wisdom of the just. He would make ready a people prepared for the Lord. Zechariah would have immediately recognized those words. They were the very last words in the Bible of his day, in the prophet Malachi. Malachi closed his book with the promise of the return of Elijah before the day of the Lord's coming. He would turn the hearts of the fathers back to their children and the children back to their fathers lest, in the words of Malachi, God come and strike the land with a curse.

What did this mean to Zechariah? It meant that his son would play a special role in God's plan, He would be the promised Elijah who would prepare the way for the day of God's coming. What was the day of God's coming? The scriptures did not give an exact description of it. It was both a day of judgment but also salvation. Elijah was to prepare the way for the great and glorious thing God had in store for his people. Zechariah may not have completely understood what all the ancient prophecies meant, but he had nine months to contemplate and consider. We can imagine that it was a time of reflection, spiritual growth, growing understanding, and deep communion with God.

Luke recounts the dedication of the child. Elizabeth gave birth, and they came to circumcise him on the eighth day as prescribed in the Law of Moses. While circumcision is a mostly medical procedure to us, for a first-century Jew, it was much more. Circumcision was the sign of membership in the people of God. When a child was circumcised, he was permanently marked with the sign of the covenant and destined for inclusion among the people of God.

Luke tells the unusual and somewhat humorous story of the naming of the child. The people assumed he would be called Zechariah, after his father, and began calling him by that name. His mother said, "No." When his father was asked, he wrote on a tablet, "His name is John." Immediately Zechariah's tongue was set free, and he praised God. Luke reports that fear came on all the neighbors as they sensed that God was at work. They reported the event throughout the hill country.

Zechariah's words, as recorded by Luke, are not only words of praise but prophecy. Zechariah had ample time to consider the role and identity of their son. He had realized that he would be the forerunner of the Messiah. Since the Messiah was to come from the line of Judah, Zechariah knew that their child was not the Messiah, since he was from the tribe of Levi. After Mary's visit with Elizabeth, he knew exactly to whom the Messiah would be born. The words Zechariah spoke were thanksgiving to God and a prophecy about the newly born child. He would go before the Messiah to prepare his way and be called the prophet of the Most High.

Jesus would later say that among people, there had not come one greater than John. It would be a testimony to his character and the important role he would play. He would, as his father prophesied, give the knowledge of salvation to the people, invite them to the forgiveness of sins, proclaim light for those in darkness, and be a guide into the way of peace. Luke concludes by saying that the child, as he grew up, was strong in spirit. He lived in the wilderness, perhaps after his elderly parents' deaths, where he was able to commune with God, hear his call, and discern the message of preparation that God would give him to deliver.

Theological insights
- Names are important in the Bible because they are seen as describing a person's character and destiny. We see, in this first chapter of Luke, that the angel designates the names of both John and Jesus. They each had a special destiny and calling, even before their births.
- God works even in difficulties for our good. It seems clear that the nine months that Zechariah could not speak did him good and greatly increased the depth of his faith. Often God deepens faith through trials. That realization should temper our complaints when we go through difficult times.
- Luke tells us that Zechariah was able to write on a tablet and his neighbors read what he wrote. It is an indication that literacy was more widespread in the first century than is sometimes supposed.
- The New Testament will later describe the church as a body with many parts. Each part has a different function and all parts are important, even ones that cannot be seen. The less visible parts may, in fact, be the most important. John had a role in the plan of God. It was a supportive role that he would be willing to fulfill. It reminds us that all roles are important, even ones that support rather than lead.

Practical application

Children grow up in families, and families have a great ability to nurture faith. God placed John in a family that would raise him in the "training and instruction of the Lord" (Ephesians 6:4). Zechariah and Elizabeth would certainly have taken great care to help their son John learn the scriptures, say his own prayers, and understand the will and purposes of God. It would be the foundation that would prepare him to hear from God in the wilderness.

Protestant reformer Martin Luther said that the home should be a "little church." It should be a place of love, fellowship, guidance, teaching, and faith. If you are a parent, remember to do everything you can to develop faith and love for God within your family.

LUKE 2

The Birth of Jesus — Luke 2:1-7

IN THOSE DAYS a decree when out from Caesar Augustus that all the world should be registered. This was the first registration when Quirinius was governor of Syria. Everyone went to register, each to his own town. Joseph also went up from Galilee, from the town of Nazareth to Judea, to the city of David which is called Bethlehem, because he was of the house and family of David, to register with Mary, who was engaged to be married to him, who was with child. While they were there, the time came for her to give birth. She gave birth to her firstborn son, wrapped him in bands of cloth, and laid him in a manger, because there was no room for them in the inn.

It has been said that those who want to be good writers should do two things. They should read, and they should write. They should read good books to see how stories are told and to learn from the writing of others. Second, they should write regularly to develop and hone their craft. We do not know if Luke considered himself a writer. Perhaps he was constantly writing letters to others. As a physician, perhaps he had written manuals on the healing arts. What we do know is that the account of the birth of Jesus is masterfully written. In just seven short verses, Luke gives us a picture of the birth of Jesus that has captured the imagination of young and old for two millennia.

Luke begins the story of the birth of Jesus with a historical reference. Jesus was born in the reign of Caesar Augustus. It is important to understand that Christianity is a historical religion. It is not just a philosophy of ideas. It is not primarily about religious concepts or even a moral code. Christianity emerges and lives in history. God makes himself known to the world, not primarily in spiritual revelations to a few holy people, but in events in history. The Old Testament is the account of God revealing himself through the nation of Israel. The New Testament is the story of God coming in

27

human form in the person of Jesus and revealing his will in the life of the early church. Luke recounts that Jesus, the Son of God, was born in a particular historical moment. It was in the days of Caesar Augustus.

What was the world like in the days of Caesar Augustus? For one thing, it was the height of the Roman Empire. After the assassination of Julius Caesar in 44 B.C., there had been a power struggle. The ultimate victor was the Roman general Octavian, who took the name Caesar Augustus. His reign would be characterized by its longevity (27 B.C. - 14 A.D.), its competence, and its stability. Although being under Roman rule was a source of great unhappiness to the Jews, it gave the world of Europe, Asia Minor, and the Middle East a stability that it had rarely experienced. It would be a stability that would not only allow for the peaceful ministry of Jesus but also the rapid expansion of the Christian church over the following 50 years. Luke gives the time of Christ's birth more precisely within Augustus's reign. It was when Quirinius was governor of Syria. Historians have had difficulty aligning this detail with ancient records. It does not mean that Luke is inaccurate, however. It is possible that our understanding of this period is incomplete.

Luke not only identifies the time of Jesus' birth but the occasion for his birth in Bethlehem. Caesar had decreed that the entire world was to be registered, and everyone had to report to the town of their birth. This was what brought Joseph and Mary to Bethlehem and occasioned the birth of Jesus in that village. It was the village in which David had been born, and Joseph was a descendant in the royal line, a descendant of David himself. Rome was always in need of money, and one of the places they got it was from the territories it dominated. The registration was to tax the people. The return to one's hometown was so that no one got missed in the taxation.

As far as we can tell from Luke's narrative, except for the registration, Joseph and Mary had no intention of traveling to Bethlehem for the birth of their child. They were living in Nazareth at that point. Joseph may have had employment there, and Mary may have had family in the village. We have no indication that they understood the biblical prophecy that the Messiah was to come from Bethlehem. At least they seem to have made no effort to be there at the time of Jesus' birth. That Jesus was born in Bethlehem was not an effort by Joseph and Mary to fulfill ancient prophecy. It only happened because of the bothersome inconvenience of the decree of Augustus. But God often works his will through events that do not fit our plan or agenda, and he did in this instance. The birth of Jesus in Bethlehem links him to the ancient prophecies about the Messiah's birth (Micah 5:2) and the promise of an eternal kingdom coming from David's line (II Samuel 7:12-16, Isaiah 9:6-7).

As part of annual nativity scenes, we imagine Mary riding on a donkey alongside Joseph on their journey to Bethlehem. Luke does not say what mode of transportation they used to get to Bethlehem or how long the couple was there before she gave birth. We might reasonably assume they were not there long before her time came due. We do know that they did not have time to find better housing arrangements. They were among a vast throng of common, mostly poor people who were required to make the journey.

Luke reports that the town of Bethlehem was crowded with travelers as evidenced by the fact that the inns were full. Whether Joseph and Mary found a stable on their own or it was a meager kindness by the local innkeeper, we do not know. Their housing arrangement was certainly an inconvenience to Joseph and Mary, but it was part of God's plan. It created a memorable setting for the birth of Jesus.

Mary gave birth in a stable, probably with the help of a local midwife. After the child was born, she wrapped her son in swaddling cloths, as was custom, to keep him warm and secure. She put him in a feeding trough, filled with hay, to let him sleep, because she had no other options. Luke's account points to the very ordinary and humble circumstances of Christ's birth. The inconvenience of Joseph and Mary, however, turned out to be the perfect place for the Savior of humanity to come into the world. It is a wonderfully poignant scene that the Son of God should come among us in such a lowly way, and it is exquisite storytelling on Luke's part that he could paint such a picture.

Theological insights
- The Bible views history as linear. Some religions, particularly Eastern ones, believe it to be cyclical. That is, life and history go around and around, things repeating themselves with no overall goal or purpose. Christianity believes history to be linear. It begins with God, and he is working out his purposes in it. The birth of the Messiah was an important event in the plan of God that moved history toward his purposes.
- What is the significance of Bethlehem as the birthplace of the Messiah? It linked him to David the king who was born there, and his birth there was foretold by the prophet Micah (Micah 5:2). It

served the purpose of providing a humble place for his birth, well away from the centers of political and religious power. That Bethlehem was insignificant kept his birth hidden from the sight of those in power, such as Herod, until the visit of the Wise Men (Matthew 2:1-12).

- Though our nativity pageants view the journey of Mary and Joseph to Bethlehem as just prior to the birth of Jesus, Luke does not say so. He only says that while they were there the time came for her to give birth. They might have traveled there earlier in order to escape the inevitable gossip about Mary, though that would not explain why they had not found adequate lodging by then.

- In the first century, it would not have been unusual for people and animals to live in close quarters. Shepherds used caves as places not only for them to sleep but their animals. Scholars believe that the place where Jesus was born may very well have been one of these caves.

- Caesar Augustus was widely hailed as the leader who brought the world peace. It was during his reign that the true Prince of Peace was born.

Practical application

What is the significance of the humble birth of Jesus? It is certainly ironic and not the way we would have done it. He was the king of Israel yet born in obscurity. He was the rightful authority in the town of Bethlehem yet found no lodging there. He was God come among us yet only a few lowly shepherds would celebrate it.

The humble beginnings of Jesus set the stage for a life of servanthood. God did not come among us to experience human luxury. He left the glory of heaven to live as we do, even as the humblest among us. This humble birth begins the great story of God's love for us in Jesus Christ. In a world where it is easy to chase after earthly comforts and luxuries, we are reminded, in the birth of Jesus that life is about much more. There will be plenty of luxuries in heaven. In this life, if we are to follow the pattern of Jesus, we are called to service to God and others. Jesus will live a life of poverty, suffering, and servanthood. His suffering and poverty begin at the moment of his birth.

The Angels and the Shepherds – Luke 2:8-20

THERE WERE SHEPHERDS in the same country staying in the field, and keeping watch over their flock by night. An angel of the Lord appeared to them, and the glory of the Lord shone around them, and they were terrified. The angel said to them, "Do not be afraid, for behold, I bring you good news of great joy which will be for all the people. There is born to you today, in the city of David, a Savior, who is Christ the Lord. This will be a sign for you: you will find a baby wrapped in strips of cloth, lying in a manger." Suddenly, there was with the angel a multitude of the heavenly host praising God and saying, "Glory to God in the highest, and peace on earth to those on whom his favor rests."

When the angels went away from them into heaven, the shepherds said to one another, "Let us go to Bethlehem and see this thing that has taken place, which the Lord has made known to us." They went with haste and found Mary and Joseph, and the baby lying in the manger. When they saw it, they made known the saying that was spoken to them about this child. All who heard it were amazed at the things the shepherds said to them. But Mary kept all these things and pondered them in her heart. The shepherds returned, glorifying and praising God for all the things that they had heard and seen, just as it had been told them.

Do people have spiritual experiences? A researcher was surprised at the results when he asked the question. When ordinary people were asked if they had ever had a spiritually significant religious experience, a surprising number of people replied, "Yes." Ordinary people, even people who did not appear to be overly religious, recounted remarkable encounters with God that shaped their views of life and faith. Luke records that a group of shepherds had an extraordinary experience on the night of Jesus' birth.

The appearance of the angels to the shepherds is one of the delightful, moving, and picturesque parts of the account of the birth of Jesus. While the life of a shepherd might seem romantic from our distant vantage point, it was not considered so in the first century. It was a lowly profession characterized by long hours, little pay, and social disdain. If you could do anything other than be a shepherd, you did so.

Some may ask why the angel did not announce the birth of Jesus to the mayor of the town, or the village elders, or the leader of the synagogue. One would suppose that the answer is obvious. It was the meek, lowly, and disregarded whom God intended to reach first with his message of salvation. For that reason, we should not be surprised that God would appear to the shepherds rather than some others. The angel's announcement to them fits in with how Christ came to this world.

That the angels appeared to the shepherds was also a way to keep the birth of his Son below the radar. While the shepherds might tell their friends and neighbors, their conversations would not make their way to the local society news or the governor's ears. As we learn in Matthew's gospel, keeping things relatively quiet would be important, since Herod would eventually search for the child to take his life. The chances are that a few short days after Christ's birth, the excitement of the shepherds would be old news. Everything would go back to normal, and the newborn baby would be mostly forgotten. That was just as God wanted it to be.

Most nativity pageants take place at night, and it is because of this story. Luke does not say that the birth of Jesus took place at night. He does say, however, that the appearance of the angels to the shepherds did. He specifically says that they were watching their flock "by night" (Luke 2:8). He also does not say that the shepherds saw the angels in the sky though we often picture the scene in that way.

The first appearance is by a single angel. He is not identified as Gabriel as in the stories of Zechariah and Mary. His first words were the same as were spoken to them, however – "Do not be afraid." His message to the shepherds was clear. Something wonderful had happened that was very good news and worthy of great joy. A child had been born that very day in Bethlehem, the city of David. He was Christ the Lord. The word "Christ" means anointed one and was a clear reference to the Messiah.

The shepherds would have understood this news as the announcement of the long-awaited Messiah's birth. The idea that the Messiah was to come from Bethlehem may not have been completely foreign to them, and there had been a sense of anticipation among the people for many years. For that reason, they may not have been totally surprised at the angel's words.

We have already noted that angels are sparing with their words, and this instance is no different. Once the angel had delivered his message, Luke records that a multitude of angels appeared. He says it was a multitude of the "heavenly host." They praised God and said, "Glory to God in the highest, and peace on earth among those with whom he is pleased" (Luke 2:14). Luke does not mention that this was a song, but we tend to think of it that way. Whatever form it took, it must have been glorious. After praising God, the angels went away into heaven. Their departure into heaven is why we tend to see them as singing in the sky above the shepherds.

The shepherds must have been stunned by the encounter. Certainly, none of them would have seen an angel before. What were they to do? The answer was obvious. They should go see the child. The angel had all but told them to do so since he announced where they would find him and how to identify him. Certainly, this was an event to be seen and experienced. They also must have desperately wanted to tell someone what they had seen and heard. Luke says that they went with haste, and it may not have taken them long to find a newborn baby wrapped in swaddling cloths and lying in a manger.

This must have been a visit that Joseph and Mary did not expect. Perhaps the happy couple was hoping for a quiet time alone after the difficulty of childbirth, but that was not to be. It was a special night, and God had something in store for them. When the shepherds told what had happened to them, Joseph and Mary must have marveled. It was confirmation of what they already knew. The child was special, and God had a special work for him. Luke indicates that the shepherds told others in the days ahead. All who heard it marveled at their story. Mary simply pondered their words. She treasured all that was said about the child, considering in herself what it might mean.

Theological insights
- The appearance of the angel to shepherds was in keeping with the lowly nature of Christ's birth since the occupation of shepherd was held in low esteem.
- The appearance of the angel to shepherds linked the birth of Jesus to David since he too had been a shepherd.
- The fright of the shepherds at the appearance of the angel mirrors Zechariah's reaction (Luke 1:12). As in his case, the angel's first words were ones of assurance.
- In the first century, babies were wrapped snuggly in strips of cloth to keep them warm, protect their hands and feet, and give them a sense of security.

Practical application

The nation had waited for the coming of the Messiah for many centuries. No doubt many wondered if it would ever happen. Finally, however, the time was right. It was, in the words of the angel, "good news of great joy." What was the appropriate reaction? The host of angels sang, "Glory to God in the highest, and peace on earth to those on whom his favor rests." God would be glorified in Christ's coming, and it was appropriate for the angels to sing his praises. His coming would bring peace on earth, at least to those who found favor with God. We will see in the life of Jesus that not everyone would receive him. For those who would, however, they would find great peace and joy. This is, of course, still true today.

Jesus Presented in the temple – Luke 2:21-40

WHEN EIGHT DAYS HAD PASSED, and it was time for his circumcision, his name was called Jesus, which was given by the angel before he was conceived. When it came time for their purification according to the law of Moses, they brought him to Jerusalem to present him to the Lord (as it is written in the law of the Lord, "Every male who opens the womb shall be called holy to the Lord"), and to offer a sacrifice according to that which is said in the law of the Lord, "A pair of turtledoves, or two young pigeons."

Now there was a man in Jerusalem whose name was Simeon. This man was righteous and devout, looking for the consolation of Israel, and the Holy Spirit was upon him. It had been revealed to him by the Holy Spirit that he should not see death until he had seen the Lord's Christ. He came in the Spirit into the temple. When the parents brought in the child Jesus to do for him according to the custom of the law, he took him up into his arms and praised God, saying, "Now Lord you are letting your servant depart in peace, according to your word; for my eyes have seen your salvation, which you have prepared in the sight of all people; a light for revelation to the Gentiles, and the glory of your people Israel."

Joseph and his mother marveled at what was said about him. Simeon blessed them, and said to Mary, his mother, "Behold, this child is appointed for the falling and the rising of many in Israel, and for a sign that will be spoken against. Yes, and a sword will pierce your own soul also, that the thoughts of many hearts may be revealed."

There was one Anna, a prophetess, the daughter of Phanuel, of the tribe of Asher (she was of a great age, having lived with a husband seven years from her virginity, and she had been a widow until about eighty-four years), who did not depart from the temple, but worshiped with fasting and prayer night and day. Coming up at that very hour, she gave thanks to the Lord, and spoke of him to all those who were looking for redemption in Jerusalem.

When they had fulfilled all things that were required according to the law of the Lord, they returned into Galilee, to their own city, Nazareth. The child grew and became strong in spirit. He was filled with wisdom and the grace of God was upon him.

There is something valuable about rituals. Psychologists encourage families to create them to build family connections. Family rituals can take many forms, such as going to the mountains every Thanksgiving, making a big deal of birthdays, or going out to lunch after church on Sunday. Nations have rituals, such as America's celebration of the July 4th holiday. Churches have rituals, such as baptism, the Lord's Supper, church anniversaries, and special services. The nation of Israel had rituals that reinforced the people's identity as the people of God and connected them. Luke mentions two of those rituals in this second chapter.

After a male child was born, he was required to be circumcised on the eighth day. The Law of Moses said, "And on the eighth day the flesh of his foreskin shall be circumcised" (Leviticus 12:3). This was also where a son was officially given his name, as we saw in the story of the birth of John the Baptist. Luke reports that Joseph and Mary did as was required by the law and named the child Jesus, as the angel had instructed. In contrast to Zechariah and Elizabeth, it was not a ceremony surrounded by family and friends. Mary and Joseph, still in Bethlehem, were strangers in a distant town that was far from home.

According to Old Testament law, all women who gave birth were ritually unclean for a period of time. The period was forty days after giving birth to a male child and eighty days after giving birth to a female (Leviticus 12:1-8). This excluded them from ritual activities in the temple until their purification. At the end of that time, the parents brought an offering to the temple to make atonement for her uncleanness and as a sign of her restoration. Luke mentions that two turtledoves or two pigeons were required for the offering, which was what the poor, such as Mary and Joseph, offered. This required a trip to the temple in Jerusalem and could not be done elsewhere. Luke reports what happened when Mary and Joseph entered the temple for Mary's purification.

Luke records two encounters in the temple, the first with a man named Simeon. He was righteous and devout, and the Holy Spirit was upon him. Luke says that God had revealed to Simeon that he would not die until he had seen the Christ. He took the child in his arms and blessed him, saying: "Now Lord you are letting your servant depart in peace, according to your word; for my eyes have seen your salvation, which you have prepared in the sight of all people; a light for revelation to the Gentiles, and the glory of your people Israel."

Luke also records an encounter with a woman in the temple whose name was Anna. She was notable for her age, having been a widow for many years. She was a prophetess, eighty-four years old, who worshipped God night and day. She spoke to all those, says Luke, who had been waiting for the redemption of Israel. These must have been surprising and remarkable affirmations for Mary and Joseph. Extraordinary events seemed to follow the life of their child.

But not all the words they heard that day were comforting. Simeon had a personal word for Mary. He said to her directly: "Behold, this child is appointed for the falling and the rising of many in Israel, and for a sign that will be spoken against. Yes, and a sword will pierce your own soul also, that the thoughts of many hearts may be revealed."

Those words certainly had an ominous tone to them. From our vantage point, we understand them. Jesus would certainly cause the rise of some, like the common men who became apostles, and the fall of others, like the religious leaders who opposed him. That rise and fall would not be in the eyes of society but in the sight of God. Jesus, during the time of his ministry, would certainly be opposed, as Simeon foresaw. What was the purpose of the direct and sometimes controversial nature of Jesus' ministry? It was so that the attitudes, thoughts, and desires of many hearts would become known. Many ordinary people would respond in faith to the call of Jesus. Other high religious officials would refuse it. Those who were last in the eyes of society became first and the first became last.

When they returned home, Luke recounts that they did not return to Bethlehem, however, but to Nazareth. Luke here appears to "telescope" the account of the life of Jesus because he leaves out an important story that is recorded in the gospel of Matthew, the visit of the Wise Men and the flight into Egypt. It is an account that Matthew found important because it enabled him to show an aspect of how Jesus fulfilled Old Testament prophecies (Matthew 2:13-15).

There were perhaps many parts of the life of Jesus that could not be recorded for the sake of brevity. The Gospel of John admits such (John 21:25). What seems most likely is that the visit of the Wise Men occurred after the purification of Mary and their return to Bethlehem. Matthew reported that the Wise Men came to Jerusalem looking for the newborn king.

How soon after his birth did the Wise Men arrive? Most scholars believe it was six to eighteen months. It is reasonable to assume that it would have taken some significant amount of time to organize an expedition and travel from the east to Jerusalem. When Herod tried to kill the child, he targeted boys two years old and under, an indication that the Wise Men did not visit immediately after the child's birth. We assume then, that Mary and Joseph returned to Bethlehem after her purification. They lived there until Joseph was warned to flee to Egypt after the visit from the Wise Men. They lived in Egypt until Herod died, and Joseph was instructed to return to Israel (Matthew 2:20). Matthew records that Joseph settled in Nazareth because of his fear of one of the heirs of Herod, Archelaus, who ruled the region around Bethlehem. Luke excluded the account of the visit of the Wise Men and the family's journey to Egypt. He did indicate, however, that the family ended up in Nazareth where Jesus would spend most of his time growing up.

Luke only has a brief comment about the life of Jesus from his birth up until age twelve. Luke says that Jesus grew up, was full of wisdom, and showed the favor of God in his life, even as a child. We would love to know more about the childhood of Jesus, but that is not important for the story of his saving work. That he grew up in a family was part of the journey and process of God living among us. He did not simply appear as a fully grown man. Rather he grew up as everyone does, from infancy to childhood, through adolescence into adulthood. This is God's affirmation of human life, the family, and ordinary existence. Jesus did not live an isolated life apart from ordinary experience but lived in it as we do. That he lived without sin is even more remarkable considering that he lived in a family, had siblings, and had to endure the trials, problems, and indignities that come with being human. Luke simply indicates that Jesus experienced all this. As we will learn later, he did so without sin. That is a feat only God could achieve and which makes the life of Jesus even more amazing.

Theological insights
- The Gospel of Matthew tells how an angel of the Lord instructed Joseph not to be afraid to take Mary as his wife since the child with which she was pregnant was from the Holy Spirit. Matthew says that Joseph had no marital relations with her until after Jesus was born (Matthew 1:25). She would have been unclean after the birth until her purification forty days later. Although the Old Testament did not specify, it was general practice for husband and wife to wait for marital relations after the birth of a child until her purification. After that, normal marital relations would have been allowed.
- Even in the most corrupt of times, some people are righteous and devout. Simeon and Anna are among those, as are Mary and Joseph. They stand in sharp contrast to many in Israel who will have little true faith at the time when Jesus begins his public ministry.
- Though Joseph and Mary understand the special nature and destiny of their child, they continue to be amazed at the things that are said about him. When we see God at work, it often surprises even the most devout among us.
- Simeon and Anna signal a resurgence in the prophetic office which had been silent for 400 years. It will peak with Jesus who will be the greatest of all the prophets. The gift will also be present in the life of the early church in various ways.

Practical application
There can be good and bad traditions. Sometimes we hold on to traditions and practices long after they have lost their effectiveness. Traditions bring back memories of good times, and we fear that we will lose the memories when we lose the tradition. The church is sometimes quick to change its theology but slow to change its practice. It should be slow to change its theology but quick to change its practice.

Traditions are good when they point us to worthy goals. It is good to make a habit of being in church on Sundays. This positive tradition puts us in a place where the community of believers can nurture our faith. Joseph and Mary did not disdain the traditions of Judaism. Those traditions helped keep them connected to God and his people. We do well to follow in their example.

The Boy Jesus – Luke 2:41-52

HIS PARENTS WENT EVERY YEAR to Jerusalem at the feast of the Passover. When he was twelve years old, they went up to Jerusalem according to custom. When the festival was over, as they were returning, the boy Jesus stayed behind in Jerusalem. Joseph and his mother did not know it, but supposing him to be in the group, they went a day's journey. Then they began looking for him among their relatives and acquaintances.

When they did not find him, they returned to Jerusalem, looking for him. After three days they found him in the temple, sitting among the teachers, listening to them and asking them questions. All who heard him were amazed at his understanding and his answers. When his parents saw him, they were astonished. His mother said to him, "Son, why have you treated us this way? Your father and I were anxiously looking for you." He said to them, "Why were you looking for me? Did you not know that I must be in my Father's house?" They did not understand the saying that he spoke to them.

He went down with them and came to Nazareth and was subject to them, but his mother pondered all these things in her heart. And Jesus increased in wisdom and stature, and in favor with God and everyone.

Everyone loves a vacation. It is good to get away for a week or more and do nothing, do something you have not done, have an adventure, or simply do nothing in an exotic location. Does the Bible allow for or even authorize vacations? If we look at the Old Testament, the answer is, "Yes." To begin with, the Bible specifies that we must not work every day of the week. One day in seven is a Sabbath to God. It is a day of rest, recuperation, and worship. In addition, the Old Testament specified three national "vacation weeks" called festivals. During these weeks, the people were to stop their work, travel to Jerusalem, and remember God's blessings. The three festivals were: 1) the Passover, celebrated in the spring, remembering the nation's exodus from Egypt; 2) the Feast of Weeks, called Pentecost, a festival of thanksgiving, celebrated 50 days after Passover; and 3) the Feast of Tabernacles, celebrated in the fall, remembering God's provision for the people during their time in the wilderness. These were both religious festivals and national vacations. The Old Testament law understood people's need for rest, recreation, and community building. The festivals provided those. The most important and well-attended of the festivals was the Passover. If a family could not make other festivals, they tried at least to be in Jerusalem for the Passover.

Luke records an incident that happened when the family attended the Passover when Jesus was about twelve years of age. He says that it was the custom of the family to go to Jerusalem every year for this event. This signifies that the family was faithful to the religious practices and customs of the law, which should not surprise us. Attending the Passover festival was a national ritual and an important family ritual for Joseph, Mary, and their children.

On that particular occasion, as they made their way home, Mary and Joseph realized, about a day's journey from Jerusalem, that Jesus was not among the group. How could they not know Jesus was with them? This seems to indicate that they traveled to and from these festivals in large groups, probably made up of extended family. This would have made the group less likely to be attacked by robbers. It would also have made for a more pleasant journey both for the adults and the children. One of the enjoyable parts of the ritual would have been the time to socialize with family, neighbors, and friends as they journeyed.

Mary and Joseph had other children by the time Jesus was twelve. They must have assumed he was playing with other children in the crowd. Their own younger children needed attention and may have distracted them. Eventually, however, perhaps at dinner that first evening, they realized Jesus was not to be found. We can imagine the panic they felt. It is bad enough to lose one of your children. To lose the Messiah was a catastrophe!

Luke says that they found him after three days. He was in the temple sitting among the teachers. He was "listening to them and asking them questions" (Luke 2:46). We might imagine that a crowd had gathered around him. Everyone who heard him was amazed at his understanding and the way he answered questions.

We can also imagine that Mary and Joseph were surprised to see Jesus sitting with the teachers. He had been soaking in his religious training, but apparently not shown to others the depth to which he understood it. That he could converse with the religious leaders of the nation must have been unexpected for Mary and Joseph. Luke simply says that they were "astonished."

Mary's second reaction is not surprising, however. "Son, how could you treat us this way? Why didn't you tell us you wanted to stay behind? Didn't you know we would be worried to death?" That would be a mother's natural reaction. We might also wonder why Jesus did not alert his parents. Of course, they would not have allowed him to remain behind. Jesus' reply is both respectful and independent. "Why were you looking for me? Did you not know that I must be in my Father's house (Luke 2:49)?" Jesus indicates two things in the comment. It acknowledges God as his true Father in heaven. It also foreshadows a higher priority than even family. Jesus has a destiny to fulfill. Even the commitment to family will not get in the way of it, as his family will discover later on. Luke notes that his parents did not fully understand his response.

We learn from this story that Jesus had indeed been absorbing his lessons well. He would have received religious training as part of the village synagogue. His life of faith was, no doubt, nurtured in the family as well. That Jesus could converse with the teachers in the temple indicates, not only the divine understanding that was emerging but also the good job Mary and Joseph had done with him. He was learning the faith at home and in his community, and he was learning it well.

Luke concludes by saying that Jesus went home with his parents and was obedient to them. As with many other unusual events surrounding the life of this special child, Mary continued to ponder it all, trying to discern what it meant, how to raise Jesus best, and what his destiny might be. Jesus continued to grow up and was approved by all, says Luke. We wish we had more stories like this from the childhood and youth of Jesus. After this story, however, we will not hear about Jesus for another eighteen years when he begins his public ministry.

Theological insights
- While this passage highlights the emerging wisdom of Jesus, even at a young age, it is more importantly about his awareness of his nature as the Son of God. The real revelation in this story is that Jesus had a unique relationship with God as "my Father." God in heaven was his true Father, and he was God's only begotten Son.

- Part of the sinless perfection of Jesus was his obedience to Mary and Joseph. Luke notes that he went home and was subject to them.
- The Gnostic Gospel of Thomas contains a story about Jesus as a boy turning clay pigeons into living birds. That story and others like it have no historical support and were fashioned for the Gnostic purpose of seeing Jesus as the revealer of hidden knowledge and promoting his ability to transform inferior material things, such as humans, into liberated spiritual beings.

Practical application

If we think that children cannot make significant strides toward learning the things of faith, this passage tells us otherwise. Our children will not reach the level of understanding that Jesus had, but they can often learn much more than we realize. We send them to school for other things. We should make sure they learn to know, understand, and love God as well. The years between infancy and the teenage years are the great window of opportunity that God has given parents. This is when they have the most influence in their children's lives. Parents should use those years to teach them about God, help them learn to pray, and begin them on a routine of reading the Bible.

LUKE 3

The Preaching of John the Baptist– Luke 3:1-9

IN THE FIFTEENTH YEAR of the reign of Tiberius Caesar, Pontius Pilate being governor of Judea, and Herod being tetrarch of Galilee, and his brother Philip tetrarch of the region of Ituraea and Trachonitis, and Lysanias tetrarch of Abilene, during the high priesthood of Annas and Caiaphas, the word of God came to John, the son of Zechariah, in the wilderness. He went into all the region around the Jordan, preaching a baptism of repentance for the forgiveness of sins.

As it is written in the book of the words of Isaiah the prophet, "The voice of one crying in the wilderness, 'Make ready the way of the Lord. Make his paths straight. Every valley will be filled. Every mountain and hill will be brought low. The crooked will become straight, and the rough ways smooth. All flesh will see God's salvation.' "

He said therefore to the multitudes who came out to be baptized by him, "You offspring of vipers, who warned you to flee from the wrath to come? Produce fruits worthy of repentance, and do not begin to say among yourselves, 'We have Abraham for our father;' for I tell you that God is able to raise up children to Abraham from these stones! Even now the axe lies at the root of the trees. Every tree therefore that does not produce good fruit is cut down and thrown into the fire."

Beginnings can be exciting. We might think of the beginning of a new school year for students, our first job out of college, or a move to a new city. There is anxiety but also enthusiasm for what is ahead. Some moments are particularly important, such as our wedding or the birth of a child, because they mark monumental shifts in life. Such was the appearance of John the Baptist and his preaching ministry for the nation of Israel. It marked a theological and cultural shift that captured not only the attention but also the imagination of the nation.

43

As Luke did for the birth of Jesus, he places the appearance of John in a historic moment. It was the fifteenth year of the reign of Tiberius Caesar. Tiberius had succeeded Caesar Augustus after his death. Since Tiberius began to reign in 14 A.D., this would make the beginning of John's ministry about 28-29 A.D.

Luke also notes that Pontius Pilate was governor of Judea, Herod was tetrarch of Galilee, and Philip was tetrarch of Abilene. After the death of Herod the Great in 4 B.C., his kingdom was divided among his sons. Herod Antipas was given Galilee, Philip a region to the northeast of Israel, and Herod Archelaus the region around Jerusalem – the region of Judea, which was the southern part of the nation. None of the sons were given the title of king but rather "tetrarch" which was a lower title and meant the ruler of a region. Since Israel was a client state of Rome, these all were appointed by and ruled at the pleasure of Caesar. Herod Archelaus ruled his region until 6 B.C. when Augustus deposed him for his incompetence. Instead of appointing another son or a grandson of Herod the Great in his place, Augustus made the region a province under direct Roman authority. Pontius Pilate, who ruled Judea from 26-36 A.D., was the Roman governor when John's ministry began.

There was only one high priest at any given time. Why then does Luke mention two – Annas and Caiaphas? Annas was appointed high priest when Archelaus was deposed and served in that role until 15 A.D. Though his son-in-law Caiaphas was serving as high priest when John's ministry began, Annas continued to be highly influential in Jewish politics and religious life. For this reason, Luke mentions them both. Caiaphas would serve as high priest from 18-36 A.D.

The crucial event that took place at that time was that the word of God came to John, the son of Zechariah, in the wilderness. This phrase used by Luke is reminiscent of how God spoke to the prophets. The Old Testament characterized the ministry of the prophets as one of receiving a word from God to proclaim to the people. For example, the scriptures say that the word of God came to Samuel, Nathan, Elijah, Jeremiah, and Ezekiel (I Samuel 3:21, II Samuel 7:4, I Kings 17:2, Jeremiah 1:2, Ezekiel 1:3). After many years of prophetic silence, something remarkable happened. Once again God spoke clearly and prophetically to someone. In the wilderness, John the son of Zechariah heard from God and came into Judea preaching. His appearance caused great excitement among the people.

We can imagine the keen interest that John aroused. If you thought someone had truly heard from God, you would want to know what he had to say. John gave the impression of someone who had authentically heard from God, and that brought people from far and wide. John was someone not swayed by fashion or who sought political favor. He did not come with a message of comfort but rather urgency. It was time to repent and be baptized for the forgiveness of sins.

The practice of baptism seems to originate with John. That is, we see no real parallels to it in the Old Testament or the intertestamental period. That people were to be baptized as a symbol of their repentance seems to have been part of the word from God that John received. The symbolism of it would have been obvious. If one truly wanted one's sins washed away, then washing with water would symbolize it. Down into the water would go the sinner. Clean and renewed one would arise. Though baptism would be a practice that would carry through the ministry of Jesus and the life of the church, it did not originate with Jesus. The mission of Jesus was not primarily as a religious innovator. John would be given that privilege where baptism was concerned.

Luke notes that John's message fulfilled the words of the prophet Isaiah (Isaiah 40:3-5). The prophet Isaiah had proclaimed a coming time of comfort. When that time came, a voice would cry out in the wilderness. It would call for a straight path to be made before the revealing of God's glory. All people would see what God was doing. He would raise the valleys and lower the mountains so that his coming might be known by all. The crooked would become straight and God's salvation would appear.

People came from "all the region around Jordan" to hear the word from God that John proclaimed. Luke gives us some glimpses of John's preaching. He did not come to make people feel better about themselves but to call them to repentance. Those who thought themselves righteous, he especially warned. "Don't think that it is enough to be a physical descendant of Abraham," said John. "God could raise up children of Abraham from the stones around you. If you say you repent, then bear the fruit of your repentance. Know also that a time of judgment is at hand. The axe is ready for every tree that does not bear good fruit. It will be cut down and thrown into the fire." John's words remind us of the words that Simeon spoke to Mary at the time of her purification. He told her that her son was set for the rising and falling of many people. His coming would reach even to the thoughts of their hearts. John foresaw the judgment that the coming of Christ would bring. His message was one of preparation for it. He was like a farmer tilling the soil so that the seed would grow. John's message of repentance prepared the way for the good news of hope that Jesus would bring.

Theological insights
- How does the word of God come to people today? It comes to us through the written word found in scripture, and it is illuminated by the Holy Spirit.
- The ceremony of baptism is considered a Sacrament by much of the Christian church. It marks one's entrance into the family of God. The sign that accompanies it is water; the promise contained in it is our forgiveness and salvation in Jesus Christ.
- Repentance is part of the practice of Christian discipleship. It is part of the work of sanctification, which is the work of living in greater degrees of holiness as we mature in faith.
- While God's judgment takes many forms, it begins in the heart. God looks upon the heart; for that reason, nothing can be hidden from him.

Practical application

When we have company coming to visit, we prepare for their arrival. We clean the house, shop for food, and make various arrangements. What then should we do for our house to be in order as a place of God's residence? Do we present less than our best to God? Do we ask God to live in moral squalor? John's ministry reminds us of the importance of tilling the soil of our lives, hearts, attitudes, and desires so that Christ can take root there. God continues to work in the world in Jesus Christ; let us make ourselves ready so that his work can take place through us.

The Baptism of Jesus – Luke 3:10-22

THE MULTITUDES ASKED HIM, "What then must we do?" He answered them, "He who has two coats, let him give to him who has none. He who has food, let him do likewise." Tax collectors also came to be baptized, and they said to him, "Teacher, what must we do?" He said to them, "Collect no more than that which is appointed to you." Soldiers also asked him, saying, "What about us? What must we do?"

He said to them, "Extort money from no one by violence, neither accuse anyone wrongfully. Be content with your wages."

As the people were in expectation, and all men reasoned in their hearts concerning John, whether perhaps he was the Christ, John answered them all, "I indeed baptize you with water, but one is coming who is mightier than I, the strap of whose sandals I am not worthy to untie. He will baptize you in the Holy Spirit and fire. His winnowing fork is in his hand, and he will cleanse his threshing floor. He will gather the wheat into his barn, but he will burn up the chaff with unquenchable fire."

Then with many other exhortations he preached good news to the people. But Herod the tetrarch, being reproved by him for Herodias, his brother's wife, and for all the evil things Herod had done, added this also, that he locked up John in prison.

Now when all the people were baptized, Jesus himself was baptized. As he was praying, the heavens were opened, and the Holy Spirit descended on him in bodily form like a dove. And a voice came out of the heaven saying, "You are my beloved Son. In you I am well pleased."

Most good sermons end with a practical application. No matter how compelling the biblical analysis or the theological insights, the listener wants to know, "What should I do? How should I apply what you have said? Make this clear for me!" John's hearers voiced that same sentiment. They wanted to know how to apply John's message of repentance in practical terms.

Luke does not give us a detailed accounting of John's preaching. John's practical applications, however, must have stood out, since Luke records them. Like any good preacher, his applications were things people could do. He encouraged kindness and mercy toward others. If you have more than you need – specifically two coats – share with someone who has less, said John. Do the same if you have food you can share. This guidance was certainly in line with Old Testament instructions, such as the one later emphasized by Jesus, "You shall love your neighbor as yourself" (Leviticus 19:18).

John's words to tax collectors and soldiers emphasized justice. Tax collectors were to require no more than they were appointed to collect. To be a tax collector in that day meant you were willing to endure the disdain of the people. Both Rome and local rulers drew their wealth from taxation. The responsibility for collecting what was due to Rome fell to the local and regional authorities, such as Herod Antipas. While there was recognition of the need for some taxation, just as today, no one liked the process, especially when it was viewed as unjust. The Roman taxes were particularly distasteful because they reminded the nation of Rome's dominance of them.

John's words to the tax collectors were remarkably restrained. They did not need to quit their jobs only do them fairly. They were not to enrich themselves, as most tax collectors did, off the backs of the people. Collect what was authorized and live modestly from your means, not at the expense of others. While this might sound simple to us, it would have been a real sacrifice for those who were living richly from their unjust gain.

Soldiers were also touched by John's preaching and wanted to conform to God's call. But what were they to do? We might suspect that the soldiers were a particularly difficult ethical problem. How could a soldier, who might be called upon to do battle, conform to God's purposes? John was again practical. Do not use your authority to extort money from people. Do not coerce people by false accusations, and do not complain about what you are paid.

We marvel at the wise, practical, and reasoned insights of John. They remind us of the exhortation of the prophet Micah who instructed people to "Do justice, love mercy, and walk humbly with God" (Micah 6:8). John's preaching fit well into that pattern. Do justice toward others. Show mercy where you can. Repent and turn your hearts back to God.

We can imagine the excitement John's preaching aroused. Was this possibly the Messiah? Had he finally appeared? John was clear about his role. He was the forerunner, not the Messiah. The Messiah was close at hand, and when he appeared, said John, it would be a momentous day. However impressed people might have been by John's preaching, the Messiah's message and purpose were much greater. He was so much greater, said John, that he was not even worthy to untie his sandals. John was baptizing with water, but the one to come would baptize people with the Holy Spirit. He would also come in judgment on people's hearts, words, and actions. His coming would signal a harvest where the grain would be gathered but the chaff burned in unquenchable flame. People must have wondered at John's words. How would the Messiah's coming be a day of judgment, and what might it be like to be baptized with God's Holy Spirit?

Thus Luke describes in brief the message of John. He warned the people, but the heart of his message was good news. Get ready for something great that God is ready to do. Then Luke recounts the shortening of John's ministry by Herod. John had rebuked Herod for his adulterous marriage to Herodias, his brother Philip's wife. It was not lawful for you to marry her, said John. This angered Herod, and as we learn in other gospel accounts, especially his wife. Herod therefore put John in prison. Luke records that it was characteristic of Herod to act wickedly. His imprisonment of John was one in a long line of such cruelties. We see in the preaching of John a theme we will also find in the words of Jesus. Herod was a wicked ruler whose ways and purposes were opposed to God.

Luke culminates this section with a short recounting of the baptism of Jesus. True to his style, he paints a compelling picture in a few short sentences. After the people had come, Jesus also came. When Jesus was baptized, something unique happened. The heavens were opened and the Holy Spirit descended on Jesus in the form of a dove. A voice came out of heaven and said, "You are my beloved Son. In you, I am well pleased."

It is important to note the words of the voice from heaven. What does the Father in heaven do? He affirms his Son. "You have done well," says Jesus' heavenly Father. "I am proud of you." This is an example that every parent should note. Every parent should, at appropriate moments and in appropriate ways, tell their children that they love them and are proud of them. There are few affirmations more important to a child than the approval of their parents. The Father in heaven affirms his Son. Jesus had indeed done well up to that point. He had lived in a family for thirty years and done so without sin. He had passed the first part of his spiritual test. There would be many more ahead, but at that point, the Father expressed his approval. Jesus had done all that the Father had asked and done it well. He was indeed ready for the task that was before him.

One important thing to note about the baptism of Jesus is that Jesus prayed. Luke's gospel is the only one that records it. We will see many instances of the prayers of Jesus in his life. Here is the first of them in the gospel of Luke. At this pivotal moment when his public ministry was beginning, Jesus approached it with prayer. It is the reminder that prayer, though appropriate at all times, is especially appropriate in our moments of decision, difficulty, and new beginnings. Especially then, we should not neglect to pray.

Theological insights

- The baptism of Jesus is considered the official start of his public ministry. The event revealed him as the promised Messiah (at least to John and others present at his baptism) and began his official ministry.
- It is easy to get out of balance in one's spiritual perspective, either being too detached from the world or too attached to it. Wisdom, common sense, and good judgment are signs of a mature, healthy, and balanced life of faith. John exhibited all those factors.
- That John the Baptist was not afraid to criticize Herod shows his fearless confidence. He is a worthy biblical example of someone who spoke truth to power.
- John predicted that Christ's ministry would "separate the wheat from the chaff." Jesus still separates people, groups, and perspectives today. His words clarify the truth, break down human traditions, proclaim a higher kingdom, and call people to holiness. People fall into the categories of those who receive him and those who do not.
- The baptism of Jesus in a place in the gospel where we see the presence of all three members of the Trinity. The Father speaks from heaven. The Spirit descends, and the Son is baptized.

Practical application

Can a person know, understand, and experience the presence of God's Holy Spirit? The answer of the New Testament is, "Yes." The Holy Spirit is the way that we know God. God gives the Holy Spirit to those who have faith in Jesus Christ so that he not only is with us but also indwells us. This is the great blessing that Christ brings us and is how, in the new covenant, God puts his laws within us and writes them on our hearts (Jeremiah 31:31-34). It is how the universal experience of God's people is a deep and intimate knowledge of the living God.

What does it mean that Jesus baptizes with the Holy Spirit? We may tend to think of this as an emotional state. A careful consideration yields another definition, however. Being baptized with God's Spirit is not merely an emotional high. Rather, it is when all aspects of our person, such as our minds, hearts, attitudes, words, affections, and actions are devoted to God. To be baptized with the Spirit is for every dimension of our lives to be impacted, influenced, and filled by him.

The Genealogy of Jesus – Luke 3:23-38

JESUS HIMSELF, WHEN HE BEGAN to teach, was about thirty years old, being the son (as was supposed) of Joseph, the son of Heli, the son of Matthat, the son of Levi, the son of Melchi, the son of Jannai, the son of Joseph, the son of Mattathias, the son of Amos, the son of Nahum, the son of Esli, the son of Naggai, the son of Maath, the son of Mattathias, the son of Semein, the son of Joseph, the son of Judah, the son of Joanan, the son of Rhesa, the son of Zerubbabel, the son of Shealtiel, the son of Neri, the son of Melchi, the son of Addi, the son of Cosam, the son of Elmodam, the son of Er, the son of Jose, the son of Eliezer, the son of Jorim, the son of Matthat, the son of Levi, the son of Simeon, the son of Judah, the son of Joseph, the son of Jonan, the son of Eliakim, the son of Melea, the son of Menan, the son of Mattatha, the son of Nathan, the son of David, the son of Jesse, the son of Obed, the son of Boaz, the son of Salmon, the son of Nahshon, the son of Amminadab, the son of Aram, the son of Hezron, the son of Perez, the son of Judah, the son of Jacob, the son of Isaac, the son of Abraham, the son of Terah, the son of Nahor, the son of Serug, the son of Reu, the son of Peleg, the son of Eber, the son of Shelah, the son of Cainan, the son of Arphaxad, the son of Shem, the son of Noah, the son of Lamech, the son of Methuselah, the son of Enoch, the son of Jared, the son of Mahalaleel, the son of Cainan, the son of Enos, the son of Seth, the son of Adam, the son of God.

Genealogies are not very important to most people. We know we come from ancestors, and it is likely that some originally came to this land as immigrants. But determining exactly who they were does not affect our ownership of property, our marriage prospects, or our social status. Knowing about our past may, however, give context to our lives. It may help us to realize that we are the result of a long line of people who engaged in occupations, struggled with problems, and made their way in the world. Some of who we are is because of who they were.

Family heritage was very important to first-century Jews. They kept meticulous records to a degree that would astonish us today. This was not without reason. Every Jew was a part of some tribal family descending from one of the sons of Jacob. It was important to be able to prove one's heritage, especially for members of certain tribes such as Levi. Within tribes, some families had particular privileges and responsibilities, such as the family of Aaron within the line of Levi. Marriages were supposed to be arranged within tribal families to keep property within the clan. One's family heritage was a source of pride and an important piece of information to be passed along to one's descendants. It is no surprise that the genealogy of Jesus would be known and a source of important information to Luke and his readers.

Two gospel accounts contain genealogical information – Matthew and Luke. Their genealogies have similarities and differences. One difference is that Matthew's has fewer generations. That is, there are fewer names listed in his genealogy. Scholars have suggested that he "telescopes" the genealogy and only reports the most important parts. The lineages are not the same. This is because lineages may be traced in several ways and both converge and diverge at some points.

One glaring difference is that the genealogies name different fathers for Joseph, the husband of Mary, to whom Jesus was born. Matthew calls him Jacob and Luke calls him Heli. There are several possible reasons for this. People sometimes had two names. We see this in the Bible in such names as Simon Peter. The scriptures sometimes call him Simon, sometimes Peter, and sometimes Simon Peter. This might have been the case for Joseph's father. We also see an example of this in Mark, who is also called John and John Mark.

It is also possible that something more complicated was involved. If a woman's husband died without leaving a male heir, his brother was required to marry the widow. This was back in the days when more than one wife was allowed. Their firstborn male child was to be counted as belonging to the line of the original husband. It is possible that the first husband of Joseph's mother was not his biological father. One genealogy may use the name of his legal father, the other his biological one.

We might ask why the genealogies trace the line of Jesus through Joseph rather than Mary since none of Joseph's DNA was in him. The answer is that this was how family lines were traced in Judaism at that point. It was through the father's line. That Mary was married to Joseph made Jesus a member of the tribe of Judah, since Joseph was from that tribe. As devout Jews who would have tended to marry within their tribes, Mary was most likely also from the family line of Judah.

Both Matthew's and Luke's genealogies converge to agree that Jesus came through David, from whom the prophets said the Messiah would come. Matthew, however, traces David's line through his son Solomon. Luke traces it through David's son Nathan. Both genealogies converge again at Zerubbabel, the son of Shealtiel, who was the governor of Judea after the return from exile. Since people married within their tribal relatives, genealogical lines converged more often than they do today.

One important thing to note about the genealogies is that while Matthew traces Jesus back to Abraham, Luke goes back to Adam. This is not unexpected. Matthew's audience was primarily Jewish. They would want to know that Jesus could be traced back not only to David but also to Abraham. Luke was writing to a different audience, which was primarily Greek. He thought it more important to trace Jesus back to Adam since Jesus did not come just for the Jews but all people.

Luke reports the age of Jesus as being "about thirty." While family lineage was kept meticulously, exact ages were not. Birthday celebrations are a more recent practice. Most scholars believe the birth of Jesus was about the year 4-5 B.C. This is because we can accurately date the death of King Herod to 4 B.C. We know that Herod was alive when Jesus was born because he would seek his death as a child. If John's ministry began about the years 28-29 A.D. (see page 44), then Jesus would have been about thirty, or just slightly older, at his baptism, which was probably around 28-30 A.D.

Theological insights
- The genealogies in the Bible are another indication of the historical nature of Christianity. It is not just about moral or philosophical ideas but God's revelation of himself in history.
- The apostle Paul will portray Jesus as the new Adam (I Corinthians 15:42-49). Through the original Adam, sin came into the world and with it death. Through Christ, the second Adam, salvation came to the world and brought eternal life.
- The genealogies in Luke and Matthew demonstrate the truth of God's promises. God told David that a descendant of his would sit on the throne of Israel forever. Jesus Christ fulfills that prophecy and the genealogies demonstrate that Jesus was a descendant of David.

Practical application

Many names make up the genealogy of Jesus. Some are recognized and well known, but many are not. This reminds us that God's plan is worked out through many people and over many generations. You do not have to be famous to be important. Those who may not attain fame or reputation still play a part. Only God knows how valuable is each person's contribution. Who knows how we might play a part in God's grand plan if we will faithfully do our part?

LUKE 4

The Temptation of Jesus – Luke 4:1-13

JESUS, FULL OF THE HOLY SPIRIT, returned from the Jordan and was led by the Spirit into the wilderness. For forty days he was tempted by the devil and he ate nothing during that time. Afterward, when they were completed, he was hungry. The devil said to him, "If you are the Son of God, command this stone to become bread." Jesus answered him, saying, "It is written, 'Man shall not live by bread alone, but by every word of God.' "

The devil, leading him up on a high mountain, showed him all the kingdoms of the world in a moment of time. The devil said to him, "I will give you all this authority and their glory, for it has been delivered to me, and I give it to whomever I wish. If you therefore will worship me, it will all be yours." Jesus answered him, "Get behind me, Satan! For it is written, 'You shall worship the Lord your God, and you shall serve him only.' "

He led him to Jerusalem and set him on the pinnacle of the temple, and said to him, "If you are the Son of God, throw yourself down from here, for it is written, 'He will put his angels in charge of you, to guard you;' and, 'On their hands they will bear you up, lest perhaps you dash your foot against a stone.' " Jesus answering, said to him, "It has been said, 'You shall not tempt the Lord your God.' " When the devil had completed every temptation, he departed from him until another time.

It has been said that easy times create weak people, and hard times create strong people. We might expect that, if God sent his Son to live on earth, he would make things easy on him. After all, was it not enough of a sacrifice just to become human? Why make things more difficult? Why make the life of Jesus more difficult than it was already going to be?

We see in the gospels, however, that Jesus did not come to live a life of comfort and leisure. Nor did the Father spare him from the troubles and

55

difficulties of life. In fact, much of his life was more difficult than most of us will ever endure. One such instance is the temptation of Jesus.

The first thing to note about the temptation of Jesus is that it was the Spirit, not the devil, who led him into the wilderness. We might ask what the purpose of such a time of temptation would be. One obvious purpose was for Jesus to resist temptation and demonstrate his ability to do so. The children of Israel had spent forty years in the wilderness, failing repeatedly in their efforts to trust God. Would Jesus be able to do better? He would, passing in forty days the test that the children of Israel could not pass in forty years.

We can also imagine that this was a time of prayer, meditation, and preparation for Jesus' ministry. John the Baptist had heard from God during his time in the wilderness. We assume no less for Jesus. If we ask when Jesus developed his remarkable teachings and parables, one answer is during his time in the wilderness. What better time to thoughtfully consider his ministry, think of practical ways to teach about the kingdom of God, and bring the ways of God to life with everyday illustrations? If we assume that the various parables, lessons, and teachings of Jesus were not merely spontaneous inspirations, we can believe that some of them originated in his time alone with the Father in the wilderness.

It is significant that Jesus spent forty days in the wilderness. In the Bible, the number forty signals testing and trial, such as the forty years the children of Israel spent in the wilderness (Numbers 14:33-34). It signals judgment, as when it rained for forty days and forty nights (Genesis 7:4, 12) and as when God gave Nineveh forty days to repent (Jonah 3:4). It marks a time of preparation, as when Elijah traveled for forty days to hear from God (I Kings 19:8) and when Jesus appeared to the disciples over forty days after his resurrection (Acts 1:3). Forty years also serves to mark the passing of a generation, as when the Israelites wandered forty years until a new generation grew up. In the case of Jesus, the number forty signals a complete period of testing.

Though God tests people for their good as in this instance, the devil seeks to harm and destroy. The devil sought to deter Jesus from his appointed path. Nowhere does the Bible say that Satan is omnipresent. That is, he is not everywhere at the same time, as God is. He works most often in the world through other evil spirits under his command. That Jesus would garner the attention of Satan himself, signals Jesus' great importance. If the devil had not known with certainty who the Messiah was before Jesus' baptism, he did after it.

Both Matthew (Matthew 4:1-11) and Luke record the temptation of Jesus. The three recorded temptations may be illustrative of many temptations during the forty days. Matthew's account switches the order of the second and third temptations.

Theologians have seen various patterns in the temptations:

- Physical needs: Turn stone into bread.
- Power and ambition: Worship Satan in exchange for worldly kingdoms.
- Pride and glory: Prove your identity as the Son of God.

- Lust of the flesh: Satisfy physical hunger.
- Lust of the eyes: Strive after power.
- Pride of life: Seek fame and applause.

- Bread: The children of Israel demanded bread in the desert.
- Idolatry: The children of Israel worshipped a false god, the golden calf.
- Testing God: The children of Israel grumbled and tested God.

- Appetite: Use your power for personal gratification
- Ambition: Gain wealth, power, and control.
- Approval: Receive validation from your heavenly Father.

- Prophet: Perform a miracle for your benefit.
- King: Take worldly power.
- Priest: Demonstrate that you are God's representative.

- Economic: Provide for physical needs miraculously.
- Political: Assert political power.
- Religious: Show the world that you are God's Messiah.

- Obedience: Fail to trust in God.
- Kingship: Seek Lordship over the world in one's own way.
- Messiah: Misuse your role as Messiah for spectacle and glory.

It is interesting to note that the devil used scripture in one of his temptations. This echoes what the serpent did to Eve in the Garden of Eden

(Genesis 3:1-5). As he misrepresented what God said to Adam and Eve, so he did to Jesus in quoting from Psalm 91:11-12. The verses do not promise that God will keep a person from harm, even the Messiah, should he depart from the will of God. They only promise God's provision for those who "hold fast to God in love" (Psalm 91:14). To leap from the temple would have taken Jesus outside the will of God. It would have purposely tested God. To test God is to ask him to give a sign greater than he is pleased to give.

In each case, Jesus responded with scripture. These came from what we might think a relatively obscure part of the Old Testament, the book of Deuteronomy (8:2, 6:13, 6:16), though it would not have been so from a first-century perspective. The book of Deuteronomy recounted and summarized the laws of God to the people. That Jesus quoted from this book not only indicates its importance, but it tells us that Jesus had meditated on and assimilated this book. That he was able to know and use appropriate scriptures in response to the devil's temptations is an indication of how he had given himself to its study.

What secret to resisting temptation do we learn from the example of Jesus? The passage is not given to us to give practical tips for resisting our temptations. Jesus resisted the devil's temptations because he was determined not to stray from his heavenly Father's will. There was no question as to what Jesus would do. He would not give in to Satan. For that reason, the temptations held no power over him. That we are not so committed is why temptations hold power over us.

This period of testing was an important one for Jesus' upcoming ministry. Jesus first had to defeat Satan in his own heart and soul. Only then would he be ready to begin his public ministry. This is the foundation for anyone wishing to engage in ministry with others. The temptation of Jesus in the wilderness showed his honest, pure, and authentic love for the Father's will. It would be the foundation of his ministry and what kept him true to his mission.

Theological insights
- Temptation is a common part of human experience. We should not be surprised by it.
- The Bible portrays the devil as real. We do well not to assume otherwise.
- As with Jesus, Satan tempts people in weak moments.

- Remarkably, Jesus underwent this period of testing without sinning in thought, attitude, word, or action. Consider the difficulties of doing so.
- The knowledge of scripture is a help in temptation, and we should strive to understand, know, and assimilate it into our lives. Jesus himself affirms that it is our spiritual bread and every word of it is worthy of our attention and obedience.

Practical application

The devil's promises to Jesus were lofty. Worship me and I'll give you all the kingdoms of the world! We suspect, however, that the devil was not truthful. Jesus certainly knew that the devil could not be trusted to keep even a single promise. We should understand that Satan tempts us with lofty things that never fulfill their promises. All the world's treasures do not fulfill nor do the many idols we create in our hearts. Only doing the will and purposes of God for our lives brings fulfillment. Jesus understood that there was one good way, and he would not depart from it. His example should give us hope and courage. With his help, we too can find and embrace God's ways, even when we are tempted or fall short.

Jesus Begins His Ministry – Luke 4:14-30

JESUS RETURNED IN THE POWER of the Spirit into Galilee, and news about him spread through all the surrounding area. He taught in their synagogues, being glorified by all.

He came to Nazareth, where he had been brought up. He entered, as was his custom, into the synagogue on the Sabbath day and stood up to read. The book of the prophet Isaiah was handed to him. He opened the book and found the place where it was written, "The Spirit of the Lord is on me, because he has anointed me to preach good news to the poor. He has sent me to heal the broken hearted, to proclaim release to the captives, recovering of sight to the blind, to deliver those who are crushed, and to proclaim the year of the Lord's favor."

He closed the book, gave it back to the attendant, and sat down. The eyes of all in the synagogue were fastened on him. He began to tell them, "Today, this scripture has been fulfilled in your hearing."

All testified about him and wondered at the gracious words which proceeded out of his mouth; and they said, "Isn't this Joseph's son?"

He said to them, "Doubtless you will tell me this proverb, 'Physician, heal yourself!' Whatever we have heard done at Capernaum, do also here in your hometown." He said, "Most certainly I tell you, no prophet is acceptable in his hometown. But truly I tell you, there were many widows in Israel in the days of Elijah, when the sky was shut up three years and six months, when a great famine came over all the land. Elijah was sent to none of them, except to Zarephath, in the land of Sidon, to a woman who was a widow. There were many lepers in Israel in the time of Elisha the prophet, yet not one of them was cleansed, except Naaman, the Syrian."

They were all filled with wrath in the synagogue as they heard these things. They rose up, drove him out of the city, and led him to the brow of the hill that their city was built on, that they might throw him off the cliff. But he, passing through the middle of them, went his way.

Everyone loves success. We love to be appreciated, accepted, and esteemed. The actor basks in the honor of winning the award; the athlete holds up the trophy as the confetti showers down; the commencement speaker smiles and graciously accepts the applause of the graduates. If we are honest, most of us strive to maximize the approval of others and minimize their criticism. It takes a very strong person not to be hurt by criticism.

Would the ministry of Jesus be widely embraced? The answer is both yes and no. It would be embraced by the common people, but rejected by some people and groups. As Luke recounts the beginnings of Jesus' ministry, we see both its embrace and rejection.

Luke records that Jesus began his ministry in the full power of the Holy Spirit. He had completed his time of temptation and reflection in the wilderness. No doubt it took some days to recover his strength after a long fast. Where would Jesus begin his ministry? It was not in the religious center of the nation, Jerusalem, but in Galilee, the region in which he had grown up. He began to preach in the synagogues and word spread about the new preacher in the area. His words were fresh and powerful. He was full of gifts and graces. People universally praised his teaching. As with John the Baptist, here was someone who had heard from God!

We might note that Jesus had the practice of going to the synagogue on the Sabbath day for worship. Synagogues had developed in the intertestamental period in Israel. They were the nation's attempt to teach the laws of God to the people and encourage obedience. The nation had gone into exile because of their disobedience of God's laws. The development of local synagogues was an effort to correct the people's ignorance of the commands, statutes, and precepts of God. Luke notes that Jesus made it a practice to attend Sabbath worship in the synagogues. Interestingly, it would be the synagogues that would become the model of worship for the early church rather than the temple. We might also note that Jesus attended the synagogue even when its people and worship lacked much in terms of their faith and obedience.

When Jesus came to Nazareth, he entered the synagogue and stood up to volunteer to read from scripture. We do not know if the passage he read from Isaiah was the scheduled reading for the day or if Jesus chose it himself. He opened the scroll to Isaiah 61 and read from its opening verses. Jesus' hearers would have understood those verses as Messianic. They were about the day of God's coming and about one upon whom God's Spirit would rest. God's appointed messenger would bring good news to the poor, bind up the brokenhearted, proclaim liberty to the captives, and declare the year of the Lord's favor. In addition, though Jesus did not apparently complete the reading, it would be a time of God's vengeance on all those who stood outside his grace. When he had finished reading, Jesus made a bold affirmation to the people gathered in the synagogue. "Today, this scripture has been fulfilled in your hearing." Luke says that the people marveled at the gracious words that he spoke.

There is an interesting textual issue in this passage. If you read Isaiah 61:1, 2 in your Bible today, it does not include a phrase that Jesus used. Luke records that when Jesus read from Isaiah, it included the promise of the "recovering of sight to the blind." That is because Jesus apparently read from the Greek version of Isaiah, called the Septuagint. The Septuagint's version includes the phrase whereas the Hebrew version does not.

The Hebrew Old Testament was translated into Greek in Alexandria in the third century B.C. Alexandria was a center of learning and also the home of a large Jewish population. Because Greek was the language of the empire and fewer and fewer people spoke and read classical Hebrew, the Greek version was widely used. It was apparently even used in the synagogue in Nazareth at the time of Jesus. There are a few places where the Septuagint differs slightly from the Hebrew versions. This is one of them. The differences reveal some variety in ancient Hebrew manuscript traditions. The translators of the Septuagint obviously thought that they were using the most reliable versions. Scholars today believe that our Hebrew versions of the Old Testament to be closer to the original than the Septuagint version, and almost all translations follow it. A close examination of New Testament quotations from the Old Testament reveals the widespread use of the Septuagint (Matthew 1:23, 12:21, Romans 3:10-18, 9:33, Hebrews 1:6, 10:5-7, Acts 7:14, Revelation 2:27). We see that, in several instances, Jesus uses the Septuagint when he quotes from the Old Testament (Matthew 4:4, 21:5, Luke 8:10).

Jesus' visit to his hometown of Nazareth would not be a joyous one, however. Jesus seems to go out of his way to insult the people gathered in the synagogue. We might ask why he did so. It seems that he chose to expose their lack of real faith, rather than allow them to assume they would receive some preferential treatment, in God's eyes, since they had known him from his youth. We can imagine some local pride. "We knew Jesus as a boy," some would say. "My daughter used to babysit Jesus." "I know his mother and father well." This did not constitute true faith, however.

It was this familiarity that was a hindrance to their true faith because beneath it was skepticism. That they had known Jesus as a youth increased their suspicion that he could not be the Messiah. The words of Jesus reminded the people of instances in the Old Testament (I Kings 17:7-16, II Kings 5:1-19) where God responded to the faith of outsiders rather than people in Israel. These were instances that highlighted the lack of faith in the nation. It was a way of saying to the people of Nazareth that Jesus knew they did not have authentic faith. Others, however, would believe, even if they did not.

The geographical details of the story are correct. There is a cliff on the outskirts of the town of Nazareth that would have served as a place from which a person might be thrown. The sting of the insult infuriated the people, and they intended to throw Jesus off. The cliff is some distance from where archeologists believe the synagogue was in the first century. Perhaps by the time they reached it, their ardor had cooled. Whatever the case, when they arrived, Jesus turned and walked through the middle of the crowd. We can imagine it parting as he did. He went on his way to continue his ministry.

We can imagine that Jesus' family was in the synagogue on that day. The incident must have disturbed, embarrassed, and frightened them. It may have been a part of their growing anxiety about the way Jesus was going about his ministry. We will see evidence of this anxiety as the account of his life continues.

Theological insights

- Even though the place we worship may be lacking in terms of its fellowship and purity, it is better to attend regularly than not attend at all.
- The applause of others is not always evidence that one is doing God's will.
- Jesus was not impressed by the approval of others and did not seek it for its own sake. This also characterized the life and ministry of John the Baptist.
- Jesus was full of both grace and truth. He spoke the truth, even when it was not well received.
- A person's ministry may not be appreciated by those closest to them. Others may see its value more clearly.

Practical application

There is great power in the gospel. The apostle Paul says that the gospel is the "power of God for salvation" (Romans 1:16). What power does the gospel have? In the words of Jesus, it is good news for the poor, healing for the brokenhearted, freedom for the captives, sight for the blind, and deliverance for those crushed by life's burdens. The gospel proclaims the acceptable year of the Lord, in which all who wish to come are invited, welcomed, and received. In the gospel, there is great freedom of spirit, mind, and heart. The gospel sets us free to love truly, give generously, live worthily, and serve eagerly. It gives us the grace to live out our potential to the fullest. This is good news, and it is the message the church is given to share.

Jesus Preaches and Heals – Luke 4:31-44

HE CAME DOWN TO CAPERNAUM, a city of Galilee. He was teaching them on the Sabbath day, and they were astonished at his teaching, for his word had authority. In the synagogue there was a man who had an unclean spirit. He cried out with a loud voice, saying, "Ah! What have we to do with you, Jesus of Nazareth? Have you come to destroy us? I know who you are: the Holy One of God!"

Jesus rebuked him, saying, "Be silent and come out of him!" When the demon had thrown him down in the middle of them, he came out of him, having done him no harm.

Amazement came on all and they spoke together, one with another, saying, "What is this word? For with authority and power he commands the unclean spirits, and they come out!" News about him went out into every place of the surrounding region.

He rose up from the synagogue and entered into Simon's house. Simon's mother-in-law was ill with a high fever, and they begged him to help her. He stood over her and rebuked the fever, and it left her. Immediately she rose up and served them. When the sun was setting, all those who had any who were sick with various diseases brought them to him; and he laid his hands on every one of them, and healed them. Demons also came out of many, crying out and saying, "You are the Christ, the Son of God!" But he rebuked them and did not allow them to speak, because they knew that he was the Christ.

When it was day, he departed and went into an uninhabited place and the multitudes looked for him. They came to him, and held on to him, so that he would not go away from them. But he said to them, "I must preach the good news of God's Kingdom to the other cities also. This is the reason that I have been sent." He went about preaching in the synagogues of Galilee.

Some events attract crowds. It may be a football game in a college town, or Christmas season in the shopping district, a popular singer's concert, or move-in day on a college campus. People who live in the town often avoid going out on days when they know the crowds and traffic will be heavy.

One thing we see in the gospels is that Jesus attracted crowds. This is not surprising. News of his teaching abilities and particularly his healings spread rapidly. We can understand that those with ailments or those whose family members were sick could not wait to get to where Jesus was.

If we ask where Jesus lived during his ministry, the answer seems to be the town of Capernaum. It was a fishing village on the northern side of the Sea of Galilee. Jesus did not own a home there, nor did his family, who lived in Nazareth. Several of the disciples did, however, and Jesus appears to have stayed with them when he was in town. Simon Peter owned a home there, and it was the location of several miracles by Jesus.

Luke records that after his encounter with the people in Nazareth, Jesus went down to Capernaum, which is in the region of Galilee. Israel in those days was divided into three major sections. There was the region associated with the tribe of Judah in the south. This was where the capital city of Jerusalem was located. In the middle of the country was the region of Samaria. This was the region of the old northern kingdom of Israel and was still considered mostly apostate by religious Jews. In the north was the region of Galilee. Its defining landmark was the Sea of Galilee, a large lake that is thirteen miles long by eight miles wide. Capernaum, located on this lake, was the home base for the fishing business of Simon and Andrew, and James, John, and their father Zebedee. That Jesus went *down* from Nazareth is a reference to its higher elevation compared to Capernaum.

Luke reports that Jesus' reputation continued to grow. His teachings were astonishing to the crowds. Luke also reports some especially striking healings. People brought to Jesus friends and family in great distress. Whether it would have been known that the people were possessed by demons is unclear. When the demons encountered Jesus, however, they had vocal reactions. In one instance the demon recognized Jesus as the "Holy One of God" and in another instance as the "Christ" and the "Son of God." The first to recognize Jesus' true identity were not people but unclean spirits.

Why did Jesus not allow them to speak? Why not let them proclaim his Messianic identity? We will see in the ministry of Jesus as recorded by Luke that Jesus is very cautious about publically proclaiming his Messianic identity. He let people experience him and decide for themselves. It would not be his self-proclamation that would finally identify him as the Son of God but his crucifixion and resurrection. Though Jesus slowly helped the disciples understand his identity, it would only be after his ascension and the coming of the Holy Spirit that the church would fully comprehend.

It is also important to note the authority of Jesus' word. Exorcising the demons did not require an elaborate ritual, only his command. His words, as observed by the people, had authority. In addition, he was able to heal everyone who came to him no matter how difficult their infirmity or ailment. There was no instance beyond his capability.

Interestingly, three gospels record the miracle of the healing of Simon's mother-in-law. Compared to other more spectacular miracles, it would seem fairly pedestrian. It does show the power of Jesus' healing ministry, however. We see it in that Peter's mother-in-law was immediately able to get up and serve them. We usually recover from an illness slowly. That is not the case in this instance.

This is the first time that Simon, who is Simon Peter, is mentioned in the gospel of Luke. We learn from this account that he is married. We also see the hospitality of his family, inviting Jesus into his home. Whereas there are instances in the gospels where illness seems related to the work of the devil (Luke 8:26-39, 13:16), in this instance she merely seems to have been sick. Her illness became the occasion of a miracle by Jesus.

We might imagine that Jesus would wish to stay in a place where he was experiencing such success. After all, his visit to Nazareth had been less than affirming. The next day, however, Jesus was not to be found. Mark reports a detail not included in Luke, that he had gone out early to pray (Mark 1:35-39). When the people wanted him to stay, Jesus explained that he had a mission to accomplish. As the good news had been preached to them, it must also be preached to other towns. He began to travel around the countryside preaching and healing.

There is debate about the hometown of Peter and his brother Andrew. The gospel of John identifies it as Bethsaida (John 1:44). The gospel of Luke says that Jesus entered Simon's house in Capernaum. The two villages are not far from one another – about six miles – on the northern part of the Sea of Galilee. It is possible that Simon and his brother were born in Bethsaida but eventually moved to the larger town of Capernaum as their fishing business grew.

Archeologists today believe they can identify the house of Peter in the ancient city of Capernaum. This is because there is a place in the ruins of the ancient city where a church was erected over the site of an individual home. What site would early Christians have chosen for the church in that town? There is no more likely place than Peter's house. The archeological site is an ancient home that was enlarged over the centuries to hold a congregation of people. Today pilgrims can visit the site. It is fascinating to imagine the home in which Peter lived, in which Jesus healed many people, and which Jesus considered his home base for ministry.

Theological insights

- Rabbis in the time of Jesus merely summarized the opinions of others. The teachings of Jesus were fresh and powerful. The people marveled at the wisdom and authority with which Jesus taught.
- The gospels are full of accounts of Jesus' encounters with demons. His ministry was an attack on the forces of Satan over which he demonstrated authority and power.
- Luke describes the demonic spirits as "unclean." This is in contrast to the purity of Jesus who was the "Holy One of God." The demons recognized a time of judgment coming upon them.
- Jesus healed with the power of his word. Just as God created all things by speaking them into existence (Genesis 1:3), so at the command of Jesus, healings and miracles took place.
- Luke, as a physician, takes note of the physical circumstances of the people's exorcisms. The demons left violently but did the people no harm.

Practical application

In this section, Luke summarizes the early period in which Jesus taught and healed. The book of Acts (10:38) says that Jesus went about "doing good and healing all who were oppressed by the devil." He did good in every place he went and in every circumstance in which he found himself. He also gave attention to his relationship with God, seeking him in prayer before the day began. The example of Jesus reminds us that we too have the opportunity to do good in the various circumstances of our lives. We meet people every day and have numerous opportunities to extend grace, show kindness, and represent Christ. We see that the power of Jesus was not in his earthly possessions; he did not even own a home. Rather it was in the presence of God that rested on him. We too have the opportunity to walk in God's presence and share his love with others. We too have authority from God to do good wherever we are.

LUKE 5

Jesus Calls the Disciples – Luke 5:1-11

NOW WHILE THE MULTITUDE pressed around him to hear the word of God, he was standing by the lake of Gennesaret. He saw two boats on the shore of the lake, but the fishermen had gone out of them and were washing their nets. He entered into one of the boats, which was Simon's, and asked him to put out a little from the land. He sat down and taught the multitudes from the boat.

When he had finished speaking, he said to Simon, "Put out into the deep and let down your nets for a catch." Simon answered him, "Master, we worked all night and caught nothing; but at your word I will let down the nets." When they had done so, they caught a great multitude of fish, and their nets were breaking. They signaled to their partners in the other boat to come and help them. They came and filled both boats, so that they began to sink.

But Simon Peter, when he saw it, fell down at Jesus' knees, saying, "Depart from me, for I am a sinful man, Lord." For he was amazed, and all who were with him, at the catch of fish they had taken; and so also were James and John, sons of Zebedee, who were partners with Simon. Jesus said to Simon, "Do not be afraid. From now on you will be catching people." When they had brought their boats to land, they left everything, and followed him.

If you have spent much time on a lake, you know that sound carries. One wonders why boaters on the lake are shouting so loudly since you can hear their every word. They are not shouting, of course. It is just that sound carries over water. This fact plays an important role in this account in the gospel of Luke.

One day the crowds pressed in on Jesus while he taught along the shore of the Sea of Galilee. Luke calls it the Lake of Genessaret. The New Testament uses three names to describe this large lake. The most common is the Sea of Galilee. This takes its name from the region, Galilee, in which the lake is located. Another name is the Sea of Tiberias, named after the city of Tiberias built by Herod Antipas in honor of the Roman Emperor by that name. It was the largest city on the lake, the capital city of the region, and located on its western side. The term Genessaret came from the fertile agricultural region located to the west of the lake.

Luke has already noted the large crowds that attended Jesus. On the particular occasion, because of the press of the crowd, Jesus got into a fishing boat pulled up on shore. While this might appear to be a random event, we will see that it was not. Jesus seems to have intentionally selected Simon's boat. After Simon had pushed out from the shore, Jesus taught the people, the water providing both protection from the press of the crowd and natural amplification.

What happened after Jesus finished teaching must have surprised Simon. He and his brother had fished all night, along with their fishing partners, James and John. Nighttime fishing was a customary practice for Galilean fishermen as it typically brought in the most fish. Simon must have winced when Jesus asked him to put out in the deep part of the lake for a catch. We might imagine that Peter frowned inside even if he did not show it. He was a fisherman and had been one all his life. That Jesus wanted to go fishing that morning must have seemed inconvenient for someone who knew that the fish were not biting. To Simon's credit, he did as Jesus requested. We might note the confidence in Jesus' words. They were to put out for a "catch."

That is what they got. When they pulled the nets in, they were so full that they had to call their fishing partners James and John. Even so, the fish filled both boats to the point of sinking. We can imagine that this had never happened in their extensive experience. Luke says that they were amazed at the number of fish in the net.

What happened next gives us a poignant and winsome view of Simon Peter. We see his honesty and his authenticity. He does not hide his amazement. He also recognizes that Jesus seemed to keep showing up where he was. What did Jesus want with him? Did he not know that he was only a common fisherman? What use could he possibly be to him? In a wonderfully honest moment, Simon humbles himself. "What do you want with me, Lord? Don't you know what a sinful man I am?" The reply of Jesus is full of grace. "Do not be afraid. From now on you will be catching people." Luke records that when they brought the boats ashore, they left everything and followed Jesus.

The gospels of Matthew and Mark tell the account of the call of the first disciples very succinctly (Matthew 4:18-22, Mark 1:16-20). Jesus simply walks up to their boats and calls them to follow him. Luke's gospel gives us more context. Simon and his partners would have listened to Jesus as he taught from the boat. Luke records the incident of the large catch of fish as the prelude to the disciples' calls. The gospel of John records an encounter between Jesus and Simon that came before Simon's official call (John 1:35-42). This is to say that the call to the disciples does not take place in a vacuum.

It is interesting that in Matthew and Mark, Jesus heals Simon's mother-in-law *after* he has called Simon to become a disciple (Matthew 8:14-17, Mark 1:29-31). In Luke, the healing takes place before Simon's call (Luke 4:38-39). While, in Luke, the healing serves as further context for Simon's call to discipleship, we would assume that Matthew's and Mark's accounts have greater eyewitness credibility and should be preferred. All the accounts indicate that the healing takes place early in the ministry of Jesus around the time of the call of the disciples.

The words of Jesus to the disciples are prophetic and intriguing. "From now on I will teach you to fish for people." Simon knew a great deal about fishing. He knew the fish did not always bite. He knew you had to go where the fish were. He knew you have to be diligent and crafty to bring in a good catch. These skills were not going to help Simon catch people, however. This he would have to learn from Jesus over the next years. The words of Jesus give an indication, however, of what Simon would help the early church learn to do. They would be in the business of catching people. It is the business of the church in all eras, to cast wide its net and catch people for salvation and the kingdom of God.

Theological insights
- The choice of disciples was not accidental. If we think about the attributes of people like Simon, they were hardworking people who had common sense and the ability to relate to others. These would prove very useful in their future ministries.
- Jesus did not look for perfect disciples. He looked for honest people without pretension. He knew he would mold them into what they needed to be.
- Jesus modeled catching people in his interactions with Simon and his friends. He "fished" for them until he successfully "caught" them.

- The promise of Jesus to the church is that he will enable it to "catch people." The church should not be discouraged when the fishing does not seem good. It is not merely our ability that matters but the promise, presence, and call of the Master. He is the One who enables the catch.

Practical application

We should note that the call of Jesus to the disciples was absolute. Though Luke's account does not specifically include the words "Follow me," we know from the other gospels that this call was issued. It was a call to complete and total obedience. Jesus did not negotiate with them nor did he explain the implications of his call. He did not seek to persuade them. He did not ask what objections they might have. It was a call that had divine authority; it came from God, as did the calls of the prophets in the Old Testament. Such calls are rejected at one's peril.

When Christ calls a person, it is a divine call. Most people are not called to leave their occupations, as were Simon and his friends. The call of Christ is absolute for everyone, however. Nothing can come before it. Nothing supersedes it. Nothing takes priority over it, for Christ is God and God's call is always to place him first. That was the first of the Ten Commandments in the Old Testament, to have no other god before the one true God. The same is true in the New Testament; nothing comes before God. The call of Christ takes preeminence.

Jesus Cleanses a Leper – Luke 5:12-16

WHILE HE WAS IN ONE OF the cities, behold, there was a man full of leprosy. When he saw Jesus, he fell on his face and begged him, saying, "Lord, if you are willing, you can make me clean." He stretched out his hand and touched him, saying, "I am willing. Be made clean."

Immediately the leprosy left him. He commanded him to tell no one, "But go your way and show yourself to the priest, and make the offering for your cleansing that Moses commanded, as a testimony to them."

But the report concerning him spread even more, and great multitudes came to hear and to be healed by him of their illnesses. But he often withdrew into the wilderness and prayed.

One of the great benefits of modern society is the advancement of medical science. When we come down with some illness or disease, we can be reasonably confident that some form of treatment is available – if not a complete cure then at least something to manage the condition. In the first century, there were many diseases with no cure. One of the worst was leprosy.

Leprosy is a skin disease. Today we know that it is caused by a bacterial infection. The infection leads to damage to the skin, nerves, and eyes. The damage to the nerves can lead to loss of feeling in one's extremities, which can lead to injuries and infections. Our modern understanding of the disease only came about in the 20th century with effective treatments only appearing in the second half of the century. There are about 200,000 cases of leprosy in the world today.

The book of Leviticus, in the Old Testament, gives instructions for a person suspected of having leprosy (Leviticus 13, 14). There are procedures for examining a person suspected of leprosy and declaring them either clean or unclean. There are also prescribed offerings for anyone who was declared clean from leprosy. In all the Old Testament, no one was ever cured of leprosy, except for Naaman, the Syrian (II Kings 5), whom Jesus referenced in his speech in the synagogue in Nazareth, and Mariam, the sister of Moses (Numbers 12:1-16).

In addition to serious physical problems, leprosy created another problem. It isolated a person from others, including their family. Lepers could not live among ordinary people; they had to live outside the camp or the city. This was because of the contagion risks associated with leprosy. They were also not allowed into the temple for the worship of the people. Nor would they have been allowed in the synagogue. To come down with leprosy was a deadly sentence that drove a person away from those he or she loved. It also drove them away from the worship life of the people.

Luke records an incident in which Jesus met a leper. As far as we can tell, this was a chance encounter not instigated either by Jesus or the leper. From what Luke reports, however, the leper had heard about Jesus, for he came to him with faith. "If you are willing, you can make me clean."

Why, in the man's mind, might Jesus have not been willing? There might have been several reasons. Perhaps Jesus was too busy. Perhaps lepers were not important enough for his attention. Perhaps Jesus would not find the man worthy. The man seemed sure, however, that Jesus had the power. The question was, "Would Jesus be willing?"

Jesus responded to the man's faith and did so quickly. There was no doubt that Jesus was willing. "I am willing," Jesus replied simply. With that, he commanded that the man become clean, and it was so. We can imagine the surprise on the faces of the people around the man. How, they must have wondered, can such disfigured skin become perfect? Even now leprosy does not heal quickly but only over many months. It was a remarkable miracle and one that the church remembered. To make it even more memorable, Jesus reached out and touched the leprous man. Since no one touched a leper, we can imagine that he had not experienced human touch in quite some time. Jesus' touch must have felt like the touch of God's hand. Jesus instructed him not to tell anyone but to offer the required sacrifice as a testimony of Jesus' power to the priests. Yet as much as Jesus sought to keep the publicity down, the word about him spread. As Jesus continued through the countryside, the crowds got larger and larger.

It has been noted that leprosy is, on a physical level, much like sin on the spiritual level. Leprosy is terminal and progressive. It disfigures and isolates. This is what sin does. It does not stay the same but grows worse. It ultimately ruins our relationships with others, God, and ourselves. It deforms us in spirit and separates us from God. Like the leper, we need the touch of Jesus to be cured of our sins.

Theological insights
- Luke notes that the man was "full of leprosy." That is, the disease was at an advanced stage. This highlights the power of Jesus for what would have been considered a "difficult case."
- Just as leprosy can be in its beginning or advanced stages, so can sin. While no one is without sin, those who allow it free reign become full of deceit, corruption, spiritual disease, and shame. This is why Paul encourages us not to let sin reign in our mortal bodies (Romans 6:12).
- We sometimes underestimate the power of touch. Human touch is a way of communicating kindness, concern, and care. Families should especially be intentional about extending physical touch.

- The offering to the priest and the priest's declaration of his cleansing would have allowed him to reintegrate into society. We can imagine the great joy of the healed leper.
- Jesus did not seek popularity but to fulfill the mission the Father had given him. It is a pattern in the gospels that Jesus did not seek the limelight, but people could not stop spreading the word.

Practical application

Where did the power come from for such miraculous healings? It came from Jesus' life of prayer. Luke reports that as the crowds grew, he was constantly drawing away to lonely places where he could commune with his heavenly Father. Jesus gives us a good example to follow. Our strength is not in ourselves but in God. The more we get away to pray, the more learn to hear his voice. If Jesus was not too busy to pray, we should not be either. God will also meet with us if we will allow him time to do so.

Jesus Heals a Paralytic – Luke 5:17-26

ON ONE OF THOSE DAYS, as he was teaching, Pharisees and teachers of the law were sitting there who had come out of every village of Galilee, Judea, and Jerusalem. The power of the Lord was with him to heal.

Behold, men brought a paralyzed man on a cot, and they sought to bring him in to lay before Jesus. Not finding a way to bring him in because of the multitude, they went up to the housetop and let him down through the tiles on his cot into the middle before Jesus. Seeing their faith, he said to him, "Man, your sins are forgiven you."

The scribes and the Pharisees began to reason, saying, "Who is this who speaks blasphemies? Who can forgive sins, but God alone?" But Jesus, perceiving their thoughts, answered them, "Why are you reasoning so in your hearts? Which is easier to say, 'Your sins are forgiven you,' or to say, 'Arise and walk'? But that you may know that the Son of Man has authority on earth to forgive sins," he said to the paralyzed man, "I tell you, get up, take up your cot, and go home."

Immediately he rose up before them, and took what he had been lying on, and departed to his home, glorifying God. Amazement took hold of everyone, and they glorified God. They were filled with fear, saying, "We have seen extraordinary things today."

This story introduces a group for the first time in Luke's gospel. This is the first mention of the Pharisees in Luke. The Pharisees were a religious group dedicated to the observance of the Jewish Law. They believed that the fate of the nation depended on its obedience to the laws of God. It was the nation's disobedience that had sent them into exile. The Pharisees had arisen out of the nation's desire to teach and keep God's laws. The Jewish historian Josephus said that they were highly respected by the people.

It is not surprising, therefore, that Jesus and his teachings would give them reason for investigation. They believed themselves to be the chief authorities of the Jewish law. Since Jesus was teaching and drawing great crowds, they wanted to know if his teachings were in line with theirs. We will discover that Jesus will find himself in conflict with them on numerous occasions. Luke says that a group of Pharisees and teachers of the law had come from all over the countryside and even Jerusalem to see what this new teacher was about.

In addition to introducing the Pharisees, this account introduces a new term, the "Son of Man." Jesus refers to himself as the Son of Man. This is an intriguing term that has several meanings. It seems to have been a way for Jesus to emphasize his humanity. He was a human being and a descendant of human beings. The term Son of Man identifies Jesus with humankind. Luke's gospel will show throughout that Jesus was indeed human. It will also show him as much more.

The phrase, Son of Man, also connected Jesus with the Old Testament in a way that the Pharisees would have recognized, even if others did not. The Old Testament prophet Daniel had a vision of God in his heavenly glory, as recorded in Daniel, chapter 7. As part of the vision, there appeared one "like a son of man." Daniel says:

"... and behold, there came with the clouds of the sky one like a son of man, and he came to the Ancient of Days, and they brought him near before him. Dominion was given him, and glory, and a kingdom, that all the peoples, nations, and languages should serve him. His dominion is an everlasting dominion, which will not pass away, and his kingdom one that will not be destroyed." (Daniel 7:13-14)

In Daniel's prophecy, this heavenly figure who was given an everlasting kingdom was also deeply connected to humanity. Therefore he was a "son of man." Yet he was given a kingdom that would not be destroyed. To astute biblical scholars of the first century, this was certainly a Messianic prophecy. The Pharisees would have found it highly suspicious of Jesus to use the term about himself.

The account of the healing of the paralyzed man is an important one for several reasons. It is, first of all, an account of faith. Because the crowd packed the house where Jesus was, it was impossible to get the paralyzed man to Jesus. His friends decided to lower him through the roof right in front of Jesus. Luke does not indicate the man's age. In Mark's account (Mark 2:1-12), however, Jesus refers to him as "My son," indicating that he might have been a young person. The audacity of lowering him through the roof sounds like something an enthusiastic group of young men would do. Roofs were typically thatched or tiled, so it would not have been overly difficult to remove a section to lower the man through the rafters. Jesus will commend them for their faith. It says that he spoke to the man on the cot when he saw the faith of his friends. We can imagine that it also took faith for the man to allow his friends to lower him, an adventure that must have been precarious.

The man wanted to be healed of his paralysis. Before he healed him, however, Jesus extended him a word of grace. "Your sins are forgiven you." Jesus extended spiritual healing to go along with the man's physical healing. Jesus came to heal the whole person, and we see that illustrated in this incident. We should see the statement of Jesus as addressed to us. All those who believe in Jesus will be forgiven their sins and reconciled to God.

The statement by Jesus raised the anxieties of the religious leaders. They rightly understood that only God can forgive sins. Who was Jesus to think he had that authority? The question Jesus posed to the religious leaders might be answered in a couple of ways. Which was harder, to forgive a person's sins or to heal him? It would be harder to actually forgive someone's sins. One might *say* so but to *do* so was impossible for an ordinary human being, as the Pharisees rightly understood. It was also hard, in fact impossible, to heal a paralyzed person, at least for anyone other than Jesus. Jesus uses the moment to demonstrate his spiritual authority by exercising his healing abilities. He commanded the man to walk, which he did to the astonishment of the crowd. In doing so he declared his divine right and authority to forgive sins as well.

Jesus' ministry continues to reveal aspects of his person and mission. This incident makes an audacious claim about the person of Jesus. He has prerogatives that only belong to God, such as the authority to forgive sins. Luke says that the crowd was amazed at what they were seeing. The young man went home praising God. Jesus continued to do remarkable things, and everyone but the religious leaders was excited about him.

We continue to learn more about the person of Jesus. Not only could he cast out demons, heal the sick, and teach with authority. He also had the authority to forgive sins. We continue to see, in the Gospel of Luke, Jesus' divine person revealed.

Theological insights
- Though they started with good intentions, the Pharisees had become rigid and legalistic in their approach to God. Their lack of appreciation of the healing ministry of Jesus was one evidence of a moral corruption that robbed them of ordinary human compassion.
- Roofs could typically be removed and then repaired, without damage. Jesus recognized and rewarded the determination and ingenuity of the friends.
- Luke says that Jesus spoke to the man when he saw the faith of his friends (Luke 5:20). As Jesus responded to the "intercession" of his friends for the paralyzed man, we should assume that he responds to our prayers for others. The account is an encouragement to pray for others, labor to bring them to Christ, and work for their healing.
- Every sinful and sick person needs intercessors who will bring them before God in prayer.
- There is no indication in the passage that the man's sins were the cause of his paralysis. As everyone needs forgiveness, so did he.
- To blaspheme God was a capital offense in Judaism. The assertion by Jesus that he had the authority to forgive sins would have been blasphemous to the religious leaders. They were right except that Jesus, as the Son of God, did have the authority to forgive sins.

Practical application
What is our greatest need? We might answer that it is a financial, material, physical, or social need. This account offers a different answer. In

reality, our most urgent need is forgiveness for our sins. If we have all the riches and success one can have but are not justified before God, our achievements are only temporary.

The Pharisees trusted that their own good deeds were sufficient for salvation. For that reason, their trust was in themselves, not God. The good news of the gospel is that Jesus offers us forgiveness for our sins apart from our good works. Nothing we can do merits salvation. How then can we be saved? We are saved by the unmerited grace of Christ who takes away our guilt, removes our shame, and makes us acceptable in God's sight. This is the wonderful good news of the Christian faith.

The Call of Levi – Luke 5:27-39

AFTER THESE THINGS he went out and saw a tax collector named Levi sitting at the tax booth, and said to him, "Follow me!" He left everything, and rose up and followed him. Levi made a great feast for him in his house. There was a great crowd of tax collectors and others who were reclining with them.

The scribes and the Pharisees murmured against his disciples, saying, "Why do you eat and drink with the tax collectors and sinners?" Jesus answered them, "Those who are healthy have no need for a physician, but those who are sick do. I have not come to call the righteous, but sinners, to repentance."

They said to him, "Why do John's disciples often fast and pray, likewise also the disciples of the Pharisees, but yours eat and drink?" He said to them, "Can you make the friends of the bridegroom fast while the bridegroom is with them? But the days will come when the bridegroom will be taken away from them. Then they will fast in those days."

He also told a parable to them. "No one puts a piece from a new garment on an old garment, or else he will tear the new, and also the piece from the new will not match the old. No one puts new wine into old wine skins, or else the new wine will burst the skins, and it will be spilled and the skins will be destroyed. But new wine must be put into fresh wine skins, and both are preserved. No one having drunk old wine immediately desires new, for he says, 'The old is better.' "

Change is difficult. We grow accustomed to certain routines and often prefer things to remain the same. This is especially true when it comes to significant areas of life – family dynamics, religious practices, learning new technology, or adjusting to a new boss at work. Change can unsettle our sense of security, disrupt our identity, and push us out of our comfort zones.

What changes would the appearance of the Messiah bring to Judaism and its practices? Most people expected it to be more of what they had seen in the past, more military victories, more national prosperity, and more independence. Little did they understand how radical would be the mission and program of Jesus.

One place we see the radical nature of Jesus' mission had to do with those he called as disciples. In Luke we have already seen Jesus call common, supposedly non-religious people to follow him. Simon, Andrew, James, and John were not on anyone's list of likely candidates for disciples of the Messiah. In this incident, Jesus called another unlikely person, a tax collector named Levi.

Taxes were collected by both the Romans and Herod. The Jews who helped facilitate their collection were not looked on favorably. They were seen as traitors because they helped the Gentiles, in the case of Rome, take away their livelihoods for their pagan purposes. Because the tax collectors had to interact with Gentiles, they were seen as ritually unclean. It was also widely known that they padded the amount they collected to live in luxury. A tax collector would have been the last person anyone would expect the Messiah to call as a disciple.

The name Levi makes us think that this tax collector was a member of the tribe by that name. The Levites were dedicated to the service of the temple. If Levi had come from that tribe, it would have made his occupation an act of betrayal, not just against the nation but also against God. He had forsaken his God-given calling for the sake of money.

Levi is also traditionally understood to be Matthew, as that is what he is called in the Gospel of Matthew. As with others in the New Testament, he seems to have gone by several names, like Simon who was also called Peter; Saul, also called Paul; John, also called Mark; and Nathanael, also called Bartholomew.

Luke gave his readers some background to the call of Simon at the first of this chapter (Luke 5:1-11). He gives no such context in the instance of Levi. We might wonder what interactions Levi had with Jesus before his call. We would imagine that he had listened to him preach. Perhaps he had witnessed healings. We do not know for certain. What we suspect is that Levi was dissatisfied with his life. There was a hole in his spirit that material wealth did not fill. When Jesus called him, his heart was open. He got up from his tax booth to follow Jesus. We can also assume that Levi was social by nature. His first reaction was to throw a grand party for Jesus. He invited his friends, who were other tax collectors, to meet Jesus now that he had been befriended by him.

We learn something about the mission and strategy of Jesus in this account. The Pharisees were already deciding that they did not like Jesus or his approach to religious faith. They did not complain against Jesus, however, but his disciples. "Why do you eat with tax collectors and sinners?" Jesus responded on their behalf. It was not the healthy who needed a physician but the sick. Then Jesus gave a clear articulation of his mission. He had come to call sinners to repentance. If he was going to do so, he must spend time among them.

This led the Pharisees to express another concern. John the Baptist had taught his disciples to fast as a way to strengthen their faith. The Pharisees did not like John or approve of his ministry, but it helped them make the point. The Pharisees also taught people to fast. Why did Jesus and his disciples always appear to be having a party, eating and drinking? The response of Jesus was cryptic but gave a hint of his identity. You do not fast when the bridegroom arrives. That is the time for celebration. Then Jesus indicated that a time for fasting would come when the bridegroom was taken away. From our perspective, his words are clear. Jesus was the bridegroom God had sent, but only for a while. When he went back to the Father, the church would indeed fast and pray.

Jesus then told a parable about the nature of God's kingdom. Those who did not like change would find it uncomfortable, at least at first. Just as you did not put new material on an old garment or put new wine into old wineskins, the kingdom of the Messiah would need new structures and forms. Little did people understand just how new the wineskins of Jesus would be. To some, he would appear to be overturning many sacred traditions and laws. It would be hard for the religiously trained to understand that the Old Testament was preparation for the Messiah's coming. Once he came, many of its practices would no longer be needed. Jesus also noted how hard change was. Many, he noted, would prefer the old ways. That would not stop him, however, from teaching and proclaiming the new thing God was doing. It would be much bigger and more expansive than anyone had imagined.

Theological insights
- As with the calls to Simon and his friends at the beginning of this chapter, the call to Levi had divine authority. Levi heard it as a call from God. To his credit, he responded with complete obedience.
- The joy of the feast in Levi's home is contrasted with the criticism of the scribes and Pharisees. Ironically, those who should have embraced Jesus were the most unwilling to do so.
- The Jews were obsessed with ritual purity, one part of which was separation from sinners. Jesus is going to institute a new definition of purity. It has less to do with one's associations and more to do with attitudes of the heart. By this definition, the religious leaders will be exposed as the most impure and unholy.
- Jesus' words teach that repentance is a requirement of spiritual health. Because they did not see themselves as spiritually sick, repentance was not something the scribes and Pharisees were inclined to do.

Practical application

The kingdom of God, as Jesus taught it, was indeed new. We can understand how those trained in the ways of the old covenant would find his ways difficult to accept. It was perhaps the reason Jesus called his disciples from outside the religious community.

From our perspective, we recognize that the Old Testament was preparation for the coming of Christ. The book of Hebrews calls its laws a "shadow" of things to come (Hebrews 10:1). Jesus would emphasize love over legalism, forgiveness over retribution, peace over war, and the heart over external duty. We are grateful for the new vision of God's kingdom that Jesus brought. It also reminds us to hold fast to our theology but loosely to our traditions.

LUKE 6

Jesus and the Sabbath – Luke 6:1-11

ONE SABBATH JESUS WAS GOING through the grain fields. His disciples plucked the heads of grain and ate them, rubbing them in their hands. But some of the Pharisees said to them, "Why are you doing what is not lawful to do on the Sabbath day?"

Jesus, answering them, said, "Haven't you read what David did when he was hungry, he and those who were with him, how he entered the house of God, and took and ate the sacred bread, and gave also to those who were with him, which is not lawful to eat except for the priests alone?" He said to them, "The Son of Man is lord of the Sabbath."

It also happened on another Sabbath that he entered into the synagogue and taught. There was a man there whose right hand was withered. The scribes and the Pharisees watched him, to see whether he would heal on the Sabbath, that they might find a reason to accuse him. But he knew their thoughts; and he said to the man who had the withered hand, "Rise up and stand in the middle." He arose and stood. Then Jesus said to them, "I will ask you something: Is it lawful on the Sabbath to do good, or to do harm? To save a life, or to kill?" He looked around at them all, and said to the man, "Stretch out your hand." He did, and his hand was restored as sound as the other. But they were filled with fury, and discussed among themselves about what they might do to Jesus.

Cultures have different characteristics. The most important marker of culture is language. It shapes how people communicate, express emotion, and view the world. Food and eating habits are also marks of culture. Mediterranean culture is rich in olive oil whereas East Asian cultures tend to focus on rice and noodles. Clothing varies between cultures as does music, dance, and artistic expression. Culture can even affect such things as how time is viewed. American culture tends to be punctual whereas some African cultures have a more relaxed view of time.

A notable aspect of first-century Judaism was the importance of the Sabbath. This was not just a cultural characteristic that had developed over the centuries, however. It was part of their identity as the people of God. God himself had commanded that his people keep the Sabbath. While other commands might have been disregarded, this one was sacred. To be a Jew meant to keep the Sabbath. The importance of the Sabbath was institutionalized by its being one of the Ten Commandments. The Sabbath and circumcision were the two defining marks of Jewish faith, which was faith in the one true and living God.

At the time of Christ, however, Sabbath observance had become legalistic. The Jews had sought to put a "fence" around the law. This meant that they had added regulations on top of the scriptural commands. The law said not to work on the Sabbath. The Jews defined exactly what work meant by such things as how far one could walk, what kind of fires could be lit, which items could be carried in public, and whether crops could be harvested. These helped place a fence around the Sabbath. That is, if these specific prohibitions were kept, one was more likely to keep the Sabbath well. We see one of these prohibitions in the account with which Luke begins this chapter.

One day when Jesus and the disciples were going through a field of grain, the disciples picked some of the heads of grain, rubbed them in their hands, and ate them. Matthew's account says that they did so because they were hungry (Matthew 12:1-8). We can imagine that the disciples were often hungry since they had no regular schedule for meals and traveled continuously around the countryside.

The law did not allow a person to harvest another's field (Deuteronomy 23:25), but you could pick fruit or grain for your consumption. The only problem was that it was a Sabbath day, and the Pharisees were present. When they rubbed the grain together in their hands, it was considered "threshing" and thus forbidden on the Sabbath by their tradition. "Why are you doing what is against the law," said the Pharisees to the disciples.

Jesus answered on their behalf. He referenced a story in the Old Testament where David and his men were hungry. They went to the priest and asked for the sacred bread that was kept in the Tabernacle. It represented God's provision for the people and was not lawful for anyone but priests to eat. David and his men had eaten the bread when they were hungry, without any condemnation from God (I Samuel 21:1-6). Jesus asserts that his disciples are likewise guiltless. Jesus used a term Luke introduced in the previous chapter. He asserted that "The Son of Man is lord of the Sabbath."

Why did Jesus not respect the traditions of the Pharisees? One reason was that their "fence" was not a command from God, only their human invention. Though well-intentioned, it had made the true keeping of the Sabbath more difficult. It focused people on outward legalistic duty rather than the heart of the law. The Sabbath was not intended merely to provide rest for the body but also for the heart and spirit. As the Gospel of Mark tells the account, Jesus would also add, "Man was not made for the Sabbath but the Sabbath for man" (Mark 2:27). In other words, people did not exist to keep the Sabbath. The Sabbath was given for people's nurture, renewal, and help.

There was perhaps another reason Jesus used the particular example he did. David felt justified in using the sacred bread because he was the anointed king of the nation. Saul was still technically the king, and David was in hiding from him, but God had declared David to be the next king. He waited for the time when the reality would come to pass.

The same was true for Jesus. He was the true king of Israel. As such, he had authority that others did not. Though Jesus awaited the full realization of his kingdom, he possessed all the rights of it already. One of those was to make judgments about right and wrong. The term "lord of the Sabbath" also alludes to divine authority. Since the Sabbath was a command that came from God, Jesus as the Son of God, had authority to determine its proper use.

The account about the healing of the man with the withered hand also concerns what the religious leaders considered a breaking of the Sabbath. On another Sabbath, a man was present in the synagogue who had a withered hand. We do not know whether it was by accident, such as a burn, or from birth. Though he knew the scribes and Pharisees would disapprove, Jesus would not refuse to do good to appease their misplaced sensibilities.

Already in Luke, we have heard of another group that will be associated with the Pharisees throughout the gospel; it is the scribes. They were with the Pharisees on that occasion. The scribes were a group that also developed in the intertestamental period. They had several functions. As their name indicates, they were experts in the written language who could produce legal documents, record deeds, and act as notary publics or secretaries for legal proceedings. They had also taken on an important role, which was copying the scriptures. They began by transcribing the scriptures onto new scrolls. In time, because of their deep acquaintance with the text of scripture, they became interpreters of it for the people. Like the Pharisees, they were highly respected as people who knew the law of God intimately. Also like the Pharisees they had become proud and legalistic. We see that early in the public ministry of Jesus they had turned decidedly against him.

It was not technically against Jewish law to heal on the Sabbath. No command in the Old Testament forbade doing so. The scribes and Pharisees had decided, however, that such actions constituted work and were against Jewish law. Luke indicates that on that day they particularly watched Jesus to catch him in some moral misstep. How was Jesus to defend healing on the Sabbath?

Jesus' rhetorical question put them on the defensive. To the people gathered that day in the synagogue, it would certainly be lawful to do good on the Sabbath. Any other answer would have been wrong and lacking in common sense. Jesus then acted on the principle. When Jesus instructed the man to stretch out his hand, it was instantly made whole. Luke says it became just like the other one.

We see, already in the ministry of Jesus, the emerging conflict with the religious leaders of the nation. Why was their hatred so intense? There are several reasons. Jesus was a threat to their power, status, and the respect they had from the people. There was no room, in their view, for two religious authorities. Another reason is that they were essentially godless. Though they had a show of religion, the Spirit of God did not live in them, otherwise, they would have recognized the good that Jesus was doing and the truths he taught. We marvel that they did not rejoice at the healing of a person in need. Luke records that their ensuing discussions centered on how they might find a way to bring Jesus under their authority and control.

Theological insights
- Sabbath practice was highly visible because it came every seven days and served as a public demonstration of one's religious obedience. It gave the self-righteous the opportunity to applaud themselves and disdain others.
- There was a great deal of wisdom and compassion in Old Testament law. While a person could not harvest another's field, they could eat from it to satisfy their hunger. It was part of the safety net for the poor that the law provided.

- Jesus intentionally taught a theological point by making the man stand in front of everyone. Doing good is the right thing to do when it is within your power, and it is evil not to do so. In the encounter, Jesus exposed the callousness of the scribes and Pharisees.

Practical application

The idea of putting a fence around the law might have seemed wise. It was, however, a violation of Old Testament law. In Deuteronomy, the law said, "You shall not add to the word which I command you, neither shall you take away from it, that you may keep the commandments of the Lord your God which I command you" (Deuteronomy 4:2). The theological principle is that God's word describes "perfect righteousness." We should not take away from what God has instructed. Neither should we add to it. The Pharisees had added to God's commands. In doing so, they had made them legalistic standards rather than guidance for the heart. The command in Deuteronomy also offers a principle of moderation, intended to keep the people from straying – whether well-intentioned or not – into extremes.

This was Protestant Reformer Martin Luther's objection to monasticism. It was, in his view, a set of vows that went beyond scripture. Nowhere in scripture were people encouraged to make vows of poverty, chastity, and obedience. Since scripture did not command it, we should not encourage it. We are better off sticking to the perfect righteousness that scripture describes. We always miss the mark when we imagine that our innovations are wiser than scripture.

Jesus Chooses Twelve Apostles – Luke 6:12-16

IN THOSE DAYS, HE WENT OUT to the mountain to pray, and he continued all night in prayer to God. When it was day, he called his disciples, and chose twelve of them, whom he also named apostles: Simon, whom he named Peter; Andrew, his brother; James; John; Philip; Bartholomew; Matthew; Thomas; James the son of Alphaeus; Simon who was called the Zealot; Judas the son of James; and Judas Iscariot, who also became a traitor.

If you wanted to start a great movement, how would you do it? You might seek to gather large numbers of people and inspire them with enthusiasm. Get as many followers as possible, and trust that the critical mass would be sufficient to get the effort off the ground.

Jesus did just the opposite. Instead of depending on a large number of people with low commitment, he chose a smaller group as the core of his movement. He would spend three years teaching and training them. In the end, they would be convinced that he was not only the Messiah but also the Son of God. It would turn out to be a wise decision. Instead of masses of marginally committed followers, Jesus started the church with a small group of disciples who would give their lives for his sake.

Luke says that at some point early in his ministry, Jesus chose twelve apostles. He did so after spending a night in prayer. This is an important aspect of the choice of the apostles. Jesus did not choose them lightly. He understood that the beginnings of the early church would depend on them. If they failed, all would be lost. We might imagine that the choice of Judas Iscariot was especially difficult. It seems that Jesus already knew that he would be betrayed by one of his inner circle. It seems to have been part of his choice to include someone whose heart would never fully be with him.

The names of the twelve are listed in three of the gospels (Matthew 10:2-4, Mark 3:16-19, Luke 6:14-16). The names are mostly similar with some exceptions. It seems that some disciples went by several names. Simon was named Peter, which means "Rock," by Jesus. Matthew was also called Levi. We can be certain about this because the accounts of the call of Matthew (Matthew 9:9-13) and Levi (Mark 2:13-17, Luke 5:27-28) are the same, except the name.

If we align the various lists of the apostles, we see that Bartholomew was also called Nathanael. Thomas was also called Didymus, which means "the Twin." James the son of Alphaeus is sometimes called James the Less. Thaddaeus is also called both Lebbaeus (in some ancient manuscripts) and Judas, son of James. Simon the Zealot is also called Simon the Cananaean. Only Andrew, James, John, Philip, and Judas Iscariot are called by only one name. Judas Iscariot is always listed last and is always noted as the one who betrayed Jesus.

The twelve disciples make up an unusual group. For one thing, none of them appear to come from the religious establishment. John may be an exception because we see that, in the gospel of John, he had some acquaintance with the high priest. This might mean that his family had significant religious connections in Jerusalem. Matthew, called Levi, might have been a Levite, which would have put him in the tribe charged with the religious life of the people. We might think that Jesus would have chosen some Pharisees, scribes, or priests to be apostles, but he did not.

Think about the differences among them. Simon Peter, Andrew, James, and John were fishermen by trade. Matthew was a tax collector. Simon the Cananaean is called a Zealot, which refers to a group dedicated to the overthrow of Roman occupation. A Zealot would have been immediately antagonistic toward a tax collector. Jesus had his work cut out for him in creating a harmonious group. It may have helped that there were two sets of brothers among them, although they may at times have seemed like a clique to the others. Philip and Nathanael were from the town of Bethsaida, the hometown of Simon and Andrew. This probably means they knew one another and perhaps from childhood. That does not necessarily mean that they were friends or had positive interactions. The natural leadership and impulsiveness of Peter may have been an irritation to others at times. Matthew's wealth and education may have been a source of jealousy or disdain, at least at first.

Jesus must have had many criteria for choosing the twelve. He no doubt looked on the heart more than outward matters. He needed a group that would be cohesive. For that to be the case, everyone could not be the chief. There would need to be natural leaders and some followers among the group. There would need to be some analytical people and some more creative ones. Some may have been loud, others quiet. This reality is indicated by the fact that we hear more in the gospels about some disciples than others. Some were always in the middle of things, others behind the scenes.

To be chosen as one of the twelve apostles must have seemed quite a privilege. Little did they understand the cost of their discipleship. They would spend the next three years following Jesus around the countryside with little pattern for where they would stay or when they would eat. They would leave occupations, livelihoods, and in some instances, families. They would have a remarkable opportunity, however. They would get to spend intimate time with Jesus, and he would train them for a ministry like his. It would be the adventure of a lifetime but one that would cost them their lives. From what we gather from church history, none of them ever regretted their call. The word "apostle" means one who is sent. Jesus called them to send them out into the world. They would be the foundation from which he would establish his kingdom in the world through the church.

Theological insights

- Jesus serves as a model for prayer. When faced with a difficult decision, he bathed it in prayer. We would do well to do the same.
- Not many people ever spend an entire night in prayer. Jesus did so on more than one occasion. His prayers were rewarded with the insight to choose the twelve wisely.
- What breaks down barriers between people? Christ is the one who can break down otherwise insurmountable barriers. Even today he brings together people who would never otherwise associate.
- Jesus chooses people who appear common and ordinary. The apostles must have thought themselves so. However, no one is ordinary, because we are the creation of God. God takes "ordinary" people, such as the apostles, and does extraordinary things through them.

Practical application

We see in the choice of twelve apostles that even Jesus did not attempt to fulfill his ministry alone. He called a group of people whom he could mentor, teach, travel with, and send out in ministry. Since Jesus was fully human as well as fully divine, he chose to live in close relationships with others. He no doubt enjoyed the laughter of the group, the relaxed times over a meal, and the conversations as they traveled from one place to another. His example reminds us that we need not fulfill our destinies all by ourselves. We do well to include others, work alongside friends, nurture relationships, and live life together as the people of God.

The Sermon on the Plain: The Beatitudes
Luke 6:17-26

HE CAME DOWN WITH THEM and stood on a level place, with a crowd of his disciples and a great number of the people from all Judea and Jerusalem and the sea coast of Tyre and Sidon, who came to hear him and to be healed of their diseases, as well as those who were troubled by unclean spirits; and they were healed. The entire multitude sought to touch him, for power came out of him and healed them all.

He lifted up his eyes to his disciples, and said: "Blessed are you who are poor, for the kingdom of God is yours. Blessed are you who hunger now, for you will be filled. Blessed are you who weep now, for you will laugh. Blessed are you when people hate you, and when they exclude and mock you, and throw out your name as evil, on account of the Son of Man. Rejoice in that day and leap for joy, for behold, your reward is great in heaven, for their fathers did the same thing to the prophets.

"But woe to you who are rich, for you have received your consolation. Woe to you, you who are full now, for you will be hungry. Woe to you who laugh now, for you will mourn and weep. Woe, when everyone speaks well of you, for their fathers did the same to the false prophets.

What is the best way to remember something? There are numerous techniques for memorization, including memory devices, repetition, active recall, visualization, and teaching what you wish to learn. People have asked how the early church remembered the many teachings of Jesus. We get an indication of one way in what has been called the "Sermon on the Plain." It would appear that Jesus taught important lessons repeatedly in different contexts. This would have helped the disciples remember them. The "Sermon on the Plain" is much like the "Sermon on the Mount" in Matthew (Matthew chapters 5, 6, and 7) but not exactly. If Jesus taught similar lessons and retold his important parables, it would explain how the early church remembered his teachings. It would also explain some differences in how various gospel accounts record his teachings. Both Matthew's and Luke's sermons open with a set of Beatitudes.

There are some striking differences between the Beatitudes in Luke and Matthew (Matthew 5:1-12). In Luke it is the poor who are blessed; in Matthew the poor in spirit. In Luke it is the hungry who are blessed; in Matthew, it is those who hunger and thirst after righteousness. In Luke those who weep now will laugh; in Matthew, those who mourn will be comforted. Both accounts include those who are persecuted. Matthew's account includes beatitudes about the meek, the merciful, the pure in heart, and the peacemakers. In addition, Luke includes a set of "woes" that are not included in Matthew.

Why are the accounts different? Some have suggested that Luke did not record the sermon as accurately as Matthew. He did not know the full extent of Jesus' teachings on various subjects, such as the Beatitudes. In addition, some suggest that Luke, not being an eyewitness, got the location wrong. It was not a flat place but the mountainside where Jesus gave the sermon. It is possible that both Matthew and Luke recount the same event in the life of Jesus, told differently. If that is the case, Luke's location of a "level place" may be the same as Matthew's gentle mountainside slope.

Another explanation is that Jesus taught the lessons on numerous occasions. As we have said, it seems likely that he did so. He tailored them differently for various audiences. We have a record of this when we compare Luke and Matthew. The content of the teachings varies enough to make this a possibility. In addition, in both instances, the authors may have recorded only a representative sample of what Jesus taught.

Matthew's version emphasizes being poor in spirit rather than merely poor. It is certainly possible to have wealth and also be humble before God. Matthew, as someone who may have been wealthy at one point, might have been more aware of that possibility and recorded a version of Jesus' teachings that allowed for such. Luke's version may have been one that Jesus spoke to truly poor people. It encouraged them because they were less distracted by their wealth. Though being poor was a problem in their eyes, from the point of view of faith, it was a blessing. It made them more likely to understand their true need for God.

The inclusion of woes along with blessings mirrors a set of blessings and curses found in the Old Testament book of Deuteronomy (Deuteronomy 28:1-68). God promised to bless the people with his gracious gifts if they obeyed his commandments. If they departed from them by worshipping idols, they would experience his curses. The woes spoken by Jesus focused on things ordinarily thought of as blessings, such as wealth, laughter, the praise of others, and having plenty to eat. If those good things in this life caused one to turn from God's grace, however, they would become curses instead of blessings. What is important is not riches in this life but humility before God, devotion to him, and obedience to his will.

As with the Beatitudes in Matthew, these sayings by Jesus turn ordinary human standards upside down. The kingdom of God, as Jesus taught it, is governed by a different set of values. In these few verses, we learn just how different God's kingdom is. In the world, wealth, abundance, and popularity are signs of success, but true blessing is not tied to external circumstances but a life aligned with God's purposes. Our human inclination seeks personal comfort and recognition. According to the words of Jesus, sacrificing for God and others leads to true and lasting joy. Blessed are those who admit their neediness before God, for in doing so they open themselves to his grace. Those who rely on wealth, power, and status are warned about their eventual loss. It is humility and vulnerability before God that are the marks of true greatness and signs of God's blessing.

Theological insights

- As in Matthew, Jesus directed his teaching toward his disciples, first of all. His disciples, in particular, were called to exemplify his teachings and the new values of God's kingdom. Disciples today should strive to do the same.
- Throughout his gospel, Luke gives attention to those who are the least, last, and lost. Jesus' words in Luke seem tailored to those who would have been disenfranchised from the upper layers of first-century culture.
- As in other parts of the Bible, the word "blessed" refers to more than mere happiness. It is what those who share in the salvation that comes from God experience.
- Jesus does not say that everyone should hate us, only that we should be worried when everyone speaks well of us. Those who follow God's ways will experience, to varying degrees, the scorn of those in whom God's words find no place.

Practical application

The Danish theologian Søren Kierkegaard said that the world is like a department store in which someone has rearranged the price tags. The things that are of great worth are valued cheaply. The things of little real worth of esteemed valuable. The Beatitudes of Jesus in Luke call us to account, especially in a prosperous culture. It is easy to become proud, to think that we are blessed because of our wealth as compared to others, and to turn a blind eye to those in need. As do all the teachings of Jesus, these words cut beneath our pretensions. There are great dangers in prosperity and success. Those who experience them should be always on their guard. If they lead us away from Christ, they will become curses. Our life in this world is a short span in comparison to the life to come. It is that realm in which we should strive to be rich.

The Sermon on the Plain: Love Your Enemies
Luke 6:27-35

"BUT I TELL YOU WHO HEAR: love your enemies, do good to those who hate you, bless those who curse you, and pray for those who mistreat you. To the one who strikes you on the cheek, offer also the other; and from the one who takes away your cloak, do not withhold your coat also. Give to everyone who asks you, and do not ask the one who takes away your goods to give them back again. As you would like people to do to you, do so to them."

"If you love those who love you, what credit is that to you? For even sinners love those who love them. If you do good to those who do good to you, what credit is that to you? For even sinners do the same. If you lend to those from whom you hope to receive, what credit is that to you? Even sinners lend to sinners, to receive back as much. But love your enemies, and do good, and lend, expecting nothing back; and your reward will be great, and you will be children of the Most High; for he is kind toward the ungrateful and evil.

In this section, Jesus continues to announce the values of God's kingdom. He does so with great wisdom in that he does not simply assert various principles but defends them logically. At the root of his comments is the character of God. God is extravagantly generous. You must be like God.

Think about a person with an incredible amount of money, so much that he could never spend it all. Imagine that person decided to walk through the streets handing out money to all he met. In his generosity, he did not discriminate between the rich and poor, the deserving and the unworthy, the gracious and the rude. He was overwhelmed with a sense of thankful generosity. For that reason, he dispensed goodwill and good gifts to all he met.

This seems to be the kind of attitude Jesus encourages in these verses. You have been blessed beyond measure by God; therefore give generously to all you meet. Jesus declares that this is the character and nature of God. What is God like? He is kind, gracious, and good to everyone. Even to the ungrateful and evil, God shows mercy.

Jesus teaches with remarkable wisdom and power. How are you better than sinful people if you only love your friends? How are you better than they are if you only do good to those who will repay you? No, says Jesus, you must love your enemies and do good to those who hate you.

This is a radical statement and one that even the most devout find difficult. How exactly can this be lived out? Can you love someone who harms you? Does this apply to the relationship of nations to one another? Does this forbid protecting yourself and your family? How can you love someone who has hurt you deeply?

Jesus does not give the details, and his words do not seem to be an exact prescription for every situation. Rather, he describes an attitude that is radically different from an ordinary one. It is characterized by doing to others as we would have them do to us. We tend to hate our enemies. What would it be like if we loved them instead? Might they respond differently? Might their hearts be softened toward us? These words do not seem to be intended for those who govern nations or as a prohibition of civil laws and courts of justice but for individual relations. They create the opportunity for reconciliation and healing where none would otherwise be possible.

Here is a conspicuous characteristic of Christianity – radical forgiveness. It is found in no other religious faith to this degree. Consider the importance of it. How many conflicts in the world today are driven by generational hatreds, ethnic animosities, and long-standing feuds? It is one reason international and interregional conflicts continue for centuries, even millennia in some instances. No one is willing to forgive. One group's response to aggression is an even greater one. It is the pattern of Lamech, in the Old Testament, who said, "If Cain will be avenged seven times, truly Lamech seventy-seven times" (Genesis 4:24). Vengeance can become a way of life if no one is willing to forgive. One wonders what healing might come to troubled corners of the world if these words of Jesus were put into practice. What might happen if just one group of people began to do so?

It always makes news when someone lives by these radical words of Jesus because it is so unexpected. The concentration camp survivor meets one of his tormentors and forgives him. The spouse takes back the unfaithful but repentant partner. The family forgives the person who murdered their family member. Such instances stir our emotions. We realize that vengeance would be justified and sometimes even satisfying. Yet Jesus forbids it. Our heavenly Father does good to the wicked and the ungrateful. If we are to be like him, we must do the same.

Theological insights

- These comments by Jesus are for those "who hear." Jesus did not simply mean hearing with the ears but the heart. Not everyone can hear these radical words of Jesus, only those whose spiritual ears God has opened.
- Jesus does not advocate for the abandoning of ordinary criminal or judicial punishments. He is describing a radical way of relating to others in everyday relations.
- Jesus instructs us to love, bless, pray, and give. It may be hard to love our enemies, but we can pray for them. This may be a first step. If we can do something tangible toward them as an act of love, it may be a second step. If we pray and bless and act, those things may eventually enable us to love, with true and real emotions.
- The Old Testament does not contain the call to radical forgiveness like in these words of Jesus, but it does not encourage vengeance. Leviticus 19:18 says, "You shall not take vengeance, nor bear a grudge against the children of your people, but you shall love your neighbor as yourself" (also see Exodus 23:4-5). In his teaching, Jesus is expounding on this instruction that already existed in the Old Testament.

Practical application

We see, in the life of Jesus, that he always lived out his teachings. He exhibited great patience with the religious leaders, answering their questions even when he knew they were plotting his death. Though he called out their errors, he treated them with remarkable restraint. We see the love of Jesus displayed when he wept over the city of Jerusalem as he came into it on Palm Sunday. Though he knew he would be crucified there, his heart broke over their rejection. He loved them even if they did not love him.

We truly are people who have reason to be extravagantly generous. This was certainly what enabled Jesus to act as he did. He knew that, as the Son of God, all things belonged to him. He did not have to grasp at small things. Our standing with God enables us to be generous. We have all things in Jesus Christ. If anyone can be lavish with their time, attention, possessions, and affections, we are those people. It is not those who grasp after the things of this life who are blessed but those who live by God's will. Those who do, said Jesus, will find that "their reward is great" for they will be children of the Most High who does these very same things.

The Sermon on the Plain: Fruit and Obedience
Luke 6:36-49

"THEREFORE BE MERCIFUL, even as your Father is also merciful. Do not judge, and you will not be judged. Do not condemn, and you will not be condemned. Forgive, and you will be forgiven. "Give, and it will be given to you: good measure, pressed down, shaken together, and running over, will be given to you. For with the same measure you use, it will be measured back to you."

He spoke a parable to them. "Can the blind guide the blind? Will they not both fall into a pit? A disciple is not above his teacher, but everyone when he is fully trained will be like his teacher. Why do you see the speck that is in your brother's eye, but do not consider the beam that is in your own eye? Or how can you tell your brother, 'Brother, let me remove the speck that is in your eye,' when you yourself do not see the beam that is in your own eye? You hypocrite! First remove the beam from your own eye, and then you can see clearly to remove the speck that is in your brother's eye."

"For there is no good tree that produces rotten fruit, nor again a rotten tree that produces good fruit. Each tree is known by its own fruit, for people do not gather figs from thorns, nor do they gather grapes from a bramble bush. The good man out of the good treasure of his heart brings out that which is good, and the evil man out of the evil treasure of his heart brings out that which is evil, for out of the abundance of the heart, his mouth speaks."

"Why do you call me, 'Lord, Lord,' and do not do the things I say? Everyone who comes to me, and hears my words and does them, I will show you what he is like. He is like a man building a house, who dug down deep and laid the foundation on the rock. When a flood arose, the stream broke against that house, and could not shake it, because it was founded on the rock. But the one who hears and does not do them, is like a man who built a house on the earth without a foundation, against which the stream broke, and immediately it fell; and the ruin of that house was great."

Who is the wisest person you know? Many people will point to a parent, teacher, coach, or mentor. It takes more than intelligence to be wise. The wise have often learned through the experience of being unwise. If we could learn from the wise, perhaps we would not make so many mistakes ourselves.

The teachings of Jesus display astounding wisdom, particularly for a person who was relatively young, as was Jesus. His wisdom is not just human, however, but divine wisdom. The people would often respond that they had never heard anyone speak like Jesus. That was true. They had not heard teachings before with such clarity, wisdom, and power.

Jesus continued to encourage his disciples to be like God in their interactions with others. His words give us a personal incentive. You will be treated, said Jesus, as you treat others. If you do not judge others, they will not judge you. If you do not condemn others, they will not condemn you. If you forgive, others will forgive you. Though he does not specifically say so, Jesus seems to imply that God also will show mercy, forgiveness, and grace to those who show those things to others.

Is this law of reciprocity true? Yes, said Jesus. The same measure you use will be used for you. If you give to others, they will give to you. You will receive in abundance, a full measure, pressed down and running over. Our experience confirms this. If we are hard with others, they are hard with us. When we smile and greet others, they return the favor. Disciples are not simply to do these things for their benefit, however, but because God is like this. God's children should try to imitate their Father in heaven.

Then Jesus spoke what Luke calls a parable. It is a simple one. Notice, said Jesus, that a blind person cannot lead another blind person. They will both go astray. Then Jesus tells a short aphorism. Know that a disciple is not above his master. When you are fully trained, said Jesus, you will be like me. The lives of the disciples did not feel like those of their master, at that point. In the end, their lives would become more like Jesus than they ever imagined.

The problem of judgment is complicated. It is impossible to live without making judgments, about safety, whom to trust, what is right, and many other things. Jesus certainly made judgments about many things, and so must the church. If the church is to teach, it must make judgments about right and wrong. To what then, is Jesus referring, when he said, "Do not judge?" He is pointing to those petty personal judgments we make about others that serve to disparage them and exalt us in our own eyes and the eyes of others. He is talking about the judgment that turns into gossip and disregard. This is often made worse by our projecting our faults onto others. Faults that exist in us, we particularly disdain in others. Jesus does not say that we cannot make judgments. He points us to the need to recognize our sins and work to remedy them. He does not say that we cannot work to help others with their problems, only that we must do so humbly, knowing we are subject to the same weaknesses and failures.

Luke ends this sermon with two sets of sayings that are also at the end of the Sermon on the Mount, in Matthew 7. One has to do with bearing good fruit. The other centers around the foundation on which our lives are built. What should we understand about bearing fruit? Good fruit comes from good trees. Work on developing a heart that is honest, healthy, and true. Good fruit will flow naturally from it. Corrupt attitudes, words, and actions flow from infected and unhealthy lives. People can tell what kind of person you are from the kinds of things that flow from your life.

There is, then, no other right response but obedience to Christ's words. Jesus used an example the people would have understood. Everyone understands, said Jesus, that a good foundation matters. This is true in the spiritual realm as well as the physical one. Those who put the words of Jesus into practice will be laying a solid foundation for their lives. All those who do not attend to the words of Jesus will discover their foundation shaky. It may not be evident at first, but the inevitable flood will reveal the truth.

Theological insights
- The teachings of Jesus qualify as "Wisdom Literature" along with such books in the Bible as Job, Proverbs, and Ecclesiastes. The teachings of Jesus are the highest form of such writings. In these very practical lessons, we learn the difference between wisdom and folly, right and wrong, truth and falsehood. The words of Jesus contain the most profound wisdom ever taught.
- The Pharisees were among the "blind" who led the blind. They passed their errors on to their followers. Later in Luke, Jesus will warn the disciples not to follow their teachings (Luke 12:1). Those who follow selfish teachers will be led astray. Those who follow Jesus, however, will reflect his character in numerous ways.
- We easily project our own failings on others. What we overlook in ourselves we especially disdain in others. It is better to spend time in introspection than to project our faults onto others.

Practical application

It has been said that "truth is in order to goodness." This means that we cannot live a truthful and honest life if it is based falsehoods. This reality makes the teachings of Jesus extremely valuable. His words cut through pretense. They expose not only the sins of others but our own. They help us think clearly about our lives in relation to God and others. The ways of God's kingdom often run contrary to our natural tendencies. For that reason, we need a radical reorientation if we are to align with God's values. In this sense, the words of Jesus are like a set of glasses. They focus our vision so that we can see life, ourselves, and God more clearly. The teachings of Jesus bring many aspects of life and faith into much clearer focus.

LUKE 7

Healing a Centurion's Servant – Luke 7:1-10

AFTER HE HAD FINISHED SPEAKING in the hearing of the people, he entered into Capernaum. A certain centurion's servant, who was dear to him, was sick and at the point of death. When he heard about Jesus, he sent Jewish elders to him, asking him to come and heal his servant. When they came to Jesus, they begged him earnestly, saying, "He is worthy for you to do this for him, for he loves our nation, and he built our synagogue for us." Jesus went with them.

When he was not far from the house, the centurion sent friends to him, saying, "Lord, do not trouble yourself, for I am not worthy for you to come under my roof. Therefore I did not even think myself worthy to come to you; but say the word, and my servant will be healed. For I also am a man placed under authority, having soldiers under me. I say to this one, 'Go!' and he goes; and to another, 'Come!' and he comes; and to my servant, 'Do this,' and he does it."

When Jesus heard these things, he marveled at him, and turned and said to the crowd who followed him, "I tell you, I have not found such great faith, no, not even in Israel." Those who were sent returned to the house and found that the servant who had been sick was well.

Do you like surprises? Most of us like them, at least occasionally – if they are good surprises. We enjoy a mid-morning coffee left on our desk by a coworker, a spontaneous visit from an old friend, an early birthday present, or unanticipated tickets to a sporting event or concert. When we think of the ministry of Jesus, we think of him surprising people, with his teachings, a miracle, or a statement. Luke reports an incident in which the opposite happened. Jesus was surprised by faith found in an unexpected place.

This incident took place when Jesus returned to Capernaum. We remember that he was using the city of Capernaum as a home base for his ministry. When he entered the city, he was met by a group of Jewish elders. The elders of the city would have been older, respected men. They were the group that a town looked to for leadership, wisdom, and stability. This group of elders came to Jesus with an unusual request. They wanted Jesus to help one of the Roman centurions in their town.

The region of Galilee was under the governance of Herod Antipas, but it contained Roman soldiers. They served to help Herod keep control of the population and were available in case of invasion. Though Herod ruled the region, he did so at the pleasure of Rome and could be deposed by Caesar at any time. The city of Capernaum, a relatively large town in the area, had Roman soldiers and a centurion.

Roman troops were organized in several ways. The largest group was a legion, which typically contained ten cohorts. A cohort was typically made up of six centuries. Though a century implies one hundred soldiers, they were typically made up of about eighty, along with supporting staff such as assistants and flag bearers. Thus a cohort would typically be four hundred eighty soldiers and a legion four thousand eight hundred.

A person got to be a centurion through demonstrated abilities. He would need to have excelled at military skills, including hand-to-hand fighting. Leadership qualities were important as well as managerial abilities. He would need the respect of those under his command and have demonstrated a willingness to follow orders. Thus those who achieved the rank of centurion were highly accomplished. They also would have been paid more than ordinary soldiers and so able to live a wealthier lifestyle.

It is surprising that the Jewish elders would voice such praise for this particular centurion. Jews and Romans were often at odds, particularly Jewish leaders and Roman soldiers. Instead, the elders affirmed to Jesus that this centurion was "worthy" of his help. From the passage, we learn that the centurion was a person of compassion. He had a servant of whom he was fond and went out of his way to ask Jesus for help. In addition, he had used his wealth to help the Jews build a synagogue in the town. Here was an unusual person, who broke the mold for what a typical centurion would have been like.

This request must have seemed important to Jesus, as he agreed to go to the centurion's home. He responded with graciousness to the plea for help. The key moment in the story comes with the second communication from the centurion. After reflection, he decided to send Jesus a second message. He did not want to impose on the Master. Instead, he offered an illustration from his own experience. He understood what it meant to be under authority. He told his soldiers and servants to do a certain thing and they did it. He also understood obedience because he obeyed the orders of his superiors. If Jesus would only speak the word, said the centurion, he knew his servant would be healed.

We might ask if it was possible for Jesus to be surprised. From this account, the answer is "Yes." Because he was human as well as divine, he did not know everything. Some circumstances, events, and reactions surprised him. We will see in the next chapter a time in which the disciples' lack of faith surprised him (Luke 8:22-25). The faith of the centurion did also, and Jesus remarked to the crowd about the centurion's faith. "I tell you, I have not found such great faith, no, not even in Israel."

Here is an incident in the life of Jesus that points to the future expansion of God's kingdom beyond Israel. It demonstrated that people outside the nation could have faith. Did the centurion have faith in the God of Israel? We do not know his exact beliefs or circumstances but he seems to have. The elders reported that he loved their nation. After this incident, he would certainly have had unwavering faith in Jesus, and the event foreshadows the opening of the gospel to the Gentiles through another centurion, named Cornelius (Acts 10).

What is faith? It is conviction about God. It is a deep belief in God's ability to keep his promises. It is also a work of the Holy Spirit. While there is value in raising doubts and asking questions, the gospels repeatedly encourage faith. They encourage us to believe in God's goodness, humble ourselves before him, and open ourselves to his Spirit.

Theological insights
- Good people do good works. The centurion's good works, such as helping the people build a synagogue, were a sign of his good heart. So was his faith in Jesus.
- Faith is found in unexpected places. We never know in whose heart God may be at work.
- Jesus was not impressed with the level of faith in the nation of Israel. We might wonder about how he feels about us, our churches, our communities, and our nation.
- Jesus makes no distinction between a religious leader, soldier, or servant. He was willing to help anyone in need.

- Jesus was willing to go and help someone in need. If we would follow his example, we must also be willing to go to those in need.

Practical application

   Both Jesus and the centurion are examples of compassion. The centurion cared for his servant. A man of such importance might have been too busy to take thought for those under him. He might have treated them with disregard but did not. His example reminds us not to look down on others who may be in a lower position than we are, who have a lower social status, or who are less prosperous. All people are valuable in God's eyes; they should be in ours too. Jesus is the perfect example of kindness. He did not disdain visiting the centurion's servant in order to make him whole.

Raising a Widow's Son – Luke 7:11-17

SOON AFTERWARD, HE WENT to a city called Nain. Many of his disciples, along with a great multitude, went with him. Now when he came near to the gate of the city, behold, a dead man was being carried out, the only son of his mother, and she was a widow. Many people of the city were with her. When the Lord saw her, he had compassion on her and said to her, "Do not cry." He came near and touched the coffin, and those who bore it stood still. He said, "Young man, I say to you, arise!" The dead man sat up and began to speak. Then he gave him to his mother.

   Fear took hold of everyone, and they glorified God, saying, "A great prophet has arisen among us!" and, "God has visited his people!" This report went out about him in the whole of Judea and in all the surrounding region.

We have learned a great deal about the human body. It is a marvel of creation and engineering. The body is composed of over thirty-seven million cells. They are different types such as blood cells, muscle cells, and nerve cells. If you unwound the DNA of just one cell, it would stretch to over six feet. All the DNA in a person's body would stretch to the sun and back – seventy times. The brain contains eighty-six billion neurons, each of which is connected to over a thousand other neurons. The average heart

104

beats one hundred thousand times a day and pumps two thousand gallons of blood daily. The acid in the stomach is strong enough to dissolve metal, but the stomach's lining regenerates so quickly that it maintains a secure barrier.

For all that, the human body is fragile. The brain begins to die if it is deprived of oxygen for only four to six minutes. When oxygen no longer gets to the cells they quickly die. With the stoppage of blood flow and oxygen, cell membranes begin to rupture. They release enzymes that destroy the cell from the inside out. The skin loses its pink hue and changes color within thirty minutes. Within a very short time, thirty-seven million cells are irreparably damaged at every level. We understand human biology much better today than people did in the first century. What we know today makes the raising of the young man in the city of Nain even more astounding.

The city of Nain still exists today in Israel. In the time of Jesus, it was a small town not far from Capernaum. On its western side, it is approached by a steep ascent with tombs on either side. It is probably this path that the funeral procession traveled when Jesus met them. Luke reports that Jesus met the funeral procession as they approached the gates. Except for kings and other notable people, the dead, being ceremonially unclean, were usually buried outside the city gates. This fits well with the story as Luke tells it.

In previous healings, we saw that the leper personally asked Jesus to heal him. The centurion approached Jesus through a group of elders. This miracle takes place without Jesus being asked. It is a result, says Luke, of his compassion.

The young man was the only son of a widow. That put her in an unenviable spot. Widows often had little means of supporting themselves. Her son may have been her only source of income. His loss would have been catastrophic for her and destined her for a life of poverty. In addition, there is a special grief that accompanies the loss of a child. Jesus' heart went out to her in her sorrow and plight. Since Jewish burials usually took place on the day of a person's death, her emotions would have been fresh and raw. We can imagine that it was a scene full of real and tragic grief.

Luke portrays Jesus as quite tender in this account. He tells the woman not to weep. He knows, of course, what he is about to do. When he touches the coffin, the men carrying it stop. He speaks very simply to the dead man. "Young man, I say to you, arise!" The young man sat up, which would have been proof to the crowd that he was alive. Luke also says that he began to speak. Without fanfare, Jesus gave him to his mother. We can imagine the amazement, joy, and relief she would have felt.

It is not surprising that the crowd would be astonished. Luke says that fear took hold of them. They praised God and exclaimed that truly a great prophet had arisen among them. As one might imagine, news about this incident spread throughout the region.

It is good to see joy in others. Jesus would certainly have seen it in the astonished widow. This miracle done by Jesus, as Luke records it, is not done for the sake of proving his divinity. It is simply a response of compassion. Jesus felt compassion and acted on it. In doing so, he expressed the heart of God toward his people. God is not distant or uncaring. He cares about our needs, hurts, griefs, and sorrows.

We only have three instances in the gospels of Jesus raising someone from the dead. They are this incident, the daughter of Jairus later in Luke (Luke 8:40-56), and the story of Lazarus in John (John 11:1-57). We do not know if Jesus raised others from the dead; it is certainly possible. Jesus did tell the disciples of John the Baptist (in the next passage, Luke 7:18-35) to report to him what they had seen. Part of what they were to report was that the "dead are raised up." The account of the raising of the widow's son is only found in Luke. It is the first indication that a wider resurrection of the dead was part of God's plan.

Theological insights
- John the Baptist was a powerful preacher and prophet, but he did not do miracles. Such abilities by Jesus are one evidence that he was the great prophet whom the Old Testament had foretold.
- This miracle would have reminded the people of the Old Testament prophet Elijah who raised the widow's son to life (I Kings 17:17-24). As the feeding of the five thousand showed Jesus to be at least as great as Moses, so this incident showed him at least as great as Elijah.
- The power of Jesus was that he was not only able to say, "Do not cry," but also removed the source of her sorrow.
- When we are moved by compassion, we should act on it, if we are able, as Jesus did.

Practical application
What we know about the human body makes this miracle truly astounding. Within a few minutes of death, the human body begins an internal process of decay that is both devastating and irreversible. Every cell

106

in the human body falls apart at every level. To be able to reverse such a widespread and catastrophic decay is inconceivable. Yet Jesus does so. It is a power that no human source could assert. Only God, who has the power of life, could have done so.

This resurrection from the dead is the great promise of Christianity. We too will rise to new life in Jesus Christ and enter the kingdom of God with new, resurrection bodies. Those who complain that this is a miracle too great to believe, need only consider what Jesus did to the widow's son. It too was humanly impossible. God, however, can do the impossible. He is the source of life and is able, in his mercy, to give life to all who come to him.

John the Baptist's Question – Luke 7:18-35

THE DISCIPLES OF JOHN told him about all these things. John, calling two of his disciples to him, sent them to Jesus, saying, "Are you the one who is to come, or should we look for another?" When the men came to him, they said, "John the Baptist has sent us to you, saying, 'Are you the one who is to come, or should we look for another?'"

In that hour he cured many of diseases and plagues and evil spirits; and to many who were blind he gave sight. Jesus answered them, "Go and tell John the things that you have seen and heard: the blind receive their sight, the lame walk, the lepers are cleansed, the deaf hear, the dead are raised up, and the poor have good news preached to them. And blessed is the one who takes no offense in me."

When John's messengers had departed, he began to speak to the crowds about John. "What did you go out into the wilderness to see? A reed shaken by the wind? But what did you go out to see? A man clothed in soft clothing? Behold, those who are gorgeously dressed and live delicately are in kings' courts. But what did you go out to see? A prophet? Yes, I tell you, and much more than a prophet. This is he of whom it is written, 'Behold, I send my messenger before your face, who will prepare your way before you.' "For I tell you, among those who are born of women there is not a greater prophet than John the Baptist; yet he who is least in the kingdom of God is greater than he."

When all the people and the tax collectors heard this, they acknowledged God's justice, having been baptized with John's baptism. But the Pharisees and the lawyers rejected the purpose of God for themselves, not being baptized by him.

"To what then should I compare the people of this generation? What are they like? They are like children who sit in the marketplace and call to one another, saying, 'We played the flute for you, and you did not dance. We mourned, and you did not weep.' For John the Baptist came neither eating bread nor drinking wine, and you say, 'He has a demon.' The Son of Man has come eating and drinking, and you say, 'Behold, a glutton and a drunkard, a friend of tax collectors and sinners!' But wisdom is justified by all her children."

Is it okay to have doubts? Everyone has them at times. How should we feel when we have doubts? Have we done something wrong or is our faith weak? We have an account in Luke where even someone with great faith had doubts. It is the account of John the Baptist's question.

We learned earlier that Herod had put John in prison (Luke 3:18-20) for his criticism of Herod's adulterous marriage. Luke will mention the death of John the Baptist in chapter 9 (Luke 9:9), though he does not give the details of it. Here Luke simply says that John sent messengers to Jesus.

We might be surprised that John would appear to have doubts about the messianic ministry of Jesus. Did he expect someone different? The answer probably lies in human nature. John had been in prison for some months. It would have been a very difficult place and a lonely time. He had lots of time with his thoughts. Now that he was not engaged in an active ministry, his questions surfaced. Was Jesus the one? Perhaps even John wondered when Jesus would gather the army the Messiah was expected to gather.

Apparently John's disciples had access to him in prison since they brought Jesus a message from him. Allowing visitors may have been one of Herod's kindnesses to his prisoner whom he knew to be a holy man. This may have been a question his disciples wanted answered. Perhaps they kept pressing John until he authorized it. It may also have been John's.

Jesus did not respond to the question directly. He allowed the disciples of John to observe his healing and teaching ministry. What they saw would have astounded them. In addition, they would have heard the recent story about Jesus raising a dead person to life in the village of Nain.

The message Jesus sent back to John would have been a clear reference to the promised Messiah's ministry. Jesus alluded to Isaiah 29:18 which talked about the deaf hearing and the blind being given their sight. Isaiah 35:4-6 added that the lame would walk and the mute speak. Isaiah 61 referred to God's Anointed One bringing good news, binding up the brokenhearted, and setting the captives free. John would have recognized these sayings from Isaiah as references to the coming salvation of God. That Jesus was fulfilling them would have assured John.

Jesus would rebuke the disciples on occasion for their lack of faith and would often do so sternly. Would he rebuke John? If there was any rebuke toward John in the words of Jesus, it was a mild one. Jesus certainly understood that John was suffering in prison. He answered him with a beatitude: "Blessed is the one who takes no offense in me." It was a call for John to continue steadfast in his faith and obedience.

Jesus waited until the messengers left to praise John. His words would turn out to be a kind of eulogy for John about his impending death. The first thing to note, said Jesus, was that John was a man of conviction. He was not shaken by every wind that blew. Neither was he tempted by material wealth or luxuries. He was not daunted by anyone's position and spoke the truth openly. Jesus praised him highly in the hearing of the people. Then he quoted from the prophet Malachi, who foretold the coming of the Messiah's messenger. God would send a messenger to prepare the way before he came. Who was this messenger, asked Jesus? It was John. He was this long-awaited prophet.

Then Jesus encouraged the crowd. There has not been a prophet greater than John, said Jesus. Yet the least person in the kingdom of God will be greater than he. Though John was great, said Jesus, you too can find the blessing of God, and that blessing will be very great. The kingdom of God is so great that the least person in it will be exceedingly blessed. John had revealed the coming of the kingdom. You, said Jesus, will have the opportunity to participate in it.

Verse 29 contains a phrase that has been difficult to interpret. It literally says that the people, on hearing Jesus' words "justified God." Most commentators understand this to mean that the people acknowledged God's righteousness – that he was right to send John, and wise, just, and holy in doing so. In contrast, the religious leaders, by rejecting John, were in fact rejecting God's will for themselves.

This section ends with a quaint saying by Jesus. It may have been a common proverb, but we can also imagine that Jesus created it himself. The point of the proverb is that some people are never satisfied. He addressed it to the crowd, but he seemed to have the religious leaders in mind. They said John was too strict. They said Jesus was too lax. They had rejected the purpose of God for themselves; for that reason, they could accept neither John nor Jesus.

Jesus closed his comments with a statement about which there have been various interpretations. What does it mean that "wisdom is justified by all her children?" Perhaps the best interpretation is that everyone justifies their own opinion and is righteous in their own eyes. The Pharisees and lawyers certainly were, though they were completely wrong about many things, especially Jesus.

Theological insights
- John demonstrated healthy emotional intelligence. He had a question and asked it. If he had not been willing to ask, he would not have gotten the response from Jesus that he did.
- No doubt many wanted a stronger approach from Jesus concerning Israel's political troubles. He had a different agenda, however, that would prove effective in the end.
- This passage contrasts the faith of the common people who received John's baptism and ministry with the religious leaders who did not.
- English reformer John Knox followed the example of John's strong preaching. He claimed, in the mode of John the Baptist, to "flatter no flesh." That approach often got him in trouble but also made him a powerful reformer and preacher.
- Jesus continued to do good wherever he went. Sunshine may seem weak but it heats the entire planet. Love, mercy, and truth, may not seem enough, but in God's hand, they have a powerful effect over time.

Practical application
Should we expect to be without doubts? This account suggests that even spiritual giants will have occasional questions and doubts. The Protestant reformer Martin Luther said that only fanatics have no doubts. That is, fanatics stir themselves up to an artificial state of emotion that refuses to

entertain doubt. That is not normal or healthy. Everyone has questions. When we have them, it is good to ask them.

Author Frederick Buechner said, "Doubt is the ants in the pants of faith." Doubt is one of those things that keeps us from getting too comfortable. It forces us to ask questions and seek answers. This is good for us because it is one way we grow. When a doubt or question arises, we should search for an answer. The good thing about Christianity is that it has answers to the questions we ask. The Christian faith is reasonable and does not fall apart upon examination. The more we seek and find answers to our doubts, the greater our assurance and confidence will be.

A Sinful Woman Anoints Jesus – Luke 7:36-50

ONE OF THE PHARISEES invited him to eat with him. He entered into the Pharisee's house and reclined at the table. Behold, a woman in the city who was a sinner, when she knew that he was having dinner at the Pharisee's house, brought an alabaster jar of ointment. Standing behind him, weeping at his feet, she began to wet his feet with her tears and wipe them with her hair, kissing his feet, and anointing them with the ointment. Now when the Pharisee who had invited him saw it, he said to himself, "This man, if he were a prophet, would have known who and what kind of woman this is who touches him, for she is a sinner."

Jesus answered him, "Simon, I have something to say to you." He said, "Teacher, speak." "A certain lender had two debtors. The one owed five hundred denarii, and the other fifty. When they could not pay, he forgave them both. Which of them therefore will love him most?"

Simon answered, "I suppose the one he forgave the most." He said to him, "You have judged correctly." Turning to the woman, he said to Simon, "Do you see this woman? I entered into your house, and you gave me no water for my feet, but she has wet my feet with her tears, and wiped them with her hair. You gave me no kiss, but since the time I came in, she has not ceased kissing my feet. You did not anoint my head with oil, but she has anointed my feet with ointment. Therefore I tell you, her sins, which are many, are forgiven, for she loved much. But the one who is forgiven little, loves little." He said to her, "Your sins are forgiven." Those who sat at the table with him began to say to themselves, "Who is this who even forgives sins?"

Occasionally we find ourselves in a socially awkward situation. We wave at someone who does not see us. We forget someone's name. A conversation stalls, and there is an uncomfortable silence. We smile at someone we thought was looking at us but was not. We trip in public. This story in Luke revolves around what was a very socially awkward moment.

The Pharisee who invited Jesus to a meal may been more noble than some of his group. There appears to be nothing disingenuous about the invitation. Jesus showed grace in that he accepted. We can imagine that the Pharisee invited his friends to the meal, some of whom might have been among the wealthy and influential people of the town.

The story is made possible because of how meals were typically served in Jesus' day. You did not sit in a chair at a table as we do today. The meal was served around a low table or mat at which people reclined on pillows or low couches. They typically reclined on their left side and used their right hand for eating. This stretched their feet out behind them, which kept them away from the table. No utensils were used, but people tore bread from a loaf and used it to scoop sauces, stews, and dips.

Luke records that while Jesus reclined at table in the Pharisee's home, a woman brought in an alabaster jar of ointment. Ointment was used for many purposes in the first century, from personal grooming to burial preparations. A person might save their entire lifetime to have enough ointment for their burial. Luke does not say, but the ointment may have represented a significant amount of money. Homes were much more open in the first century, which is what enabled her to simply walk in to observe the meal.

We can imagine that she intended simply to anoint Jesus' feet with ointment. When she got to where he was, however, her emotions overwhelmed her. She began to cry, to weep so profusely that her tears wet the feet of Jesus. As her tears ran off the feet of Jesus, she wiped them with the only thing she had which was her hair. She began to kiss his feet and anoint them with the ointment. Not only would the smell of the ointment have filled the room, but it was certainly a socially uncomfortable moment that drew everyone's attention. We would suspect that no one knew what to do.

To make things worse, the woman was someone of immoral character. The Pharisee knew her to be a sinful person known around town. Down through the centuries, commentators have considered her most likely a well-known prostitute in town. If that were the case, her appearance and attention to Jesus would have been scandalous. The Pharisee noted with self-satisfaction that Jesus could not be a prophet, or he would have known who the woman was. He assumed Jesus would not allow someone of such character to show him such affection. If we had been in Jesus' place, we might have felt the urge to protest: "Just to be clear – I have never met this woman before."

We might wonder how such an incident would resolve. Would the Pharisee ask her to leave? Would Jesus take notice of what she was doing? If so, what would he say to her? The response of Jesus serves two purposes. It is a teaching moment for the Pharisee if he would be willing to receive it. It would also serve to commend the woman's faith and extend grace to her.

The response of Jesus is first addressed to the self-righteousness of the Pharisee. As we see throughout the gospel, Jesus used common, ordinary illustrations to illuminate profound truths. Who would love a person more, someone forgiven much or little? The amounts used in the parable are not extravagant but would have been ones common to ordinary experience. The Pharisee responded with the obvious answer. The one forgiven more would be more grateful than the one forgiven less.

You have spoken rightly, replied Jesus. Then he began the moral of the parable. Its purpose was not only to teach the Pharisee but address the woman. Simon, the Pharisee, had not anointed the head of Jesus, washed his feet, or greeted him with a kiss. She had done all of those things, and more. Then Jesus got to his most important point. Therefore, her sins, which are many, said Jesus, are forgiven, for she has loved much. At that point, he said to her, "Your sins are forgiven." It was a remarkably kind way of commending the woman without embarrassing her. Jesus did not ignore her sins but acknowledged that they were many. But her love was great. She was truly one of the contrite of heart and broken in spirit whom God always receives graciously (Psalm 51:17). The incident ends with the Pharisees questioning in their hearts how Jesus could be so audacious as to think he had the authority to forgive sins.

Theological insights

- Some have suggested that this woman was Mary Magdalene. There is no evidence in the scriptures or early church tradition that this was the case.
- Jesus is anointed in other places in the gospels (Matthew 26:6-13, Mark 14:3-9, John 12:1-8). This seems to be a completely different incident from any of them.
- We sometimes are more gracious in giving than receiving. Here we see the ability of Jesus to graciously receive a very personal gesture of love that someone chose to bestow on him.
- The moneylender in the parable is generous. This probably intentionally mirrors that God is generous in his forgiveness.
- In this incident, like the one in Luke 3:17-26, Jesus asserts his authority to forgive sins, a prerogative of God only.

Practical application

It is good to be aware of our sinfulness. To be grateful to God, however, does not require that we were once a great sinner. While it is good when people deeply mired in sin turn to Christ, it is also good when people are spared a long downward spiral into sin's depths. Just because a person has not committed wicked acts does not mean that they are not sinners in God's sight. While the debts of some sinners are greater than others, everyone's debt is far more than they can pay. The parable of Jesus reminds us of this. If we are aware of our hearts, we know that sin and selfishness lie just below the service, waiting for an opportunity to emerge. This is why repentance is part of the Christian life. We need to continually examine ourselves in order to turn from our sins. It is why, in the Lord's Prayer, Jesus instructed us to pray that we not be led into temptation but delivered from evil. We should always be aware of our sinfulness. It is a dangerous habit to applaud our own righteousness.

LUKE 8

Women Who Accompanied Jesus – Luke 8:1-3

SOON AFTERWARDS, HE WENT ABOUT through cities and villages, preaching and bringing the good news of God's Kingdom. With him were the twelve, and certain women who had been healed of evil spirits and infirmities: Mary who was called Magdalene, from whom seven demons had gone out; and Joanna, the wife of Chuza, Herod's steward; Susanna; and many others who provided for them out of their possessions.

Most things are more complex and nuanced than they appear. The ministry of Jesus is an example. From reading the gospels, we may see Jesus as a lone prophet, with a handful of disciples, walking across the Judean countryside with little schedule or routine. While there is an element of truth in that picture, the reality is more complicated. How did Jesus pay for his ministry, for example? Did he simply hope someone would offer him food and a place to sleep? We get a small look behind the scenes into the ministry of Jesus in the opening words of Luke in this chapter. There was a group of women who followed Jesus and helped, behind the scenes, to support him in various ways.

Billy Graham was a popular evangelist in the 20th century. His crusades were well attended wherever he went, but he did not just show up in a town and expect an audience. There was a great deal of advance preparation that took place. Teams were sent ahead to organize publicity. Dates were announced. People were organized to support the event. When Billy Graham arrived, everything was ready.

We can imagine that Jesus may have done similar things. Luke says that Jesus went throughout the towns and villages of Judea preaching and bringing good news. The twelve apostles were with him and also a group of women. Jesus always attracted crowds, and almost everywhere he went, people were around. Much of the crowd would come and go depending on how close he was to their home village. But a group of women, says Luke, stayed particularly close. They had reason to – Jesus had healed them of "evil spirits and infirmities." This was a group of women who had a particular affection for Jesus because of his impact on their lives. Though they were apparently not involved in his preaching or healing ministry, they may have been quite supportive in other ways. Perhaps they attended to various details that made things run more smoothly. Luke will say (Luke 10:1-12) that on his final journey to Jerusalem, he sent the disciples as an advance team to announce his arrival in the various villages. The women may have served in making various arrangements and logistics run more smoothly.

This is the first mention of Mary Magdalene in the gospel of Luke. Her name, Mary, was a common one among first-century Jewish women. Her second name comes from her hometown of Magdala, which was near the capital city of Tiberias in northern Galilee. Luke says that Jesus had driven seven demons out of her. That is, she had been healed of a very serious infirmity. How would a person acquire seven demons? One demon would seem to be quite bad, much less seven? Some have considered her a former prostitute. Some have thought of her as the woman who anointed Jesus with ointment in Luke 7, but there is no biblical evidence to connect them. We might wonder, however, what activities she was engaged in that opened her to Satan's emissaries to such a degree. In all the gospel accounts, she is depicted as someone who loves Jesus very dearly. Her depth of love illustrates the previous story about the sinful woman who was forgiven much. Mary Magdalene may be someone who falls into that same category.

Luke also mentions a person named Joanna, who was the wife of Herod's steward. That someone connected with Herod's court would be a follower of Jesus is unexpected. It tells us, however, how popular Jesus was and how wide his reach had become, even at that stage. The Susanna mentioned by Luke is not mentioned in any other place in the New Testament. Luke takes note of her, however, as an important part of the group of women who followed Jesus. These, and others who are not named, appear to be independent women who had some financial means. They used those means to support Jesus and his ministry. They are good examples, along with the disciples, of the good soil that Jesus will describe as part of the next parable in Luke's gospel.

Theological insights

- Though Luke does not mention them, it seems that certain of the mothers of the apostles also followed Jesus around. It would have been a way for them to both follow Jesus and be near their sons. The gospels mention the mother of the sons of Zebedee, James and John (Matthew 27:56) and the mother of James the Less (Mark 15:40).
- The Herod mentioned in this passage is Herod Antipas, the tetrarch of the region of Galilee where Jesus did most of his ministry.
- Some have suggested that Mary Magdalene was a love interest of Jesus. There is no evidence for this in the gospels. His relationship with her is perfectly chaste although he does seem to be quite close to her. She is the first person to whom he appears after his resurrection.

Practical application

There are many ways to serve God. The apostles were visible leaders in the founding of the early church. Others, however, will be behind the scenes. Even among the apostles, some will be more prominent than others. The women who followed Jesus are a perfect example that many people are needed in the work of Christ. Each person has different gifts to offer. Those gifts may be spiritual, relational, or financial. While Jesus lived a life of poverty, God used people with financial means to support his work. God still does so today. God uses people with financial abilities to support the work of his church. This is a worthy service and ministry. It stands in line with the women who supported Jesus. Their example is noted to remind us that there are many ways to serve. We should use whatever means are within our capability.

The Parable of the Sower – Luke 8:4-15

WHEN A GREAT MULTITUDE came together and people from every city were coming to him, he told them a parable: "A farmer went out to sow his seed. As he sowed, some fell along the road, and it was trampled under foot, and the birds in the air ate it up. Other seed fell on the rock, and as soon as it grew, it withered away, because it had no moisture. Other fell among thorns, and the thorns grew with it and choked it. Other fell into the good ground and grew and

117

produced one hundred times as much fruit." As he said these things, he called out, "He who has ears to hear, let him hear!"

Then his disciples asked him, "What does this parable mean?" He said, "To you it is given to know the secrets of the Kingdom of God, but to the rest it is given in parables, that 'seeing they may not see, and hearing they may not understand.'

"Now the parable is this: The seed is the word of God. Those along the road are those who hear; then the devil comes and takes away the word from their hearts, so that they may not believe and be saved. Those on the rock are they who, when they hear, receive the word with joy; but these have no root. They believe for a while and then fall away in time of temptation. What fell among thorns, these are those who have heard, and as they go on their way they are choked with cares, riches, and pleasures of life; and they bring no fruit to maturity. Those on the good ground are those who with an honest and good heart, having heard the word, hold it tightly, and produce fruit with patience."

Parables are an age-old way of conveying practical lessons. From ancient times, oral cultures in particular have used everyday situations and images to illustrate moral truths. The Greek orator, Aesop, employed a form of parable. He used personified animals to teach moral lessons. His fable about the turtle and the rabbit teaches that slow and steady wins the race.

Jesus used parables in his teachings and is generally considered the most skillful user of them. Parables, as opposed to fables, tend to use human characters and aspects of nature and are often focused on spiritual lessons. The Parable of the Sower is important as evidenced by its also being recorded in Matthew and Mark. It is a parable about the proclamation of the word and its reception. Luke begins this section by noting how people came out to see Jesus from every town in the region. It resulted in great crowds of people who came to hear him. On one occasion, he told the Parable of the Sower.

A farmer sowing seed on his land would have been a familiar scene to Jesus' listeners. What might have struck them as unusual was the variety of soils on which it fell. While farmers typically would have been careful where they threw their seed, the farmer in the parable threw it more indiscriminately. It went far and wide; thus it fell in very different places.

The meaning of the parable would not have been immediately obvious to people as evidenced by the lack of understanding of the disciples. What was important was the opportunity the disciples were afforded. What others might not understand, Jesus intended to explain to his disciples. He would reveal to them secrets that others would not know.

Jesus' statement about the understanding of the crowd may seem confusing and arbitrary. Why would he not want to explain things to the crowd as well as the disciples? He explains the answer by paraphrasing from Isaiah (Isaiah 6:9). The intent of the statement seems to be that those who reject God's word will become closed to it. They may hear the word proclaimed, but it will not penetrate their hearts. This is not because of its ineffectiveness but the hardness of their hearts.

The four kinds of soil, as Jesus explains in the parable, are four different responses to God and his word. The first kind is like the path. The soil is hard and the word cannot sink deep. Even before it has a chance, the devil snatches the word away so a person cannot believe and be saved. We notice here that Jesus acknowledges a role for Satan in the rejection of the word. How does he take the word away from someone's mind and heart? He might distract them by other things so that they do not give God much thought. The devil and the world may fill them with cynicism and unbelief so that they do not give the gospel an honest hearing.

The rocky ground represents someone who believes at a surface level but eventually falls away. This person's commitment is shallow, like seed on top of rocks with little soil. Peer pressure or hardships make the commitment less attractive, and they abandon their faith when adversity comes. We might think of this person as someone whose faith does not have roots. Their life and experiences do not sink deep into the soil of the Bible, the church, or prayer. The slightest wind pulls up the plant because it does not have strong roots.

Weeds and thorns are a common problem in gardens. The seed among thorns represents the group of people whose faith never matures. If the problem of the seed on the rocky soil is adversity, the problem here is distractions. Many worldly pleasures, activities, and worries occupy their attention. Building wealth, achieving success, and fitting in with friends takes so much time that little is left for God. Jesus calls these distractions the cares, riches, and pleasures of life. The person has potential but never reaches it.

So far the farmer has not been successful. The final kind of soil redeems his efforts. Some people are like good ground. With honest and good hearts, they hear the word, hold tightly to it, and produce fruit with patience. This does not require great giftedness or spectacular abilities, only a good and honest heart. This person produces fruit *with patience.* Why with patience? The emphasis is not on impressive acts of service but on modest ones done over time. With patience and over time, everyone can bear fruit. We might find the parable depressing. Only one kind of soil out of four produces fruit, but the fruit produced is significant and makes all the sowing worth it.

Theological insights
- Who has the opportunity to know the secrets of the kingdom of God? Not only the disciples in the time of Jesus but everyone who reads the Bible. The parables and teachings of Jesus reveal those secrets.
- To what secrets does Jesus refer? Jesus is explaining the nature of God's kingdom, will, and plan.
- None of the things that choke out the seed – cares, riches, and pleasures of life – are necessarily unimportant or bad in themselves, except where they impede the growth of faith and Christian maturity.
- Anything that takes the place of God in a person's life is an idol. To place an idol above God breaks the first commandment, which says to have no other gods in place of the one true God.

Practical application

Jesus ends the parable by saying to the crowd, "He who has ears to hear, let him hear!" This is a word of exhortation with which Jesus will often end his teachings. It places the responsibility not on the teacher but on the hearer. The teacher has done his job in teaching, but the student has responsibilities too. Those who hear the word must have more than physical hearing but also spiritual ears. The message is sown for the sake of those whose hearts God opens so they can hear it.

Though Jesus does not conclude the parable with a moral, if he had done so, it might be something like, "Be careful what kind of soil you are." While the parable serves as an explanation of why some do not believe, it is also an encouragement to faith. Be like the good soil, says the parable. The rewards of doing so are great. Watch out for the weeds. Let the word sink in deep. You too can bear much fruit if you let God's word grow to maturity in your life.

Jesus Calms the Storm – Luke 8:16-25

A Lamp for Others to See – Luke 8:16-18

"NO ONE, WHEN HE HAS LIT A LAMP, covers it with a container or puts it under a bed; but puts it on a stand, that those who enter may see the light. For nothing is hidden that will not be revealed, nor anything secret that will not be known and come to light. Therefore consider carefully how you hear. Whoever has will be given more; and from the one who does not have, even what he thinks he has will be taken away.

The Mother and Brothers of Jesus – Luke 8:19-21

His mother and brothers came to him, and they could not come near him for the crowd. Some people told him, "Your mother and your brothers stand outside, desiring to see you." But he answered them, "My mother and my brothers are these who hear the word of God and do it."

Jesus Calms the Storm – Luke 8:22-25

One day he got into a boat with his disciples, and he said to them, "Let us go over to the other side of the lake." So they set out. But as they sailed, he fell asleep. A windstorm came down on the lake, and they were taking on water and were in danger. They went to him and woke him up, saying, "Master, Master, we are perishing!" He woke up and rebuked the wind and the raging of the water; then they ceased, and it was calm. He said to them, "Where is your faith?" They were afraid and marveled, saying to one another, "Who then is this, that he commands even the winds and the water, and they obey him?"

Anyone who has vision problems appreciates the value of glasses. The child who could not see what the teacher wrote on the board can suddenly see. The street signs look clear. The words on the page come into focus. It is a great advance that poor eyesight can be cured with glasses, contact lenses, and even corrective surgery.

The words of Jesus give clarity to our spiritual and moral vision. Theologian John Calvin was fond of saying that the scriptures are like a set of eyeglasses. Without them, the world is cloudy and uncertain. The scriptures enable us to see life, God, and ourselves in much clearer focus. The words of Jesus in this section do this very thing.

The first set of sayings follows from the admonition to the crowd at the end of the Parable of the Sower – "He who has ears to hear, let him hear!" Jesus begins with an illustration from daily life. When you light a lamp, you do not then cover it up. You put it on a stand so it gives light to the room. That is the purpose for which you lit the lamp. This saying is much like what Jesus says in the Sermon on the Mount (Matthew 5:14, 15), however, Jesus follows his comment differently. Instead of saying that we should let our light shine before others, Jesus uses the illustration to note that nothing can be hidden. Just as light enables everything in the room to be seen, so things now hidden will one day be revealed. For that reason, we should be careful how we respond to God and his Word.

What did Jesus mean? What secret things will be revealed? This statement makes us think of the final judgment when every person will stand before God. At that point, all secrets will be revealed, and God's judgment will be fairly meted out. It is a statement that encourages us not to live secret lives. Let God's light shine in our hearts, and live in the light because all things will one day be known.

Then Jesus says something that seems counterintuitive. Those who have will be given more. From those who do not have, even what they appear to have will be taken away. We might find this unfair, at first reading, but the ways of the kingdom of God continue to surprise us. Jesus is referring to the blessings and benefits of God's kingdom. Those who enter it will find even greater blessings. Those in whom God's words find no place will be left empty. This has a practical application. A person who uses the gifts God gives them will discover that his or her ability to use them increases. Those who neglect to use God's gifts will find them withering from disuse. The promise for those who follow God's ways and use his gifts is that they will experience more of God and a greater measure of his gifts.

The next story also cuts against our expectations. Under normal circumstances, the family takes top priority. Those who neglect families for the sake of work, hobbies, or ambition, sin against one of God's most important institutions. Yet there is something that takes priority over family

– it is God and his calling. That seems to be the motivation of Jesus in this interaction with his family.

Luke reports that Jesus' mother and brothers came to visit him. Because the crowd was large, they could not get near. When word that they stood outside wanting to see him reached Jesus, he did not change what he was doing. He used it as a teaching moment. "My mother and my brothers are those who hear the word of God and do it."

The Gospel of Mark gives us context for this incident that Luke does not. Mark reports (Mark 3:21) that the family of Jesus had great concerns about the direction of his ministry. Mark reports them, perhaps meaning his brothers, as saying, "He is out of his mind." This would offer a reason Jesus did not meet with them. It was not the time for him to be publicly scolded by his family. It was also a sign that he had a higher priority than them; it was the ministry his heavenly Father had given him.

The words of Jesus to the crowd are encouraging. We might imagine how wonderful it would have been to be a part of the earthly family of Jesus, grow up with him, and know him so intimately. The words of Jesus offer us an even greater opportunity. Those who hear the word of God and do it are also intimate members of his family. This makes the great blessings of God accessible to every person. Those who hear God's word and obey it are invited to become part of Jesus' spiritual and eternal family.

The next account is about Jesus calming a storm on the Sea of Galilee. The small lake was known for sudden violent storms that came over the surrounding hills onto the lake. Jesus and the disciples were caught in one of those storms one day, so much so that they began to take on water. What was Jesus doing? He had fallen asleep. We might imagine that he did so after a long exhausting day of healing, teaching, and ministering to people. He fell so soundly asleep that he was able to sleep through a raging windstorm.

The reaction of the disciples is not unexpected. Though they may have wanted to let Jesus sleep, at one point it was impossible. The boat was taking on water and in danger of sinking, so they awoke him urgently. What he did astonished them. He rebuked the wind and water so that, suddenly, the lake was calm. The fishermen who had spent many hours on that lake must have been stunned. They had never seen such. Luke records their reaction. Astonishment and fear came over them. Their words to one another were, "Who is this who can do such a thing?"

We see in this account a demonstration of Jesus' divinity and power. Even creation obeys his command. If God were to come to live among us in flesh and blood, we would expect him to have powers beyond ours. We would expect that he could heal diseases, do miracles, raise the dead, and control nature. Those were exactly the abilities Jesus demonstrated. The disciples recognized, in Jesus, a power that went beyond any earthly ability. It is another instance, in Luke's gospel, where Jesus' actions were consistent with his identity as the Son of God. Jesus transforms chaos into peace.

Theological insights

- What is the word of God like? It is a lamp that brings light to the world. It brings what is concealed in people's hearts into the light.
- The New Testament does not talk about faith as seeing but rather hearing. God cannot be seen but we can hear his word and obey it.
- Jesus encouraged people to be "careful how you hear." The New Testament will repeatedly affirm that spiritual hearing takes place in the heart and is made possible by the work of the Holy Spirit.
- Jesus calls his disciples to complete commitment. As Jesus demonstrated in his life, nothing takes priority over God.
- As was the case with the disciples in the story, it may sometimes be necessary for us to find ourselves in the middle of difficulties so that we recognize our weaknesses and experience God's power.

Practical application

We sympathize with the anxiety of the disciples in the boat because they were clearly terrified. The sharp rebuke of Jesus, "Where is your faith," may seem unwarranted. Was their fear not justified? His response to them, however, has a point. It was to encourage their faith, even in seemingly impossible circumstances.

What is your faith like? Does it waver? Is it small at times? Are you trying to fix things yourself instead of relying on God? Jesus might marvel at our lack of faith at times also. With God as our Creator and heavenly Father, we should not be afraid. God is with us and will not leave us. In the next storm that you face, remember this account and ask, "What would it mean for me to have more faith in this situation? Where does God want me to trust him more fully?"

Jesus Heals a Demon Possessed Man
Luke 8:26-39

THEN THEY ARRIVED AT the country of the Gerasenes, which is opposite Galilee. When Jesus stepped ashore, a certain man from the city who had demons met him. For a long time he had worn no clothes, and did not live in a house, but in the tombs. When he saw Jesus, he cried out and fell down before him. With a loud voice he said, "What do I have to do with you, Jesus, Son of the Most High God? I beg you, do not torment me!" For Jesus had commanded the unclean spirit to come out of the man. For the unclean spirit had often seized the man. He was kept under guard and bound with chains and fetters, but he broke them and was driven by the demon into the desert. Jesus asked him, "What is your name?" He said, "Legion," for many demons had entered him. They begged him not to command them to go into the abyss.

Now there was there a large herd of pigs feeding on the mountainside, and they begged him to allow them to enter them. He gave them permission. The demons came out of the man and entered the pigs, and the herd rushed down the steep bank into the lake and were drowned.

When those who fed them saw what had happened, they fled and told it in the city and in the country. People went out to see what had happened. They came to Jesus and found the man from whom the demons had gone out, sitting at Jesus' feet, clothed and in his right mind; and they were afraid. Those who saw it told them how he who had been possessed by demons was healed. All the people of the surrounding country of the Gerasenes asked him to depart from them, for they were very much afraid. Then he entered the boat and returned.

But the man from whom the demons had gone out begged that he might go with him, but Jesus sent him away, saying, "Return to your home, and declare what great things God has done for you." He went his way, proclaiming throughout the whole city what great things Jesus had done for him.

Archeologists have confirmed a number of places and events in the Bible. For example, King Hezekiah's tunnel, built to bring water into the city during sieges, as recorded in II Kings 20:20, has been uncovered in Jerusalem. Various ancient inscriptions confirm biblical kings and events, such as Kings David and Jehu. Persian artifacts describe King Cyrus's decree allowing ancient people, including the Jews to return to their homelands. Pontius Pilate's name was discovered on an inscription in Caesarea corroborating the New Testament account of his governorship. The pool of Bethesda, with five gates, mentioned in John 5:2, has been uncovered in Jerusalem. The ruins of Caesarea Maritima have been uncovered, including the palace where Paul was tried before Festus and Agrippa.

One of the biblical sites that has not been located, however, is the place of the healing of the demoniac in Luke 8. The ancient biblical manuscripts give a number of different names for the place where Jesus and the disciples landed. Matthew calls it the country of the Gadarenes (Matthew 8:28). Luke calls it the country of the Geresenes. Some ancient manuscripts list it as the region of the Gergesenes. These may not be different names of the same place but refer to different locations. Around the Sea of Galilee, there was a prominent city called Gadara in the area given to the tribe of Gad on the southeastern side of the lake. There was also a town called Gerasa about thirty miles off the coast. There was also a village known as Gergesa much closer to the shore of the sea but not the same as the town of Gadara. In some of these sites, there are steep hills and also ancient tombs, but no site exactly fits all the details of the story. It is a site whose exact location remains unknown. One important thing about the area on the eastern and southeastern sides of the lake was that it had a significant Gentile population.

This event takes place when Jesus and the disciples arrive on the other side of the lake after the storm. Upon arrival, a man possessed with demons met them. Luke's description of the man indicates how difficult was his situation. His possession had caused him to lose his dignity; he lived naked or almost so. He was socially isolated as indicated by his life in the tombs. He had a disregard for religious duty as his life in the tombs would have made him ceremonially unclean. His speech was controlled by the demons, and he spoke loudly. As evidence of his possession, he had extraordinary strength. The people of the town viewed him as dangerous since they had attempted, to no avail, to keep him bound with chains. When the demon

126

reveals his name, it is Legion. That there were a great number of them indicates the degree to which this man was possessed.

That the man fell down in front of Jesus does not seem to be an act of worship but rather a plea for mercy. The demons recognize that future torment awaits them. Luke does not give us an indication as to what is the "abyss" into which the demons did not wish to be cast, nor does he indicate why it was better for the demons to go into the pigs rather than simply be cast out.

In reflecting on the fact that Jesus allowed the demons to go into the pigs, people have asked if Jesus disregarded the property of others. Jesus, however, did not cause the pigs to rush into the lake; the demons did. It is unclear if the pigs were kept by Gentiles or Jews. Though Jews could not have eaten them, Gentiles such as Roman soldiers in the area, could have, and their keeping may have been a business venture. Whatever the case, the destruction of the pigs would have been a striking illustration of the remarkable miracle. It also makes it clear that the man was cured of demonic possession rather than a mental illness.

The reaction of the people of the city may seem surprising. Instead of rejoicing that a man in great need had been cured, their fears were aroused. If Jesus had judged them for the matter of keeping pigs, what other secrets might he expose? What other business ventures might he disrupt? This was an incident that did not, apparently, awaken a need for repentance. They simply did not think Jesus was compatible with their way of life. They encouraged him to leave, and he did.

This is one of the few instances in the gospels in which someone who wished to follow Jesus was not allowed to do so. We can understand how the man might have wanted to go with Jesus. Why would he not allow it? Perhaps the man was not ready. We can imagine that he would need time to regain his full mental, relational, and spiritual balance. Traveling with Jesus would not allow time and leisure for that to happen. Instead, Jesus gave the man a task that would prepare the region to be able, perhaps when the early church began, to hear the gospel more readily. It would also put the man back into the normal routines of life, which may have been necessary for his full emotional healing. Soon enough the gospel would come to that region when the early church started. His evangelistic efforts may have laid the groundwork for a ready reception of it. Luke says that the man did as Jesus commanded and shared his story throughout the city.

Theological insights

- If the reason that Jesus traveled to this out-of-the-way region was this single miracle, it served a worthy purpose. Some ancient commentators suggested that demonic forces may have brought the great storm on the sea in an attempt to stop the miracle from taking place.
- There are legions of ways the devil can torment us and society. We should be on our guard against them.
- That which is unclean prefers the clean. The demons preferred the pigs rather than the abyss, though they brought destruction to them.
- In Luke's account, Jesus' ministry continues to reveal his power – displaying authority over both nature and demonic forces.

Practical application

When people follow the way of the devil it disrupts their lives in a multitude of ways. It isolates us from others, opens us to destructive living, and destroys our dignity. What Christ does is make us clean. The ways of the devil may seem enticing, but they lead to uncleanness, confusion, and loss of personal stability. The sooner we realize this, the better off we are.

The man whom Jesus healed had a dramatic story to tell to the inhabitants of the city. They knew his former life and could see the change that took place in him. We also have a story to tell of God's work in our lives. It may not be dramatic, but if it is real, then it is valid. We too should look for opportunities to share the account of God's work in our lives. There may be people who will be influenced for good by it.

Jesus Heals the Daughter of Jairus and a Woman
Luke 8:40-56

WHEN JESUS RETURNED, the multitude welcomed him, for they were all waiting for him. A man named Jairus who was a ruler of the synagogue came to him. He fell down at Jesus' feet and begged him to come to his house, for he had an only daughter, about twelve years of age, and she was dying.

But as he went, the multitudes pressed against him. There was a woman who had a flow of blood for twelve years. She had spent all her living on physicians and could not be healed by any. She came behind him and touched the fringe of his cloak. Immediately the flow of her blood stopped. Jesus said, "Who touched me?" When everyone denied it, Peter said, "Master, the multitudes press and jostle you, and you say, 'Who touched me?'" But Jesus said, "Someone touched me, for I perceived that power has gone out of me."

When the woman realized that she was not hidden, she came trembling; and falling down before him told him in the presence of all the people the reason why she had touched him, and how she was healed immediately. He said to her, "Daughter, your faith has made you well. Go in peace."

While he was still speaking, someone from the ruler of the synagogue's house came, saying to him, "Your daughter is dead. Do not trouble the Teacher anymore." But Jesus on hearing it, answered him, "Do not be afraid. Only believe, and she will be healed." When he came to the house, he did not allow anyone to enter, except Peter, John, James, the father of the child, and her mother. Everyone was weeping and mourning, but he said, "Do not weep. She is not dead, but sleeping." They laughed at him, knowing that she was dead. But he put them all outside, and taking her by the hand, he called, saying, "Child, arise!" Her spirit returned, and she got up immediately. He commanded that something be given to her to eat. Her parents were amazed, but he commanded them to tell no one what had happened.

This account in Luke contains a story that has been the subject of much speculation and devotional literature down through the centuries; it is the account of the healing of the woman with the flow of blood. Her plight has been one that has garnered sympathy and her healing one worthy of great interest.

This story has been called a miracle within a miracle because the healing of the woman takes place in the middle of the story of Jairus and his daughter. This incident took place when Jesus and the disciples came back to Capernaum after the healing of the demoniac. Luke says that a crowd was waiting for him when he arrived.

Jairus was a ruler of the synagogue. This means that he was a prominent elder, respected by the people, who served to support and manage the activities of the synagogue. From all we can tell, he was a good, honest, and noble person. His plea to Jesus was urgent. He fell to his knees and begged for mercy. His only daughter, twelve years of age, was dying. Jesus went with him to his home, and the crowds went with him.

The plight of the woman who touched Jesus was serious and debilitating. Most commentators assume it to be some sort of gynecological bleeding. This would have made her ritually unclean, meaning she would not have been able to participate in the worship life of the community. In addition, it would have been embarrassing and a source of ongoing discomfort. It may have kept her from getting married and having children. That she had spent all her money on doctors and was no better indicates how serious was her malady.

Why did the woman not approach Jesus openly and ask for healing? It might be that the nature of her illness was embarrassing and too delicate for conversation with a man. "Perhaps I can merely touch him and be healed" she may have reasoned. Then everyone could avoid an uncomfortable conversation. She had been in the crowd waiting for Jesus. When he began to move to the home of Jairus, she saw her chance. She moved close behind him and touched the edge of his robe. Instantly she felt healing flow into her, and she knew that she had been healed. Her goal was to slip away quietly so no one would notice her.

Luke says that Jesus immediately felt power go out of him. The Greek word for power is the one typically used, *dumamin.* This is the word from which we get our English word "dynamite." Jesus felt that spiritual power was released. He knew someone in need of healing had touched him.

We can imagine the dismay of the woman. This was exactly what she did not want to happen. Was she in trouble? Had she done something wrong? If she kept quiet, perhaps Jesus would still go on his way. Even the disciples said, "Master, everyone has been touching you!"

But Jesus would not relent. When the woman realized that she could not hide, she admitted what had happened and told Jesus everything. Instead of being scolded, Jesus praised her. It was her faith that had made her well. Jesus blessed her and said, "Go in peace." It must have been a wonderful day for the woman. She could now start a new life – the life God had always intended her to have.

What happens next heightens the drama of the story. It also makes the miracle more pronounced. In the time it took Jairus to come to Jesus and Jesus to head toward his home, the girl had died. People from his home delivered the disastrous news, but Jesus encouraged him not to fear. Believe and she will be healed.

We see in the gospels that Jesus sometimes took a smaller group of disciples with him. It may be that there was no room for the twelve. It might have been too much of an entourage. In the girl's room, Jesus touched her and spoke to her. She immediately sat up. Luke, as a physician, is careful to include that Jesus told her parents to give her something to eat.

Why would Jesus not want this miracle publicized? It would certainly be nearly impossible to hide. Perhaps it was why Jesus said to the crowd that she was merely sleeping. The answer may be that the crowds were already larger than Jesus could manage effectively. He and the disciples were overwhelmed, at times, by the demands, and Jesus needed time to teach the disciples. In addition, he did not want his identity as the Messiah known before the appropriate time.

While this is an account of the power of Jesus, it is also a story of faith. Some commentators have suggested that the faith of Jairus was weak and the faith of the woman strong. Jairus needed Jesus to come to his home; the woman knew that she only needed to touch him. Nevertheless, in his mercy, Jesus accommodated them both. The grieving people laughed when Jesus announced that the girl was only sleeping. We can understand their skepticism, yet they represent many who still laugh at Christ, disbelieve in him, and disdain his church.

Jesus continues to show his mastery over every situation, over the elements of nature, over demonic spirits, over difficult diseases, and even over death. His words also encourage faith – "only believe." All those who place their faith in him will find him sufficient for what they need.

Theological insights
- Sometimes interruptions turn out to be from God. While we may find them irritating and unfortunate, they may be unexpected opportunities to do good.
- We see Luke's care for and attention to the plight of women in these two stories. This is a characteristic that will run throughout his entire gospel.
- Jesus may have known prophetically who the woman was, but it seems more likely that the Spirit did not reveal it. For that reason, Jesus stopped and waited until she revealed herself.

- By touching a dead body and allowing himself to be touched by a ceremonially unclean woman, Jesus risked ritual defilement, placing himself at odds with Jewish law. Yet he did not hesitate to engage with the messy and painful realities of life. In doing so, he set a powerful example for us to follow.

Practical application

The woman with the flow of blood has captured the imagination of Christians through the centuries. The fourth-century church historian, Eusebius, tells of seeing two statues in front of what was believed to be her home in Caesarea Philippi, one of Jesus and the other of her reaching out to touch him. After her death, the residents erected them as a memorial to her faith.

In the medieval period, a legend developed of a woman named Veronica who wiped the brow of Jesus with a cloth when he stumbled on the way to the cross. The legend says that the face of Jesus was miraculously imprinted on the cloth from its touching his face. In the latter medieval period, some people connected Veronica with the woman healed from the flow of blood. In her gratitude for what Christ had done for her, she showed him a small gesture of compassion amid his sufferings. Her wiping Christ's brow has become one of the fourteen Stations of the Cross that follow Jesus from his trial before Pilate through his burial.

Neither of those stories has any foundation in scripture and little in other historical facts, except for the statues that Eusebius saw. It is an example, however, of how devotional literature developed through the centuries, as people imagined the life of the woman after her healing. They wondered if she found some tangible ways to express her gratitude to Jesus. As people envisioned her paying Christ back with a small token of devotion, they imagined themselves also finding ways to show Christ their deep gratitude. It is a valid and time-honored spiritual practice to engage one's "sanctified imagination" as a way of deepening prayer. For instance, envision your own thankfulness for Christ's healing work in your life. Picture yourself offering him a simple act of service, and let that image draw you into humble, heartfelt prayer. Then, let your prayer move you to real, tangible action.

LUKE 9

Jesus Feeds the Five Thousand – Luke 9:1-17

Jesus Sends Out the Twelve Apostles – Luke 9:1-6

HE CALLED THE TWELVE TOGETHER and gave them power and authority over all demons, and to cure diseases. He sent them out to proclaim the kingdom of God and to heal the sick. He said to them, "Take nothing for your journey – no staff, nor wallet, nor bread, nor money, and do not take an extra shirt. Into whatever house you enter, stay there, and leave from there. Wherever they do not receive you, when you leave that city, shake off the dust from your feet for a testimony against them." They departed and went throughout the villages, preaching the Good News and healing everywhere.

Herod Hears about Jesus – Luke 9:7-9

Now Herod the tetrarch heard about all that he was doing; and he was very perplexed, because it was said by some that John had risen from the dead, and by some that Elijah had appeared, and by others that one of the prophets of old had arisen. Herod said, "I beheaded John, but who is this about whom I hear such things?" He sought to see him.

Jesus Feeds the Multitude – Luke 9:10-17

When the apostles had returned, they told him the things they had done. He took them and withdrew by themselves to a city called Bethsaida. But the multitudes perceived it and followed him. He welcomed them, spoke to them of the kingdom of God, and he cured those who needed healing. The day began to wear away; and the twelve came and said to him, "Send the crowd away, that they may go into the surrounding villages and farms to lodge and get food, for we are here in a deserted place." But he said to them, "You give them something to eat." They said, "We have no more than five loaves and two fish – unless we should go and buy food for all these people," for there were about five thousand men. He said to his disciples, "Have them sit down in groups of about fifty each." They did so and had them all sit down. He took the five loaves and the two fish, and looking up to heaven, he blessed them, broke them, and gave them to the disciples to set before the crowd. They all ate and were filled. They gathered up twelve baskets of broken pieces that were left over.

A time-tested model for passing along leadership is to let someone watch you do a task, then do it alongside them, and then let them do it while you watch, giving them instruction and feedback all along. Though the disciples did not realize it, Jesus was preparing them to take over his ministry after his ascension. To do that, he would need to give them opportunities to practice the ministry they would soon be doing themselves.

Luke reports that Jesus sent out the disciples in two stages. First, he sent out the twelve. Later, as reported in Luke 10:1-20, he would send out others in addition to them. The disciples had certainly watched Jesus as he taught, healed, and performed miracles. We can suppose that they never imagined doing such things themselves, but that is what Jesus sent them to do. They too were to preach about the kingdom of God, cast out demons, and heal the sick. The idea must have excited and terrified them.

What exactly were the disciples to proclaim? How were they to preach? They had not had a seminary course on preaching. Nor had they been given a class on public speaking. The answer is that Jesus had given them ample parables and other teachings for them to communicate to others. Why did Jesus use parables? One reason was that it gave his disciples material for their preaching. They too could tell the parables and explain them as Jesus had done for them. They could relate his common sense moral teachings to others just as he had done to them. They could also tell people about Jesus and all the things he did. Every preacher and teacher, even today, is grateful for the teachings of Jesus. They are marvelous material that one can never exhaust. The parables and teachings of Jesus are rich and densely packed so that a multitude of lessons can be drawn from just a single parable or story.

How were the disciples to heal and do miracles? Jesus gave them both the power and authority to do so. That is, they had the authority to heal people in his name and cast out demons. Their words also had power. When they prayed for people to be made well, the healing miracles took place.

How was that possible? How could ordinary people, such as fishermen and tax collectors do such things? It was a special dispensation, and God honored their prayers. As God had used such signs to validate the ministry of Jesus, in the days that were ahead, he would use them to validate the ministry of the early church as well.

The instructions of Jesus to the disciples would not be standard procedure for church ministry in the future. Even the early church would give thought to how its ministry was to operate and be supported. But this first mission was a special time, and Jesus wanted the apostles to rely totally on God. They were to take nothing with them except the barest of essentials. Whatever else they needed, God would provide. The instruction about staying in one house only was a practical one. Jesus did not want the disciples to be constantly seeking better accommodations at the risk of insulting their former hosts. Whatever hospitality was offered to them, they were to accept with grace.

Jesus warned, however, that not every town would be welcoming. We see an instance of that later in this chapter. What were they to do? Was it a sign of failure on their part? Jesus gave them instructions. They were to leave the town and shake the dust off their feet as a witness against them. They were to consider it the town's inability to hear God's word rather than something wrong they had done. Luke reports that the disciples did as Jesus had instructed, going throughout the villages in that region.

The region in which Jesus did most of his ministry was the northern region of the nation, the region of Galilee. We might wonder why Jesus seemed to want to stay below the radar, both in his identity as the Messiah and his popularity. One reality of his situation was that Herod the Tetrarch ruled Galilee. He was a wicked and ruthless ruler. It would not have been good for Herod to become antagonistic toward Jesus. If he had wished to do him harm, he certainly had the power to do so.

It was impossible, however, for Herod to be unaware of Jesus. He would have heard stories about him, many of which recounted remarkable miracles. Luke says that Herod was perplexed by what he heard. No one had ever done the things Jesus did. Even the great prophets had only done occasional miracles; Jesus seemed to be doing them with regularity. Like many people, especially the religious leaders, Herod wondered how such things were possible. Being superstitious he may have wondered many things. Herod had killed John the Baptist. Who then was this doing such astounding miracles?

Luke says that Herod sought to see Jesus. The Greek language of this verse indicates that Herod actively sought to see him. Jesus, however, was hard to locate. You never knew where he and the disciples would be. He often went to out-of-the-way places. Provoking a hostile reaction from Herod was one reason Jesus did not want the enthusiastic crowds to publicly proclaim him king. Nor was he ready to publicly affirm his Messianic identity. He would have an encounter with the political authorities at the appropriate time, but that time had not yet arrived. Herod did not want the antagonism of the crowds so he did not force the issue. As it would turn out, however, Herod would get an opportunity to see Jesus, when, during his trial, Pontius Pilate sent Jesus to him (Luke 23:6-12).

Of all the miracles in the Old Testament, some are notable. One of those is the manna that the children of Israel ate in the wilderness. The wanderings of the people in the wilderness were a difficult time. It was made worse by the fact that food and water were scarce. In addition, the number of people was large. It would have been an impossible task to feed such an army of people by ordinary means, so God did a miracle to provide for them. In addition to bringing quail into the camp for the people to eat, every morning a white substance appeared on the ground (Exodus 16:13-21). It could be baked like bread and had a sweet taste. At its first appearance, the people said, "What is it?" That phrase became its name – Manna. The feeding of the nation with manna became one of the important miracles that God did under the leadership of Moses.

The feeding of the five thousand by Jesus was a miracle that showed that Jesus was at least as great as Moses. He did not do the miracle for that reason, however, but out of compassion for the people. We see evidence of Jesus' organizational ability in this account. If there were five thousand men in the crowd, the total number of people might have been twice that with women and children. How would one organize feeding them? Jesus took thought for how to do so efficiently. By sitting them in groups of fifty, the disciples could go to the various groups. It would go much smoother than requiring long lines, which would have been tedious and tiring. It is an instance in which we see the wisdom of Jesus. It reminds those who work with others to give thought to organizing matters for smooth operation. It was an example for the disciples to follow in their leadership and management of the early church.

What would it have been like for the disciples to observe the miracle of the loaves and fish? How would several loaves and fish become enough to

136

feed a multitude? We do not know, but it must have been an experience that increased their faith. The magnitude of the miracle is emphasized by the fact that everyone ate all they wanted with twelve baskets left over.

We might observe that Jesus did not ordinarily do miracles for daily nourishment. In the wilderness after his temptation, for example, he did not turn the stones into bread. When he and the disciples were without food, they experienced hunger. When he raised the young girl to life, he told the parents to give her something to eat (Luke 8:55). Why did Jesus not do miracles for daily bread? It was because the disciples and others would not be able to do so after he was gone. Jesus did not live in a way that would be impossible for others to follow. He trusted God to provide, which he did. Jesus relied on his heavenly Father in the same way he taught people to pray: "Give us this day our daily bread."

Theological insights
- Jesus gave the twelve apostles power and authority to preach and heal. He gives this same authority and power to the church today. The church uses it to proclaim the word and has the authority of Jesus to do so.
- An important part of the work of the apostles was preaching and teaching. God calls particular people today into this ministry for the health of the church and the advancement of the gospel.
- There is no indication in the scriptures that the church today does not also have the authority to heal. What it seems to lack is not the authority but the power, or perhaps the faith, to do so.
- The words used in the feeding of the five thousand are similar to those used at the Last Supper. Jesus took the bread, blessed it, broke it, and gave it. As the Lord fed the five thousand with physical bread, so he feeds his church today in the Lord's Supper with spiritual sustenance.

Practical application
The words of Jesus to the disciples seem puzzling: "You give them something to eat." This was a miracle beyond their power to perform. What then was the reason for Jesus' comment? It would seem to be an encouragement for their future ministries. It is easy to wait for someone else to take care of a problem. We might hope someone else will take matters into their hands. Here Jesus encourages initiative and courage. The disciples

would face many difficulties in starting the church. Instead of hoping someone else would solve them, the words of Jesus urge them to take responsibility. They would be charged with feeding the church with spiritual food. They should not wait for someone else to do it.

These words are instructions for us also. We too may often hope someone else will solve the problem. Jesus puts the responsibility on us. You give them something to eat. You do what needs to be done. You trust God and do what you can. It may be that God will enable you to do far beyond what you imagine.

Peter's Confession – Luke 9:18-27

Peter's Confession – Luke 9:18-22

AS HE WAS PRAYING ALONE, the disciples were near him, and he asked them, "Who do the multitudes say that I am?" They answered, "John the Baptist, but others say, 'Elijah,' and others, that one of the ancient prophets has risen." He said to them, "But who do you say that I am?" Peter answered, "The Christ of God." And having strictly warned them, he commanded them not to tell this anyone, saying, "The Son of Man must suffer many things, and be rejected by the elders, chief priests, and scribes, and be killed, and the third day be raised."

The Cost of Discipleship – Luke 9:22-27

He said to all, "If anyone desires to come after me, let him deny himself, take up his cross, and follow me. For whoever wishes to save his life will lose it, but whoever will lose his life for my sake will save it. For what does it profit a man if he gains the whole world, but loses or forfeits his own self? For whoever is ashamed of me and of my words, of him will the Son of Man be ashamed when he comes in his glory, and the glory of the Father, and of the holy angels. But I tell you the truth: There are some standing here who will not taste death until they see the kingdom of God."

Novels often have a pivotal turning point in which a character's choice, a sudden revelation, or a dramatic change in situation alters the direction of the story. Harry Potter discovers that he is a wizard, and it starts his life on a new trajectory. Katniss Everdeen volunteers for the Hunger Games in place of her sister, Prim. At the Council of Elrond, Frodo takes on the burden of the One Ring. The gospel of Luke has a turning point in what is often called the "confession" of Peter. The term is not used to describe an admission of guilt but an affirmation, or confession, of faith.

The account starts with Jesus at prayer. Luke says that Jesus was praying alone. This is an important glimpse into the life of Jesus. He was almost always surrounded by people, often large crowds. Yet he thought it vital to get time alone with his heavenly Father. Since Jesus was fully human, he related to his Father through the Spirit as all humans do. Though he certainly lived in the presence of God at all times, he needed to get away from the crowd for quiet moments. There were things to say and the Father's voice to hear that had to be done in quiet. His example reminds us that, even though we may sense God's presence in our daily activities, we too need time in quiet. This is our time to bring our praises and petitions to God. It is also time for God to nurture our spirits and nudge us with his Spirit. If Jesus found time alone in prayer crucial, we should too.

It was one of those times alone in prayer that prompted Jesus to ask the disciples a critical question. Up until this point, Jesus had not required the disciples to make a declaration about his identity. The time had finally arrived. Perhaps he knew that they were ready to answer rightly. When Jesus asked who they thought he was, Peter, spoke for himself and the group. "You are the Christ of God." Matthew's gospel describes a conversation that took place after Peter's declaration (Matthew 16:13-20), but Luke does not. What is important is not only Peter's public assertion but Jesus' acknowledgment. Peter had spoken correctly, and Jesus acknowledged it.

What made this a turning point in the ministry of Jesus was two things. First, it is the gospel's explicit recognition that Jesus is the Messiah. Peter affirms it and Jesus acknowledges it. Second, from that point onward, Jesus began to warn the disciples about his destiny. It was not going to be glamor and glory. Rather, it was the way of suffering.

Luke says that Jesus warned them not to reveal what they knew. Why were they to keep it secret? Because something unexpected was going to happen – the Son of Man was going to suffer many things, be rejected by the elders, chief priests, and scribes, and be killed, but rise on the third day. The disciples must have thought those words by Jesus impossible for the Messiah. The meaning of his words did not register in any significant way in their minds.

Jesus also began to teach them that the way of discipleship was not an easy path. He described it in the most difficult terms. For a person to follow him meant denying himself. That was bad enough. Who wanted to deny himself? Does that mean denying needs as well as wants? How is that service to God?

But there was more, and Jesus raised the stakes. To follow him meant that a person had to take up their cross and follow him. The disciples must have wondered what that could mean. A cross was not an inspiring religious symbol at that time. It was an instrument of torture. To take one's cross was a fate to be avoided at all costs. It was the most terrible of situations. How, the disciples must have wondered, would that serve the purposes of God?

Then Jesus characteristically gives a compelling rationale. It is possible to save your life but lose your soul. Those who try to save their lives will lose them. Only those who lose their lives will save them. Then Jesus adds another example. Consider a person who gains the whole world but loses his own self. How tragic would that be?

Jesus is looking at things from an eternal perspective. A person might have everything the world offers, but lose it all in eternity. One might grasp after life's most treasured possessions and experiences, but wander from God in the process. A person might seem to have gained everything but in reality, lose it all.

Jesus then makes another comment that may seem unrelated. Part of gaining one's life concerns one's feelings about Christ. To gain one's soul is related to Jesus. Those who will not acknowledge him in public will not be acknowledged by him in heaven. There will be a day when Christ will return in victory with the holy angels. Only those who acknowledge him, even amid an unbelieving world, will be acknowledged and rewarded by him.

The tone of the statements by Jesus is a warning, but he ended them with a promise and encouragement. Some of those hearing his words will see the kingdom of God come. It is not far away but soon to arrive. Be patient and faithful. Good things from God are just around the corner.

We might think that Jesus would have invited people to become his disciples with the promise of an easy, carefree life. He did not. He makes the path for a disciple appear hard. We might suppose it was his way of keeping the casual follower from joining in. He did not portray a false picture of discipleship. The way would be hard, but the reward was great. Everyone should consider the cost. Jesus was going to suffer. Disciples of Jesus will have to follow in the way of their Master.

Theological insights
- The word *Christ* means anointed one. As kings and priests were anointed by God in the Old Testament, the promised Messiah was to be the Anointed One who would surpass them all.
- Psalm 2:2 talks about the Lord's anointed, saying, "The kings of the earth take their stand and the rulers conspire against the Lord and his Anointed …"
- The Greek word *Christ* is the equivalent of the Hebrew word for "Anointed One." *Jesus Christ* means "Jesus the Anointed One." Peter called Jesus "the Christ of God."

Practical application

Peter's confession is an affirmation of his faith in Jesus as Christ. How is it that a person comes to faith in Jesus Christ? There are many ways God works in people's lives. This is part of the mystery of faith. God works in a person's life to soften their heart, open their understanding, convince their minds, and move their wills. This is the work of the Holy Spirit. Martin Luther, the Protestant reformer, said that faith was the only work that God does within us without our help. God does all other works with our involvement and cooperation. Faith, however, is God's gift. God's Spirit works in our hearts until we are confidently able to say that Jesus is indeed the Christ of God.

Some people have dramatic conversion moments like the apostle Paul. Others gradually grow in faith and understanding; they may not be able to point to a specific moment of turning. Peter seems to be of this latter type. His ability to confess Jesus as the Christ of God came over time and from his ongoing acquaintance with Jesus. The experience of Jesus is life-changing. The Spirit creates faith in us and then rewards that faith with his love and presence. It is truly a blessing and a great privilege to be granted the gift of faith in Jesus Christ.

The Transfiguration – Luke 9:28-36

ABOUT EIGHT DAYS AFTER these sayings, he took with him Peter, John, and James, and went up on the mountain to pray. As he was praying, the appearance of his face was altered, and his clothing became dazzling white. Behold, two men were talking with him, Moses and Elijah, who appeared in glory and spoke of his departure, which he was about to accomplish at Jerusalem. Now Peter and those who were with him were heavy with sleep, but when they were fully awake, they saw his glory, and the two men who stood with him. As they were departing from him, Peter said to Jesus, "Master, it is good for us to be here. Let us make three tents: one for you, one for Moses, and one for Elijah," not knowing what he said. While he said these things, a cloud came and overshadowed them, and they were afraid as they entered into the cloud. A voice came out of the cloud, saying, "This is my Son, whom I have chosen. Listen to him!" When the voice had spoken, Jesus was found alone. They kept quiet and told no one in those days anything that they had seen.

One of the extraordinary stories in the Old Testament concerns Moses on the mountain. When the people of Israel arrived at Mount Sinai, where God had appeared to Moses in the burning bush, Moses went up on the mountain to receive God's commandments. He spent 40 days there in God's presence, communing with him. It was there that God gave Moses the Ten Commandments and the other laws for the nation. Moses would spend several extended times with God on the mountain. The book of Exodus says that when Moses came down off the mountain his face shone from having been in the presence of God (Exodus 34:29).

Luke recounts a story that also appears in Matthew (17:1-8) and Mark (9:2-13). It is what has come to be called the Transfiguration. As Moses communed with God on the mountain, so did Jesus. Moses' face only shone, but Jesus was completely transfigured. The incident begins with Jesus going up the mountain for a time of prayer. As he had done on one occasion previously (Luke 8:51), he took with him only three of the disciples, Peter, James, and John. Why did he only take the three? One obvious reason might be that Jesus was not publicly proclaiming his Messianic identity, and it kept the experience somewhat private. It was hard enough for three disciples to

142

keep a secret, much less twelve. It may also be that he did not want Judas to have the experience. Peter, James, and John would play important roles in the leadership of the early church; at times, such as this, he gave them special training and experiences.

That the face of Jesus was altered is reminiscent of Moses, yet more takes place than Moses ever experienced. Jesus was completely transfigured, so that his clothing becomes dazzling white. The two people who appeared with him, Moses and Elijah, were considered among the greatest in the Old Testament. They also appeared in heavenly glory. In this context, they seem to represent the two great sections of the Old Testament, the Law and the Prophets.

The dullness of the disciples is represented by their drowsiness. What are they doing while Jesus prays? Naturally, they are falling asleep. The appearance of Jesus and the two awaken them from their slumber, however, and they become fully alert. Luke says that the two were talking with Jesus about his upcoming departure that he would accomplish in Jerusalem. It is of note that this conversation was prophetic; Jesus would indeed fulfill his mission in Jerusalem.

Much has been said about the comment of Peter. In this context, it comes across as foolish and inappropriate. When he suggested building tents, he probably had in mind the kind of temporary shelters that were built each year during the Festival of Booths. It is not surprising that Peter would be the first to speak, given his impulsive nature, even if what he says is foolish. Luke says that he spoke as the two were departing. Perhaps he wanted to prolong the experience and stay in the holy moment. One ill-advised part of his comment was that it seemed to put all three on an equal level, something the voice from the cloud rejected.

This experience seems to happen quickly. Even as Peter is making his foolish comment, a cloud overshadows them. This is reminiscent of the time of Moses in the wilderness when the cloud hovered over the Tabernacle and led the people in their wanderings. But the cloud's presence is ominous, and Luke reports that the disciples were afraid. Of course, the presence of God is often unnerving, and that is what the cloud symbolizes. From it, a voice came. "This is my Son, whom I have chosen. Listen to him!" It serves as a rebuke to Peter's comment and instruction for the disciples.

What does the voice from the cloud indicate? It elevates the authority of Jesus, even in relation to the two great Old Testament saints. When the disciples open their eyes, no one is standing there except Jesus. What does the voice of God say about him? He is God's Son. God has chosen him for a special role in his plan. The disciples are to listen to him, even above Moses and the prophets.

The experience will serve as a teaching moment for the disciples. It is confirmation from above for what they have sensed in their spirits. Jesus is indeed the Christ of God, God's Son, who is God's Messiah. They not only hear the voice but also get a glimpse of Jesus in his heavenly glory as the Son of God. Jesus has the approval of two great figures from the Old Testament and even supersedes them. If the disciples had any doubts about Jesus, this should have dispelled them. Jesus was not only the promised Messiah but also the very Son of God.

The Old Testament had given hints about the identity of the Messiah, but they were obscure. Most thought him to be a warrior king like David. That he would be more than just a great leader and prophet, however, was surprising. No one imagined that he would be God himself, the Son of God and third member of the Trinity. Jesus was slowly revealing his identity and purpose to the disciples. He was, indeed, the Son about whom Psalm 2 had hinted when it said, "The Lord said to me, 'You are my son. Today I have become your father. Ask of me, and I will give the nations for your inheritance, the uttermost parts of the earth for your possession' ... Kiss the Son, lest he be angry, and you perish on the way, for his wrath will soon be kindled. Blessed are all those who take refuge in him" (Psalm 2:7, 8, 12). Jesus was the prophet that Moses foretold, the one to whom the people would listen (Deuteronomy 18:15). He was also beginning to reveal to them that his path would involve suffering. With his life, he would fulfill the mysterious words of Isaiah about God's Suffering Servant (Isaiah 52:13-53:12).

Theological insights
- The transfiguration of Jesus confirms his identity as the Son of God, reveals his preexistent glory, and foreshadows his exaltation at the right hand of the Father after his ascension (Philippians 2:9-11).
- The figures of Moses and Elijah do not seem to be visions but the actual people. That they are alive in heaven and able to appear with Jesus gives credence to the promise of the resurrection to eternal life.
- Peter wanted to build booths for Jesus, Moses, and Elijah to stay on the mountaintop. Discipleship, however, does not consist of staying

in sacred moments. It means going, doing, and following Christ's lead into the world.

- It is this incident that Peter seems to refer to in II Peter 1:16, 17. He mentions that he was an eyewitness to the majesty of Christ, heard the voice from heaven while with him on the mountain, and listened as Jesus was declared the Son of God.

Practical application

If God were to say only one thing to us, what might it be? It might be the words of the voice on the mountain: "This is my Son, whom I have chosen. Listen to him!" The identity, role, and purposes of Jesus certainly puzzled his first-century listeners. How did his words align with the laws of the Old Testament? It was especially puzzling when the pattern of life Jesus exemplified seemed to contradict Old Testament patterns and convictions. The voice gave the disciples instruction. Listen to Jesus over all other voices.

Many voices vie for our attention today. They are voices in the news media, social media, entertainment, advertising, politics, career, friends, and family. What weight do we give them, especially when they guide us differently? The words from the cloud are still reliable guidance. Above all the voices that call to us, the words of Jesus are the most truthful, take precedence, and can be trusted. We are blessed to have his words readily available in scripture. They are indeed words of life, full of guidance, and truth. We do well to give them our faithful and consistent attention.

Jesus Heals a Young Boy – Luke 9:37-45

ON THE NEXT DAY, when they had come down from the mountain, a great crowd met him. Behold, a man from the crowd called out, saying, "Teacher, I beg you to look at my son, for he is my only child. Behold, a spirit takes him, he suddenly cries out, and it convulses him so that he foams at the mouth; and it hardly departs from him, bruising him severely. I begged your disciples to cast it out, and they could not." Jesus answered, "O faithless and perverse generation, how long shall I be with you and bear with you? Bring your son here." As he was coming, the demon threw him down and convulsed him violently. But Jesus rebuked the unclean spirit, healed the boy, and gave him back to his father. They were all astonished at the majesty of God.

But while everyone was marveling at all the things that Jesus did, he said to his disciples, "Let these words sink into your ears, for the Son of Man will be delivered up into the hands of men." But they did not understand this saying, and it was concealed from them, that they might not perceive it; and they were afraid to ask him about this saying.

There is a special bond between parents and children. This is exactly the way God designed it. His plan is for all children to be born into the arms of parents who love them, have their best interests at heart, and think they are the most precious thing in the world. That it does not always happen this way is a great tragedy. Yet even parents whose lives are disordered feel a natural bond with their children. God has placed that affection in them.

The account of the transfiguration emphasized the love of God, the Father, for Jesus his Son. When Jesus and the three disciples came down from the mountain, they found a father in distress because of his son, his only son. We see echoes of the bond between Jesus and his heavenly Father in this story. In this case, the bond between father and son had been broken by an illness that threatened the very life of the son. The illness had, no doubt, left his family in disarray. We see in the father's words that he is desperate for help.

It was great for the disciples to experience the mountaintop. Their euphoria was short-lived, however. When they came down from the mountain with Jesus, they rejoined the world of sickness, sin, and unbelief. Not only was a family in great need of healing, but the disciples who remained behind were unable to handle the problem. They had done miracles when Jesus sent them on their missionary journey, but this problem proved beyond their abilities. Luke, as a physician, seems to give extra attention to relating the details of the boy's physical condition.

The frustration of Jesus has puzzled theologians through the centuries. When he remarks, with apparent annoyance, "O faithless and perverse generation, how long shall I be with you and bear with you," his meaning is not clear. What was the object of his displeasure? Was it the disciples for their inability to perform the healing? Jesus had certainly expressed his frustration to them previously about their lack of faith. When the storm came

146

upon them, he said, "Where is your faith" (Luke 8:25). Was Jesus irritated at the devil for tormenting this family and child? Or was it something else? Commentators have noted that the father seems to call out to Jesus rudely, without humility and respect. Was his lack of faith the source of Jesus' annoyance?

We might ask how a young boy would become demon-possessed. Under normal circumstances, we cannot imagine such a thing happening to someone young and innocent. There were many pagan practices, however, even in first-century Israel. The family's lack of religious devotion and their pagan practices may have opened the boy to dark forces. That Jesus had to clean up their mess may have been the source of his frustration. We may also hear, in the words of Jesus, an echo of the frustration Moses felt at times leading the children of Israel in the wilderness (Numbers 11:11-15). Moses sought to lead, in the evaluation of God, a stiff-necked people (Exodus 32:9-10). We wonder how often Jesus felt the same way.

When the father brought the boy to Jesus, the unclean spirit convulsed him. For Luke, this was a sign of the boy's possession and the devil's power. At the sight of Jesus, it engaged in one last violent act against the boy. Jesus rebuked the spirit, however, and gave him back to his father. Luke says that the crowd was astonished. The man and his family would certainly have been very grateful.

In his ministry, Jesus continues to deal with a troubled world. The mountaintop experience was not real life. The life of even the disciples was messy, frustrating, and filled with difficulties. People from all walks of life desperately needed a Savior because their sins had overwhelmed them. God knew how desperately the world needed his Son.

This healing is followed by Jesus' second announcement about his upcoming sufferings. Once again Jesus had done well, and the crowds were astonished at his power. But Jesus understood that he would enter into his glory, not through worldly success but suffering. Though he knew the disciples could not fathom such a future, he told them anyway. With his closest friends, he shared honestly. He was going to be "delivered up into the hands of men." These words of Jesus provided new information if the disciples could have processed it. Not only was he to suffer many things; he would be "delivered up."

From our vantage point, his words point to his betrayal. Though Jesus knew it would happen, we can imagine that he found the idea difficult. He felt human affection even more deeply than we do. In his humanity, it must have hurt to think that someone in whom he had invested so much, who ate with him every day, whom he had sent out in ministry, and who was among the chosen twelve would turn against him. The nation's religious leaders would be the ones most eager to see him killed. Jesus would be delivered into the hands of men. It was part of his path of suffering that he would be subject to the whims of sinful human beings who would not provide him the justice he deserved.

Luke says that the saying by Jesus about his upcoming fate was concealed from the disciples so that they did not understand it. Some suggest that the devil darkened their understanding, but it is more likely that their preconceived notions about the Messiah were too strong to be changed. To understand the work of Christ, they would have to undergo the agony and distress of Good Friday before they could appreciate the glory of the Easter.

Theological insights
- At times down through the centuries, epilepsy has been wrongly thought to be a sign of demon possession. Though this boy's illness resembles epilepsy, the passage is clear that demonic forces, not a physical ailment, caused his symptoms.
- The disciples of Jesus, even today, are not always able to do as Jesus did. While Christ is able to do all things, we, as his disciples, are sometimes lacking in faith. The church needs more prayer and faith.
- Satan looks for opportunities to find a foothold in people's lives. For that reason, we should never dabble in the occult, experiment with dangerous drugs, or habitually lie. Yet Jesus can deliver even those in Satan's deepest bondage.

Practical application
Luke calls the spirit that possessed the boy an "unclean" spirit. Jesus in the gospels brings order to people's lives. Satan brings disorder, distress, and difficulty. We recognize the devil's work by its uncleanness. He brings confusion, chaos, and squalor. He instigates and encourages the works of the flesh.

The apostle Paul contrasted God's work in our lives with our sinful inclinations as the conflict between the flesh and the Spirit. When we walk in the Spirit, we do not fulfill the desires of the flesh. The Spirit brings peace and protects us from unclean spirits. If we want order and peace, we should follow the Spirit. Sin seems appealing but always leaves us unclean.

Who Is The Greatest? – Luke 9:46-62

Receiving a Little Child – Luke 9:46-50

AN ARGUMENT AROSE among them about which of them was the greatest. Jesus, perceiving the thoughts of their hearts, took a little child, and set him by his side, and said to them, "Whoever receives this little child in my name receives me. Whoever receives me receives him who sent me. For whoever is least among you, this one will be great." John answered, "Master, we saw someone casting out demons in your name, and we forbade him, because he does not follow with us." Jesus said to him, "Do not forbid him, for he who is not against you is for you."

Jesus Rejected By a Samaritan Village – Luke 9:51-56

It came to pass, when the days were near that he should be taken up, he steadfastly set his face to go to Jerusalem and sent messengers before his face. They went and entered a village of the Samaritans, in order to prepare for him. They did not receive him, because he had set his face toward Jerusalem. When the disciples, James and John, saw this, they said, "Lord, do you want us to command fire to come down from heaven and destroy them?" But he turned and rebuked them; and they went to another village.

A Disciple's Commitment – Luke 9:57-62

As they went along the way, a certain man said to him, "I will follow you wherever you go." Jesus said to him, "The foxes have holes and the birds of the air have nests, but the Son of Man has no place to lay his head." He said to another, "Follow me!" But he said, "Lord, allow me first to go and bury my father." But Jesus said to him, "Leave the dead to bury their own dead, but you go and announce the kingdom of God." Another also said, "I want to follow you, Lord, but first allow me to say good-bye to those who are at my home." But Jesus said to him, "No one, having put his hand to the plow and looking back, is fit for the kingdom of God."

One of the realities of life, even for people of faith, is that relationships can get messy. Misunderstandings happen between people. Expectations do not get met. Communication can be less than honest. Someone does not respect your boundaries. Differing priorities come into play. Conflicts arise because people carry emotional baggage. Those in power take advantage of others. Insecure people get jealous. It is one of the reasons Paul urged grace toward others in the church: "Bear with one another, and forgive one another if anyone has a complaint against someone; even as Christ forgave you, so also you must do" (Colossians 3:13).

What is true for us was true for Jesus. God did not shield him from everyday problems, irritations, and conflicts. He was dealing in close relationships with many people, and he was the only one without sin. Luke details several incidents in which Jesus had to deal with messy human relations.

We might think that the disciples were becoming humble servants of Christ and others after spending several years with Jesus. We see, in their ambitions, how hard a task Jesus had in training them. Just when Jesus was beginning to see his death on the cross looming larger in front of him, the disciples were imagining their worldly glory. As ordinary people, they may not have seemed ambitious, but the more they imagined a Messianic kingdom on earth, the more their inner aspirations emerged. Even Christian leaders are vulnerable to temptations. One day the ambitions of the disciples erupted into a discussion among them about their own greatness.

We see Jesus, in this account, as the preeminent teacher. He does not scold them but gives them an object lesson. What could be more humble than a child? Yet a humble child was an example of the kind of greatness God desired. In addition, whoever received a child in Christ's name received him. This reminds us of the parable in Matthew 25 in which we do good to Christ by doing good to others (Matthew 25:31-46). What is good about receiving a child? It is that they cannot repay you. They offer you no benefit in return. One must receive a child simply out of the goodness of one's heart. But, said Jesus, if you receive a child in my name, you receive me. And those who receive me, said Jesus, receive the one who sent me – God in heaven. This last statement is very important. Anyone who wishes to know God can find him through Jesus Christ. As we will hear him say in John's gospel, to come to Jesus is the only way to know God (John 14:6). Then Jesus drove home the point to the disciples. The one who is least among them is the one who is the greatest.

The response of Jesus to the comment of John is instructive: "He who is not against you is for you." This is an important reminder for Christians. It is easy to be critical of other churches and Christians who do life together and ministry differently. The words of Jesus remind us that others who are not against Jesus may be working for him also, only differently than we are. Our criticism may reveal our jealousy of others who do things, not only differently, but also better. If they "cast our demons" in the name of Jesus differently than we do, we should nevertheless rejoice that they do.

The account of Jesus' rejection by the Samaritan village begins with an important comment. Luke says that Jesus realized that the time had come for his sacrifice at the Passover in Jerusalem. Up to that point, Jesus had been traveling around Judea, often in the region of Galilee, going to the regular festivals in Jerusalem, and then going back through Samaria to Galilee. At a certain point, however, Jesus began his final journey toward Jerusalem. It begins in Luke 9:51 and will continue until he arrives, as recorded in Luke 19:27. Luke says that Jesus steadfastly set his face toward Jerusalem. He had a mission to fulfill, and even though it was a difficult one, he set about to complete it.

Luke says that the Samaritan village rejected Jesus' visit because his face was set toward Jerusalem. This statement does not give us much information to discern their specific attitude. The Samaritans were often at odds with the Jews. Though they were technically Israelites, the Samaritans were also of mixed heritage and people with a wide variety of religious practices. One source of tension between them was the regular festivals that were so important to the Jews. When the northern kingdom of Israel split off from the southern kingdom after the death of Solomon (I Kings 12:16-24), it created political, social, and religious tensions. Because the northern kings did not want their people to seek reunion, they discouraged them from traveling to Jerusalem for annual festivals. Instead, they set up their own national worship sites and promoted them. For that reason, the Samaritans had little sympathy for Jews traveling to Jerusalem for festivals and sometimes hindered them if they could.

We see the apparent aggressive natures of James and John in this story. Jesus had given them the nickname "Sons of Thunder" (Mark 3:17). In their suggestion about calling down fire from heaven, they may have remembered how Elijah called down fire from heaven on the messengers of King Ahaziah (II Kings 1:1-16). Jesus rebuked them, however, for their suggestion.

This is the only account in all the gospels of this story, and it contains several textual variants. When the King James Version of the Bible was translated in 1611, it used the best Hebrew and Greek manuscripts available. At that time there was one widely accepted and authoritative Greek text of the New Testament; it was called the Textus Receptus, or the received text. Its reading of verses 54 and 55 said, "Lord, do you want us to command fire to come down from heaven and destroy them as Elijah did? But he turned and rebuked them and said, "You do not know what manner of spirit you are of, for the Son of Man came not to destroy people's lives but to save them." Since the 19th century, several more ancient Greek manuscripts have been discovered. The best of them do not include these additional words. Though they are explanatory and may be authentic to Jesus, they seem to have been added later, perhaps by scribes wishing to explain the rationale behind the suggestion of the brothers and the rebuke of Jesus. Most Bible translations today put them as a footnote at the bottom of the page and note that some manuscripts contain the addition.

Luke records three instances of failed discipleship. To the first person, who asserts that he will follow Jesus anywhere, Jesus states that the Son of Man has nowhere to lay his head. The path of discipleship will be uncertain, says Jesus. The statement also highlights the kind of life Jesus lived during his ministry; it was one of poverty and suffering.

The second potential disciple wanted first to bury his father. Since burials were typically done quickly after death, we assume that the father had not died. It might be some extended time before that took place and the person was ready to become a disciple. The time was now, replied Jesus, because the kingdom of God must be announced.

The final person had biblical authority for his request. When Elijah tapped Elisha as his successor, Elisha said, "Let me please kiss my father and my mother, and then I will follow you" (I Kings 19:19, 20). After he did that, Elisha became Elijah's assistant and successor. Yet the call to follow Jesus is a greater one than to follow Elijah. It requires a deeper commitment and nothing, either care for self or family, takes precedence over it.

Theological insights
- Though the church today may not often literally cast out demons, we do so in many ways. Any time we bring healing to a broken person, help people recover from an addiction, or shine light into a dark life,

we defeat the power of darkness. This is the work to which Christ has called the church, to set the captives free in his name.

- The rebuke of Jesus to James and John reminds the church that violence is never a means to promote the gospel. The methods of the church are persuasion, love, and service.
- Jesus uses another simple but brilliant illustration to explain the need for a disciple's full commitment. Those who look back while plowing cannot plow a straight row. In the same way, said Jesus, wavering discipleship will not do. Such a lack of commitment is not fitting for the greatness of the kingdom to which a Christian is called.

Practical application

What is the life of a disciple like? It is not a charmed, idyllic life without care or trouble. No, it is life in the real world, lived among real people. It can be messy and difficult. There will be successes and failures. Humility will be required. Christ's love is proclaimed through acts of service to others. People cannot be forced, only invited, but the work is important because Christ's kingdom must be announced.

For the disciple, nothing can stand above Jesus Christ. Disciples often live out that commitment imperfectly, however. Other priorities get in the way and call for our attention, but the words of Jesus call us back to him. He is worthy of total commitment, and nothing less will do. God's reward for disciples is great because those who lose their lives for Christ will save them for eternal life (Luke 9:24).

LUKE 10

Jesus Sends Out Seventy-Two – Luke 10:1-16

NOW AFTER THESE THINGS, the Lord also appointed seventy-two others, and sent them two by two ahead of him into every city and place where he was about to come. Then he said to them, "The harvest is indeed plentiful, but the laborers are few. Pray earnestly therefore to the Lord of the harvest, that he may send out laborers into his harvest. Go! Behold, I send you out as lambs among wolves. Carry no purse, nor wallet, nor sandals. Greet no one on the way. Into whatever house you enter, first say, 'Peace be to this house.' If a son of peace is there, your peace will rest on him; but if not, it will return to you. Remain in that same house, eating and drinking the things they give, for the laborer is worthy of his wages. Do not go from house to house. Into whatever city you enter and they receive you, eat the things that are set before you. Heal the sick who are there and tell them, 'The kingdom of God has come near to you.' But into whatever city you enter and they do not receive you, go out into its streets and say, 'Even the dust from your city that clings to us, we wipe off against you. Nevertheless know this, that the kingdom of God has come near to you.' I tell you, it will be more tolerable in that day for Sodom than for that city.

"Woe to you, Chorazin! Woe to you, Bethsaida! For if the mighty works had been done in Tyre and Sidon that were done in you, they would have repented long ago, sitting in sackcloth and ashes. But it will be more tolerable for Tyre and Sidon in the judgment than for you. And you, Capernaum, will not be exalted to heaven, but will be brought down to Hades. Whoever listens to you listens to me, and whoever rejects you rejects me. And whoever rejects me rejects him who sent me."

Most people like adventures, at least if they are not dangerous. Though it is possible to attempt impressive and daring adventures, like climbing Mount Everest, many adventures are simple and accessible, such as: hiking a trail, kayaking in the river, exploring a new city, going camping, driving to a new place, going snow skiing, visiting a historic or interesting site, experiencing new cuisines, or taking a stimulating class. While the old is comfortable, we need excitement and adventure to keep life fresh and interesting.

We see in the Gospel of Luke that Jesus did not envision a stagnant life for his followers. One evidence was the expansion of the missionary endeavors of the twelve to include others. As he had sent the twelve out to proclaim the good news, so others would join them in that venture. There is also a sense of urgency in his doing so. The time was fast approaching for the starting of the Christian church. Many hands would be needed for the work.

Only Luke tells the story of the sending of the seventy-two. There is a discrepancy in ancient manuscripts as to the exact number. Some manuscripts say seventy, others seventy-two. Most current translations believe seventy-two to be the more likely original number. Both numbers had significance in the biblical and historical record for first century Jews. Moses took seventy elders with him up on the mountain (Numbers 11:16, 25) to commune with God. The Hebrew version of the Table of the Nations, in Genesis 10, lists seventy nations, although the Greek Septuagint lists seventy-two. According to the tradition of the Talmud, seventy-two scholars were chosen, six from each tribe, to translate the Old Testament Law from Hebrew to Greek in the third century B.C. Miraculously they completed the five books of the Law in seventy-two days. It came to be called the Septuagint, which interestingly comes from the Latin word for seventy. Jesus may have chosen the number for its symbolic purposes, or it may simply have been the number of trusted followers with him at that time. It is possible that the manuscript discrepancy came about because well-meaning copyists changed the number from seventy-two to seventy because it aligned better with the Old Testament. Luke would have known the number seventy-two from the Septuagint Table of Nations; a later scribe may have corrected it to align with the Hebrew version's seventy.

The instructions Jesus gives them are similar to those he gave the twelve (Luke 9:1-6), with some additions. Like with the twelve, they were to take nothing else with them, except what they wore. They were to stay in the same home during their visit. If a town did not receive them, they were to shake the dust off their feet when they departed. As John the Baptist had done, they were to prepare the way for Jesus' coming. Jesus also noted that the laborer is worthy of his wages. This would be a pattern for the church in the future. Those who preach the gospel would make their living from the gospel (I Corinthians 9:14, I Tim 5:17, 18).

There is a sense of urgency in their instruction from Jesus. They are to greet no one on the way. That is, they are not to be distracted from their task. Jesus encourages them; the harvest is plentiful, but there will be difficulties. They will be like lambs among wolves. Not every town will receive them, but their rejection will not negate the truth of their message. Any who do not receive them should understand that the kingdom of God has come near them.

An addition to the instructions is the greeting of peace to a household. To greet with "Peace" would have been a typical greeting. Jesus said, "Peace be with you" when he appeared to the disciples after his resurrection (Luke 24:36). Jesus also notes the possibilities of finding a "son of peace" in the villages. It is this verse (10:6) that has provided a framework for missions in some unevangelized countries. In every village the evangelist looks for a "person of peace" who is open to the gospel. From that person they begin to reach out to the community. It is an approach that has proven quite effective in some places.

There is a serious warning in the words of Jesus. It will be worse for a town that rejects the disciples' message about him than for Sodom. The biblical city of Sodom (Genesis 19:1-29) was considered an example of great wickedness and terrible judgment. To be considered worse than Sodom was a serious condemnation. It signals, in the words of Jesus, how important was his person, message, and kingdom.

Jesus also issues a set of woes to towns in Judea. If they thought they would escape judgment, they were very wrong. Even towns that might boast that Jesus had done many miracles in them would not escape. Jesus mentioned towns in the region of Galilee where he had spent a great deal of time, Chorazin, Bethsaida, and Capernaum. His point is that their response had been less that exemplary. Even the pagan cities of Tyre and Sidon would have responded better if he had done his miracles in them.

Why was the warning of Jesus so urgent? His messengers were coming with a message of peace, but peace was going to be elusive for the nation. In fact, within 40 years, the Romans would come into Judea and ravage the nation, taking many captives and burning Jerusalem. What would cause such a drastic Roman response? It was that the Jews rejected peace, rebelled against Rome, and paid the price for doing so. The trajectory of the nation was not peace, but turmoil, trouble, and destruction. Historically, had the nation accepted Christ, a different outcome would certainly have taken place. From a merely earthly standpoint, there was great urgency. Jesus' words also point to the greater judgment of God. That will be the most serious judgment of all, and not to be prepared for it will be disaster.

The disciples whom Jesus sent were to act as agents in his name. As a legal agent has the authority of the person who sent him, so did the disciples. Those who received them, received Christ. To reject them was to reject Christ. Christ also had come in the name of the Father. To reject Christ was to reject God himself. In the words of Jesus, the stakes were high. If people want to know God and live in his purposes, they must receive the messengers he sends.

The words of Jesus emphasize hearing – "Whoever listens to you listens to me" (10:16). As Jesus noted in the Parable of the Sower, it is those who hear the word, hold it fast in a good heart, and bear fruit with patience who are the good soil. The gospel is a set of promises from God that are to be heard, believed, and practiced. Blessed are those who do so. Woe to those who do not.

Theological insights
- As Jesus sent out the disciples to heal, the church today is also called to heal the sick. One way to find avenues for ministry is to ask, "Where are there people in need of healing?" It is to those places that the church is called.
- Peace and justice go together. It is hard to have peace without justice. The peace of Christ creates justice, however, because it brings healing, creates reconciliation, and fosters goodwill among people.
- Like when Jesus sent out the twelve, he sent out the 72 in pairs. This will be a pattern for ministry that we see in the early church: Paul and Barnabas, Paul and Silas, Barnabas and Mark. Doing ministry with others provides needed support and help.

Practical application
Harvest time is a time of urgency. When harvest time comes, many hands are needed, and time is of the essence. The proclamation of the gospel

158

is also urgent. In this passage, Jesus gives some important principles for ministry:

- We have Christ's authority to engage in ministry – "After these things, the Lord also appointed seventy-two others, and sent them."
- There are great opportunities for those who do ministry – "The harvest is plentiful."
- Effective ministry should be bathed in prayer – "Pray earnestly therefore to the Lord of the harvest."
- Many hands are needed for the work – "The Lord also appointed seventy-two others."
- Ministry is better done with others – "And he sent them two by two ahead of him."
- The Lord will provide what you need – "Remain in that same house, eating and drinking the things they give."
- He calls us to bring healing to others – "Heal the sick who are there."
- There will be dangers and difficulties – "I send you out as lambs among wolves."
- We should not be distracted by lesser priorities – "Greet no one on the way."
- You will not always find success – "Whenever they do not receive you."
- Know that when you are rejected, they are not primarily rejecting you, but God – "Whoever rejects you rejects me."
- Be confident in God's presence – "Know that the kingdom of God has come near."

The Seventy-Two Return – Luke 10:17-24

THE SEVENTY-TWO RETURNED WITH JOY, saying, "Lord, even the demons are subject to us in your name!" He said to them, "I saw Satan fall like lightning from heaven. Behold, I give you authority to tread on serpents and scorpions, and over all the power of the enemy, and nothing will in any way hurt you. Nevertheless, do not rejoice in this, that the spirits are subject to you, but rejoice that your names are written in heaven."

159

In that same hour, Jesus rejoiced in the Holy Spirit, and said, "I thank you, Father, Lord of heaven and earth, that you have hidden these things from the wise and understanding, and revealed them to little children. Yes, Father, for so it seemed good in your sight. All things have been delivered to me by my Father. No one knows who the Son is, except the Father, and who the Father is, except the Son, and anyone to whom the Son chooses to reveal him." Turning to the disciples, he said privately, "Blessed are the eyes that see the things that you see, for I tell you that many prophets and kings desired to see what you see, and did not see them, and to hear the things you hear, and did not hear them."

There are many things that bring us joy in life. Relationships are a source of joy. It is great when the whole family is together at Thanksgiving or Christmas. Accomplishing a goal can bring a sense of satisfaction. Being outside in nature can be a source of peace and wonder. Engaging in creative activities such as music, painting, or writing often gives people personal joy. Such things as: physical activity, learning a new skill, serving someone in need, having a good laugh, spending time in prayer, practicing gratitude, and having an early morning cup of coffee on the deck can give us a deep sense of peace, contentment, and joy.

When the disciples returned from their missionary journey, they had a deep sense of joy. Their preaching had been received, people had been healed, and even demons had departed from people in Jesus' name. Luke's gospel is the only one that records the return of the seventy-two.

The comment by Jesus about Satan's fall from heaven is part of Christianity's understanding of the origin of evil and the role of the devil in the world. Christianity's understanding of evil has roots in the biblical narrative and the church's theological reflection. Early church theologians Tertullian and Augustine laid the groundwork for the church's understanding. They interpreted passages like Isaiah 14:12-15, and Ezekiel 28:12-17 as allegories of Satan's fall from grace due to his pride. God made everything good, even Satan, but moral failure on his part, particularly his desire to be equal to God, caused him to rebel against God. When he did, he was cast out of heaven. God gave the angels free will, and some chose to join Satan in his rebellion. Thus, when Satan fell, a host of angels fell with him. Augustine interpreted Revelation 12 as an account of Satan's fall from heaven at the beginning of history and his ongoing battle against God and the church.

Though the New Testament does not contain a fully developed doctrine of evil, the words of Jesus reveal a number of aspects of Satan's activity. The devil is the one who tempted Jesus in the wilderness (Luke 4:1-13). He told him, "Be gone, Satan" (Matthew 4:10). Jesus calls him a murderer and the father of lies (John 8:44). In the parable of the Sower (Luke 8:12), it is the devil who takes the word away from people's hearts. In the Parable of the Weeds (Matthew 13:39), the devil sows weeds in the field. Jesus confirmed Satan's influence over people when he rebuked Peter saying, "Get behind me, Satan" (Matthew 16:23). He also called Satan the "ruler of this world" (John 12:31). He prayed for Peter and told him that Satan wanted to "sift him like wheat" (Luke 22:31-32). The declaration by Jesus that he saw Satan fall "like lightning from heaven" is a foundational statement in the Christian view that evil is related to the fall of Satan and his ongoing activity in the world.

One characteristic of the ministry of Jesus was his power over Satan, as shown in his ability to cast out demons. The disciples, on their return, marveled that the same authority had been given them through Jesus' name. But Jesus quickly refocused their attention. While he had indeed granted them power to confront and overcome evil, their joy was not to rest in their victories over the forces of darkness. Instead, they were to rejoice that their names were written in heaven.

The idea that the names of those who are saved and receive eternal life are written in heaven appears in several places in the Bible. God told Moses that whoever sinned would be blotted out of his book (Exodus 32:32-33). Daniel talked about people who were spared God's judgment because their names were written in his book (Daniel 12:1). Paul talked about those whose names are written in the "book of life" (Philippians 4:3). In Revelation, Jesus promised the faithful that their names will never be blotted out of the book of life (Revelation 3:5). Revelation 13:8 refers to the "Lamb's book of life." At the final judgment, says Revelation, the books will be opened and the dead judged according to their deeds. All those not found in the Book of Life will be thrown into the lake of fire (Revelation 20:12-15). In addition, only those whose names are written in the Lamb's book of life will be able to enter the New Jerusalem (Revelation 21:27). The biblical idea of a book of life symbolizes God's knowledge, justice, and grace. Being written in the Book of Life testifies to one's relationship with God through faith and is assurance of the gift of eternal life. Jesus assures the disciples that they have great reason for joy, not because the demons are subject to them, but because their names are written in heaven.

Luke records an instance of Jesus rejoicing. Luke says that he rejoiced in the Holy Spirit and thanked his Father in heaven. The source of his thanksgiving was the faithfulness of his disciples who, though they were ordinary people, had responded to his teaching. The words of Jesus point to one of the great mysteries of the faith. God hides his will from some and reveals it to others. The Bible does not unveil the mystery of election. In this statement, however, Jesus affirms one aspect of it. God reveals himself to those who are like little children, open, naïve, and trusting. As the Parable of the Sower taught, to others he hides his truths in parables (Luke 8:10). Paul himself will say that God calls the weak and foolish more often than the wise and noble (I Corinthians 1:26-29). Those who, like Satan, are full of pride will not see or understand God's gracious will or precious truths.

The words of Jesus in Luke continue to reveal his nature, identity, and purpose. In his words to his disciples, we learn of the unique relationship of Christ with God. He is the only one who has known the Father. We learn about the role of Christ; all things have been delivered to him. That includes authority and power over Satan. We learn that only Christ can reveal the Father. We learn that he is greater than the prophets and kings, who longed to see the day of his appearing. We learn that Jesus is the sole pathway into the knowledge and presence of God in heaven.

This section concludes with a beatitude. The disciples are blessed because of what they have seen and heard. They have seen the appearance of the long-awaited Messiah. They have heard the promises of God proclaimed, and they have believed them. Despite whatever struggles and problems they may experience, they are truly blessed. Though they have very little in terms of material wealth, they have the true riches, which is the knowledge of God and his Savior. They are truly blessed and have a reason for great joy.

Theological insights
- That Jesus gives the disciples authority over the devil indicates that there is an enemy. Satan works against all that is good, but God's power is greater.
- Why was Jesus able to speak and teach with authority, unlike the scribes and Pharisees? It was because Jesus truly knew the Father.

Thus he was able to speak authoritatively about him and make him known.

- In what sense is Satan a murderer (John 8:44)? He is a murderer in that he led a host of other angels into eternal damnation with him and continues to ruin the lives of all he can.
- What does it take to enter the kingdom of heaven? Does it take intelligence, money, education, or training? No, God reveals himself to "children" with naïve, open, and trusting hearts.
- What will make the disciples capable witnesses to Jesus and God? It will be, in the words of Jesus, what they have seen and heard. We also give witness to our own experience of forgiveness, grace, and new life in Jesus Christ.

Practical application

The Christian life is characterized by joy. Joy is different from happiness in that happiness of often tied to circumstances. For that reason, our happiness may go up and down. Joy, however, is a deep river that runs underneath our lives. It comes from the presence of the Holy Spirit who makes God known to us, assures us of his presence, and fills us with inner peace. Through Jesus Christ, we come to truly know the Father in heaven because Jesus reveals him to us.

Luke recounted Mary's song of joy in the Magnificat (Luke 1:46-55). She too rejoiced in the Holy Spirit and thanked God for his many blessings. We may not always be filled with praise. Life may weigh heavy on us at times. But just as nothing can separate us from the love of God (Romans 8:37-39), so nothing can steal the Christian's joy. At times we too find ourselves rejoicing in God's amazing love and mercy. Just as with Mary and Jesus, this is the work of the Spirit. It is evidence of his presence and that our names are, indeed, written in the Lamb's Book of Life.

The Parable of the Good Samaritan
Luke 10:25-37

BEHOLD, A CERTAIN LAWYER stood up and tested him, saying, "Teacher, what shall I do to inherit eternal life?" He said to him, "What is written in the law? How do you read it?"

He answered, "You shall love the Lord your God with all your heart, with all your soul, with all your strength, and with all your mind; and your neighbor as yourself." He said to him, "You have answered correctly. Do this, and you will live."

But he, desiring to justify himself, asked Jesus, "Who is my neighbor?" Jesus answered, "A certain man was going down from Jerusalem to Jericho, and he fell among robbers, who stripped him and beat him, and departed, leaving him half dead. By chance a certain priest was going down that way. When he saw him, he passed by on the other side. Likewise a Levite also, when he came to the place and saw him, passed by on the other side. But a certain Samaritan, as he traveled, came where he was. When he saw him, he was moved with compassion, came to him, and bound up his wounds, pouring on oil and wine. He set him on his own animal, brought him to an inn, and took care of him. The next day, he took out two denarii, gave them to the host, and said to him, 'Take care of him. Whatever you spend beyond that, I will repay you when I return.' Now which of these three do you think was a neighbor to him who fell among the robbers?" He said, "The one who showed mercy to him." Then Jesus said to him, "Go and do likewise."

In the year 249 A.D. a plague broke out in northern Africa and Europe. Researchers today believe it was smallpox or some form of measles. It lasted about twenty years and at its peak was devastating. At one point, five thousand people a day were dying in Rome. The population of Alexandria, in Egypt, is said to have gone from 500,000 to 190,000. During this time, the North African Christian bishop of Carthage, Cyprian, took a courageous stance. He told his congregation that rather than fleeing the plague, it was their Christian responsibility to tend to the sick, even at the danger of their own lives. Since Christ had granted them eternal life, they did not need to fear death. The Christian mandate was clear. We cannot ignore those in need, even non-Christians. The church set about to do as their bishop commanded. Their example would have a tremendous impact on how the pagan culture in that area viewed Christians and their religion.

From where does the imperative of Christian compassion come? Why are Christians not able to ignore those in need, even those outside their social group or even religious faith? It is because of teachings like the Parable of the Good Samaritan. This parable by Jesus makes it impossible for Christians to ignore those in need. It sets the standard for how Christians are to relate to others, whether it is convenient or not.

The telling of the parable comes in response to a question by a lawyer. "What must I do to obtain eternal life?" A lawyer was someone trained in the laws of God. The question of what it took to obtain eternal life would have been a common topic of discussion in that day. Jesus wisely asked the man to answer his own question, and by all indications, he answered well. It was common wisdom to recognize the importance of the Old Testament "Shema," found in Deuteronomy 6:5. It taught that God should be loved with heart, soul, and might. It was not common, however, to link the love of God with loving one's neighbor as oneself (Leviticus 19:18). Both Matthew and Mark have Jesus make the linkage in response to a question about the greatest commandment during the final week of his life (Matthew 22:34-40, Mark 12:28-34). The linkage is made in Luke by the lawyer, and Luke omits the story about the great commandment in later chapters.

Jesus affirmed the lawyer's answer. If a person loved God and their neighbor, it was the path to God's approval and eternal life. While Luke says that the lawyer asked the question to test Jesus, his question may not have been hostile. It may have been one teacher asking another what he thought. Jesus responded that if he did those things, he would live. It is important to note the importance of *doing* the commandments, not just understanding them.

Luke says, however, that the lawyer wished to justify himself. That may mean that he wished to get the best of Jesus in their discussion of spiritual matters. Jesus had won the first round, so the lawyer went further. It may mean that the lawyer wanted to be sure that he was doing all that was necessary. Religious people often set limits to religious practices to reduce their own responsibility. The lawyer may have wanted to continue to see himself as righteous and not in need of further duty. He pressed Jesus with what was, in fact, a good question. If we are to love our neighbor, who exactly is my neighbor?

The road between Jerusalem and Jericho was widely known to be dangerous. It descended 3,000 feet over 17 miles, as it sloped toward the Jordan River. The parable is geographically accurate in that Jesus said that a certain man went "down" from Jerusalem to Jericho. That is how someone in the first century might have described the road. The path between the two towns ran through narrow passes that offered many hiding places among the rocks for robbers. A person traveling alone on the road would have been in particular jeopardy. That someone had been attacked, beaten, and left for dead would not have surprised any of Jesus' listeners.

Jesus makes the first two travelers people with religious training and authority, a priest and a Levite. Their defense for not wanting to get involved might have been their religious status. If the person were dead, which was unclear, touching a dead body would have made them ritually unclean. But then, if they had religious duties, they had completed them since they were going away from Jerusalem not toward it. What is clear in the parable is that they should have been moved by compassion to help, but they chose not to.

If the person who was moved by compassion had been an ordinary Jew, the parable might have been understood as a condemnation of religious hypocrisy. That Jesus chose a Samaritan as the hero of the story widens its application. The Samaritans were viewed as social and religious outcasts for several reasons. From the time that the northern kingdom split from the southern kingdom, in the 10th century B.C., the northern kingdom had engaged in novel and corrupt religious practices. In addition, the Assyrians, after their conquest of the northern kingdom, in 722 B.C., had deported the Jews and resettled pagan people in the area. Returning Jews had intermarried with them through the centuries, making them a mixed race that most Jews thought incompatible with true Judaism. By the time of Christ, there had developed a long-standing disdain for the Samaritan region and people. That Jesus would make a Samaritan the hero of the parable would have been shocking to his listeners, especially those within the religious establishment.

What makes the Samaritan different from the religious people is his compassion. Whereas their hearts were not touched, the Samaritan was moved by the man's distress and was willing to interrupt his schedule to help. The Samaritan assists the man at some cost to himself. That he sets him on his donkey means he would have to walk the remaining way. He does not ask the innkeeper to trust his financial commitment but pays him in advance. He used his garments to clothe him and bind his wounds. He used his wine to cleanse his wounds and his oil to soothe and soften them. In addition, the inconvenience would have cost him time and energy, making him late and also putting him in danger from robbers.

This is a brilliant parable. The lawyer is left with a multiple-choice question. "Which of the three was neighbor to the man in need?" The answer is obvious though distasteful. We see this in that the lawyer will not say the word "Samaritan." He answers, "The one who showed mercy." As he was instructed to *do* the commandments to live, again the lawyer is instructed to go and *do* likewise. The will of God is not fulfilled by knowing it but by doing it. As was true for the lawyer, the parable does not leave us in a place of comfort. It teaches us that if there are people in need, Christian compassion requires us to help.

Theological insights
- Jesus affirmed the value of the commandments. Understood rightly, they lead one on the path to God. What the Jews often missed was that the law was meant to align one's heart toward God not just promote religious ritual.
- The first commandment requires that we love God with our entire person. The fourfold pattern of loving God with heart, soul, mind, and strength is an indicator of this.
- The command to love others as we love ourselves assumes that all people love themselves. Rightly understood, we are to love God, others, and ourselves, in that order.
- In many ways, the disdain between the Israelites and Samaritans of the first century continues today in the animosity between the Jews and Palestinians. As it was in the first century, it is animosity over religion, heritage, land, and grievances.
- Compassion is a distinctly Christian virtue, rooted in the heart of the gospel. Often, it is those who have suffered the most who show the deepest compassion toward others. This parable leaves no room for closing our hearts to those in need – it calls us to respond with mercy and love.

Practical application
The encouragement of bishop Cyprian for Christians to help their neighbors was difficult. Close contact with the ill meant an increased likelihood of catching the plague yourself. Christians throughout northern Africa responded to his instruction, however. They began to take care of others, some of whom had been discarded by their own families for fear of contracting the plague. Because little was known about medicine in those days, people did not realize that a person had a much greater chance of survival with care, food, water, and rest. Christians gave people this care, and those attended to by them survived at much higher rates. It resulted in a new respect for Christians in the pagan culture. It also resulted in many

people becoming Christians because of the care they had received and the example they had seen. The moment of crisis increased the credibility of the church in the communities of northern Africa and Europe.

What sets the Christian church apart? One thing is its compassion. We are compassionate toward others because God has been compassionate toward us. Jesus is, in many ways, the Good Samaritan, who has seen us in our need, stopped to help and restored us to health. He is the One who went out of his way for our sakes. When we are compassionate toward others, we reflect his character and show his heart to the world. Christians are called to compassionate care for others who are wounded and in need of help. It does not matter if they come from our social group, or not. We are called to a standard of obedience that demands radical compassion – especially toward those whom others ignore.

Martha and Mary – Luke 10:38-42

AS THEY WENT ON THEIR WAY, he entered into a certain village, and a certain woman named Martha received him into her house. She had a sister called Mary, who also sat at Jesus' feet and listened as he taught. But Martha was distracted with much serving, and she came to him, and said, "Lord, do you not care that my sister has left me to serve alone? Tell her therefore to come help me." Jesus answered her, "Martha, Martha, you are anxious and troubled about many things, but one thing is necessary. Mary has chosen the good part, which will not be taken away from her."

There are some stories in the Bible that are particularly memorable, intriguing, and relevant. The account of Martha and Mary is one of them. Over the centuries there have been a variety of interpretations of it. Some of them are listed below.

- It portrays the difference between the active and the contemplative life. Mary prioritizes prayer and devotion; Martha, active service. Though service is good, it is secondary to prayer and devotion.

- The incident displays two different temperaments. Mary is an introvert who is renewed by quiet activities. Martha is an extrovert whose world is focused externally.
- Both service and devotion are necessary ingredients to a balanced Christian life. Though Mary's devotion takes priority, Martha's active service is also important. Both should receive attention in a healthy Christian's life.
- Distractions easily take us away from the spiritual life. Like the thorns in the Parable of the Sower, lesser things can divert us from our true calling. We become like Martha, anxious and worried about many things, when our devotional life is weak.
- The role of women is affirmed in this parable. Mary chooses a role that was ordinarily reserved for men. Jesus does not refuse her that role but commends her for it. It is a gospel indication that women can also have a role in ministry.
- Hospitality was an important role and expectation in first-century Judaism. The parable shows, however, that there is something more important – listening to the words of Jesus.
- The parable shows the priority of the spiritual over the material. It is easy to give priority to material concerns over the spiritual. Even though everyday responsibilities are important, the spiritual is most important.
- The words of Jesus to Martha are often viewed as a rebuke. They are, however, also instructional and kind in their tone. While Martha's activity has a place, Jesus encourages her to recognize that she misses the best when she becomes anxious and worried about doing it.
- The parable illustrates that people have different interests and temperaments. Some like active service; some are more reflective. Everyone should use their gifts without neglecting to balance life with the other.

There are many compelling and poignant aspects to this story. Most people have a natural tendency either toward the active life or the more reflective one. We do one more naturally and easily than the other. The reality is that the world needs both. Jesus and the disciples had been invited for dinner. If they were to eat, someone had to prepare the dinner, and Jesus certainly understood that. The comment of Jesus was about Martha's anxiety and irritation. Had she done her role with grace and acceptance, no such statement would have been made.

We can understand, from Martha's point of view, how she may have viewed Mary's absence from the kitchen. Perhaps it was a repeated pattern that had long-standing family roots. Mary's absence, from Martha's point of view, may have been just another instance in a long list of lazy and irresponsible acts.

What makes Mary's activity acceptable is the presence of Jesus himself. There would only be limited opportunity to literally sit at the feet of Jesus and listen to him. Once he ascended into heaven, no more opportunities would present themselves in that way. Mary had indeed chosen wisely, and Jesus would not take the opportunity from her.

Theological insights
- Protestant reformers understood that the active vocational life was important. Without it, society would not function successfully. Every person should work hard at their God-given vocations. The reformers said that one time when people should be like Mary is when listening to sermons. Then they should let nothing distract them so that they might focus entirely on God's Word.
- We notice how Jesus reacts to Martha in this story. She is a beloved member of God's family. Jesus does not rebuke her work but only her worry. He points out her fault so she might correct it. As far as we can discern, she responded to his admonishment with humility and grace. We too should learn from God's correction.
- The account emphasizes the importance of hearing the word of God. It is only through doing so that we come to faith, trust God's promises, and receive eternal life. Jesus is the supreme bearer of God's words to humanity.

Practical application

While there are many things we can draw from this story, one reasonable application is to recognize that both reflective devotion and active service are important. God has given us work as his good gift. Through our work we use our talents, provide for ourselves, build society, and serve others. God has ordained that we must work to eat, and this requirement is good for society and us.

Work, however, must be kept in proper perspective. The greatest commandment is to love God with all our heart, mind, soul, and strength. This requires that we sit at his feet, listen to his word, and give him our undivided attention. Though we cannot do so all the time, we must do so some of the time. Marthas must also be Marys. It is by first being a Mary that we are able to work as Marthas – without being overwhelmed by worry.

LUKE 11

The Lord's Prayer – Luke 11:1-13

WHEN HE FINISHED PRAYING in a certain place, one of his disciples said to him, "Lord, teach us to pray, just as John also taught his disciples." He said to them, "When you pray, say, 'Our Father in heaven, may your name be kept holy. May your Kingdom come. May your will be done on earth, as it is in heaven. Give us this day our daily bread. Forgive us our sins, for we also forgive everyone who is indebted to us. And lead us not into temptation.'"

And he said to them, "Which of you, if you go to a friend at midnight and tell him, 'Friend, lend me three loaves of bread, for a friend of mine has come to me from a journey, and I have nothing to set before him.' And he from within will answer and say, 'Do not bother me. The door is now shut, and my children are with me in bed. I cannot get up and give it to you'? I tell you, although he will not rise and give it to him because he is his friend, yet because of his boldness, he will get up and give him as many as he needs.

"I tell you, keep asking, and it will be given you. Keep seeking, and you will find. Keep knocking, and it will be opened to you. For everyone who asks receives. He who seeks finds. To the one who knocks it will be opened. Which of you fathers, if your son asks for a fish, will give him a snake instead? Or if he asks for an egg, will give him a scorpion? If you then, being evil, know how to give good gifts to your children, how much more will your heavenly Father give the Holy Spirit to those who ask him?"

If you were to ask a group of people, "How many of you are good at prayer," how many hands would be raised? Most people do not consider themselves accomplished when it comes to prayer. We do not always connect with God when we pray, and we sometimes fail to get answers to important concerns. We would like to pray better and more effectively. The disciples of Jesus felt this way too. Jesus was quite effective at prayer. His prayers were powerful and always got answered. The disciples wanted their prayers to have the same effect. So they asked Jesus to teach them to pray.

We might have expected Jesus to focus his response on techniques. When should a person pray? Is there a best posture? What are the rules for good prayer? How can we get more prayers answered? Though Jesus does not respond as we might expect, he has given the disciples and the church since then a pattern for prayer. The Lord's Prayer is typically divided into six petitions: 1) May your name be kept holy; 2) May your kingdom come; 3) May your will be done on earth as in heaven; 4) Give us this day our daily bread; 5) Forgive us our sins as we forgive others; and 6) Lead us not into temptation, but deliver us from evil.

We notice that the first three petitions are for the advancement of God's kingdom in the world. As is generally considered good practice in prayer, the Lord's Prayer begins with a focus on God. We recognize God first, give him thanks, and pray for the success of his will on earth. This includes the honor of his name, the coming of his kingdom, and the doing of his will. If these three petitions were answered, many problems in the world would be resolved. If everyone honored God's name, submitted to his reign, and did his will, injustice, oppression, and unbelief would disappear. There could hardly be a better prayer to pray for the world. There is hardly anything that would benefit people more.

The final three petitions are for our needs. If you ask if it is okay to pray for your personal needs, the Lord's Prayer answers, "Yes." It is appropriate, and Jesus gives us a pattern for doing so. We notice that these are not prayers for wants. They are not prayers about financial needs, relationship problems, or upcoming decisions. The petitions Jesus teaches are basic but important. The prayer for bread is for sufficient food for today. Tomorrow's needs will be the subject of tomorrow's prayers. The prayer for forgiveness reminds us of our ongoing need for grace. The prayer about temptation reminds us that we are called to holiness of life.

There is a textual variant found in verse 4 of Luke's version of the Lord's Prayer. Matthew's version of the prayer concludes with the petition: "And lead us not into temptation, but deliver us from evil" (Matthew 6:13). Most new translations of Luke leave out the phrase, "but deliver us from evil." This is because important manuscripts today, such as Codex Sinaiticus and Codex Vaticanus do not include the phrase in Luke's version. Though some ancient manuscripts, such as the Codex Alexandrinus and the texts used to translate the King James Version include the text, scholars believe the most ancient and authoritative reading did not include the phrase. The longer phrase is certainly original to Jesus because it is found in Matthew's version. An early scribe may have inserted it to harmonize Luke's version with Matthew's.

Interestingly, there is a textual variant in Matthew's version of the Lord's Prayer. The most ancient versions of Matthew 6:13 do not include the final doxology of the prayer, "For yours is the kingdom and the power and the glory forever. Amen." As with the phrase in Luke, this sentence was included in the King James translation but is excluded in modern versions. While this may be an authentic saying of Jesus, it is not in the most ancient and authoritative manuscripts. If it is not an authentic saying of Jesus, it may reflect the liturgical practice of the early church. The abundance of ancient manuscripts allows us today to determine, with great accuracy, the most reliable readings for the Bible, particularly the New Testament.

One thing we notice in this prayer is its corporate nature. It says, "*Our* Father," and "Give us *our* daily bread." The prayer recognizes that we live in community with others. When we pray these things for ourselves, we pray them for our friends, neighbors, and the world. We pray these prayers for others and ourselves, but we pray that they will start with us. This is implicit in the prayer. "Lord, let your kingdom come in *my* life, and let your will be done in *my* life first of all."

There is one important thing about this prayer that should not be missed. All the petitions are according to God's will since Jesus taught us to pray them. When we wonder what is the will of God, we have it here. When we do not know how to pray, this is a prayer that is always appropriate. The Bible says that God hears us when we pray according to his will (I John 5:14-15). Here is a prayer that is always in the will of God. For that reason, we should use it often as we pray for the world and ourselves.

The Parable of the Friend at Midnight is only found in Luke. It suggests a scenario in which the neighbor lives in a small, perhaps one-room home. Everyone is in bed, and getting up will awaken the entire family. It will cause significant inconvenience for the person to do so. Yet, in the end, it turns out to be easier to give the friend everything he needs than put up with his continued knocking and pleading. The friend gets what he wants because of his supplication despite its inconvenience.

The Greek word used to describe the friend's action means, "without shame." Though the idea can carry a negative connotation in Greek, Jesus uses it positively to commend persistent prayer. The word can be translated in various ways, including shameless audacity, impudence, importunity, persistence, shameless boldness, brazen persistence, shamelessness, unrelenting tenacity, or simply boldness. It is not so much his persistence but his shameless boldness that gets him what he wants. The parable seems not so much aimed at persistent prayer but audacity in it. Though we, as humans, have no right to access the throne of grace, we approach God anyway, because of the invitation of Christ. The implication is that if the neighbor will answer because of his inconvenience, how much more will a generous, loving God answer readily and willingly?

Jesus follows up the parable with a set of sayings that encourage persistence and reinforce the idea of God's generosity. For emphasis, Jesus repeats the saying three times. Ask and it will be given to you. Seek and you will find. Knock and it will be opened. Then Jesus uses the example of earthly fathers. They will not give something bad to their child who asks for something good. No one could imagine such. If then human fathers are that way, how much more is God, your heavenly Father?

From a merely rhetorical point of view, this final section is wonderful material. Jesus was a marvelous speaker. No wonder people hung on his words. Jesus urges persistence three times, each in slightly different ways. He then reinforces each of them again, "For everyone who asks receives." His use of outlandish examples only highlights the generosity of God. Whereas Matthew, in his recounting of this saying (Matthew 7:11), says that God will give "good gifts," Luke emphasizes the Holy Spirit. One certain outcome of prayer is the gift of God's presence that comes through the Holy Spirit. That is the best answer of all and the best sign of God's generosity. He gives us more of himself. This should be a great incentive to pray, be persistent and bold in it, and engage in prayer with enthusiasm. It is the first and most accessible way to draw near to God.

Theological insights
- The use of the term "Father" by Jesus was revolutionary in first-century Israel. It characterized the warm and intimate relationship with God that Jesus both exemplified and encouraged.
- To pray for "daily bread" includes spiritual nourishment. The friend is in need of loaves of bread, and the one who prays will receive the Holy Spirit. When we pray the Lord's Prayer, we ask for sustenance for our physical and spiritual needs.

- The prayer not to be led into temptation reminds us that we can be greater sinners than we currently are. We are always subject to temptation. Therefore, we should pray to be kept from temptation greater than we can bear and not to fall prey to the evil that is around us.
- Both the parable and the sayings about prayer argue from the lesser to the greater. If the sleepy neighbor will aid the friend, how much more will a generous God do? If sinful parents will give generously to their children, how much more will God in heaven do?
- The instructions of Jesus assure us that God answers prayers; they do not say that God will answer exactly as we ask. When we pray as Jesus taught, however, we can know the presence of the Holy Spirit will be given to us.

Practical application

Martin Luther's barber once asked him for advice on prayer. In response, Luther wrote a treatise in which he described his "fourfold strand." It was a way of meditating on scripture and engaging deeply in prayer. Luther noted that it was particularly useful as a way to pray through the Lord's Prayer, the Ten Commandments, and the Apostles' Creed. The way to use the fourfold strand was to take a phrase in the Lord's Prayer, such as "Our Father in heaven," for example. Think about what was learned from that phrase. Next, consider things for which the phrase makes you thankful. Then consider what you need to confess. Finally, use those reflections to form your prayers.

From "Our Father in heaven," for example, we learn that God is like a father, gracious, strong, and good. We should give thanks for his protection, generosity, and care. We might confess that we doubt his care too often. We neglect to come to him in time of need. All this could form a prayer such as, "Heavenly Father, thank you for your gracious care. I am reminded how great is your love, how certain your protection is, and how good your will is. Thank you for the many times you have watched over me and protected my family and me. Forgive me for doubting your care and help me be stronger in faith. May I love you more deeply and share your love with those around me. You truly are my Father in heaven and I am grateful for your care." Luther went through the Lord's Prayer phrase by phrase. It gave him guidance for his prayers and made scripture the framework for them.

Jesus and Beelzebul – Luke 11:13-26

HE WAS CASTING OUT A DEMON, and it was mute. When the demon had gone out, the mute man spoke, and the people marveled. But some of them said, "He casts out demons by Beelzebul, the prince of demons," while others, to test him, kept seeking from him a sign from heaven. But he, knowing their thoughts, said to them, "Every kingdom divided against itself is brought to destruction, and a house divided against itself falls. If Satan also is divided against himself, how will his kingdom stand? For you say that I cast out demons by Beelzebul. But if I cast out demons by Beelzebul, by whom do your sons cast them out? Therefore they will be your judges. But if I cast out demons by the finger of God, then the kingdom of God has come upon you.

"When a strong man, fully armed, guards his own house, his goods are safe. But when someone stronger attacks him and overcomes him, he takes from him his whole armor in which he trusted, and divides his plunder. He who is not with me is against me, and he who does not gather with me scatters.

"The unclean spirit, when he has gone out of a person, it passes through dry places seeking rest. Finding none, it says, 'I will return to my house from which I came.' When it returns, it finds it swept and put in order. Then it goes and takes with it seven other spirits more evil than itself, and they enter and dwell there. The last state of that person is worse than the first."

The question of the origins of evil has been asked throughout history. The Greek myth of Pandora's box was an explanation for the world's sickness, pain, and suffering. Because of her curiosity, Pandora opened the jar that contained all the world's evils. Realizing what she had done, she closed it quickly, but it was too late. Everything had escaped except for one thing. Only hope was left inside.

The fifth-century theologian, Augustine, writing from a biblical perspective, sought to explain the existence of evil. In his classic work, *City of God*, he traced evil back to the fall of the angels. In the beginning, God gave the angels free will. Some willfully rebelled against God and were eternally banished from his holy presence. As the Bible depicted it, said

Augustine, the angels who fell, with Satan as their leader, became the source of the evil, temptation, sickness, and trouble in our world.

Luke records an incident in the life of Jesus that gets him into a conversation about the devil, Satan's work, and the source of Jesus' amazing power. There was a man who was possessed by a demon. We do not know what other symptoms he may have exhibited except that he was mute. When Jesus cast out the demon, the man was able to speak. This would have been evidence, for those witnessing the miracle that the demon had been cast out. When the man suddenly began to speak, the people marveled at what they saw and the power of Jesus.

This began a discussion among some gathered there that perhaps the power of Jesus was not from God. Perhaps he could cast out demons because he was in league with Satan himself! The Gospel of Matthew records that it was the Pharisees who made the accusation (Matthew 12:24). The term *Beelzebul* had a long history in first-century Judaism. Its root word is *Baal*, who was the primary Canaanite god. In II Kings 1, a variation of the name appears as *Baalzebub*, which means "Lord of the Flies." *Beelzebul* derives from *Baal-Zebul*, which means Baal the Prince. In the minds of Jesus' hearers, Beelzebul would either have referred to Satan himself or one of his chief princes.

How would Jesus respond to such criticism? We see the divinity of Jesus displayed in that he knew what they were thinking. We also see his wisdom in that he did not respond angrily, but calmly and rationally, refuting them with a reasoned argument. His first response was that a house divided cannot stand. If Satan is divided against himself by casting out his own demons, certainly his reign will not endure. Here again, we see the remarkable use of a simple illustration to make the point.

Then Jesus makes a further point by asking a question. If he casts out demons by Beelzebul, by whom do their sons cast them out? There are two possible meanings to this statement. If there were Jewish exorcists who were able to cast our demons, then the question should be asked if they too were casting out demons by Beelzebul. Another possible meaning of Jesus is that their sons were not casting out demons. They had no such power. That Jesus had powers far beyond theirs was an obvious indication, for those with understanding, that God was at work. Then Jesus made an illusion to the account of Moses and the Exodus. When God brought the third plague on the land, the plague of gnats, Pharaoh's magicians were unable to replicate it. They said, "This is the finger of God" (Exodus 8:19). If, said Jesus, I cast out demons by the finger of God, then certainly God's kingdom has come among you.

Jesus, then, gives another simple illustration. You cannot plunder a strong man's house unless you overcome him first. Satan represents someone strong and difficult to overcome, but Jesus is stronger even than Satan. He can fully overcome him, take his armor from him, and plunder his kingdom. The work of Jesus was not simply to battle with the devil but to overcome him, drive him out, and destroy his work.

We saw, earlier in Luke, that Jesus told the disciples not to forbid the person they met who was casting out demons in his name. In that instance Jesus told the disciples that whoever was not against them was for them (Luke 9:50). Here Jesus puts a different slant on things. Whereas his focus was on those doing ministry in the previous saying, here it is on those not with him. Whoever is not with me is against me, says Jesus; and whoever does not gather with me scatters. This addresses the question of discipleship. It is not enough just not to work against Jesus. If we do not work for him, we are essentially hindering his work. If we do not gather, we effectively scatter.

At this point in the ministry of Jesus, some, such as the religious leaders, had decided to be against him. Others may have been indifferent. It was hard, however, to sit on the sidelines. One was either an enthusiastic supporter of Jesus or working against him. Everyone would have to decide, and the person of Jesus was at the heart of that decision. Was God at work through him or not? Had he come from God or not? Would one place one's trust in him, or turn away? As Simeon told Mary when Jesus was brought to the temple, his coming would indeed cause the rise of some and the fall of others. As Simeon indicated and we see in this passage, he would indeed be a sign that was spoken against (Luke 2:34).

Jesus concluded his comments with a statement about the work of evil. A person from whom an evil spirit has gone out is like a house that is neat and clean. Though a spirit has gone out, it does not mean he will not look for an opportunity to return. What better place to enter than a clean and well-swept house? When he enters again, he will do so with a vengeance and create more havoc than before so that the person is worse off.

To what kind of situation does Jesus refer? Evil seeks to disgrace and destroy. Though we may conquer it once, it will seek to gain dominion over us again. When that happens, we may fall into even deeper sin and corruption. For that reason, we should not be lazy or neglect our spiritual disciplines. We should guard our house against the devil and not give him a foothold. He is never satisfied until he has destroyed a person. Only the power of Jesus can set us free, and we should lean on him to guard us against the devil's persistent attacks and corruptions.

Theological insights
- The issue in this account is the authority and power of Jesus. Throughout Luke, the miracles of Jesus are a witness to his identity as the Messiah and Son of God.
- The devil seeks to usurp God's property, which is the human soul. It is within Christ's authority to redeem and safeguard what belongs to God against the attacks of the devil.
- What was the "finger of God" by which Jesus cast out demons? It was the Holy Spirit through whom his miracles were done. Jesus's use of the phrase enables him to avoid saying, "I have cast out the demons by my own power," a statement that would have made him subject to additional questions and criticism.
- Every person must make their decision either for or against Jesus as the Messiah, the Son of God, and the Savior of the world.

Practical application

The devil attacks people in many ways. In addition, sin blinds our understanding and corrupts our hearts. The medieval church identified seven root sins that were are the heart of human corruption – pride, greed, lust, envy, gluttony, anger, and laziness. Some were sins of the body, such as gluttony and lust. Others were sins of the emotions, such as greed, anger, and laziness. Others were sins of the mind, such as pride and envy. It also identified seven capital virtues – the three theological virtues: faith, hope, and love, and the four cardinal virtues, expressed in a variety of forms: self-control, purity of heart, kindness, and gratitude.

There are two sides to the Christian life: avoiding evil and doing what is good. Theologians have asked which of these is most important. Should a person focus on avoiding evil or on doing good? Where should one's emotional and spiritual energy be spent? The answer, in the history of the church, is that both are important. Neither can be neglected. There is great value in focusing on doing as much good as possible; it leaves less time for evil to take root. The saying is credited to John Wesley: "Do all the good you can, by all the means you can, in all the ways you can, in all the places you can, at all the times you can, to all the people you can, as long as ever you can." This is good advice. We also remember that the devil tempts us to evil, and our sinful natures follow easily. For this reason, we should be watchful and pray as Jesus taught – "And lead us not into temptation, but deliver us from evil" (Luke 11:4).

The Sign of Jonah – Luke 11:27-36

Who Is Blessed – Luke 11:27-28

IT CAME TO PASS, as he said these things, a woman in the crowd lifted up her voice and said to him, "Blessed is the womb that bore you, and the breasts which nursed you!" He said, "No, rather, blessed are those who hear the word of God and keep it!"

The Sign of Jonah – Luke 11:29-32

When the crowds gathered around him, he began to say, "This is an evil generation. It seeks after a sign, but no sign will be given to it except the sign of Jonah. For as Jonah became a sign to the Ninevites, so also will the Son of Man be to this generation. The queen of the South will rise up in the judgment with the men of this generation and condemn them, for she came from the ends of the earth to hear the wisdom of Solomon; and behold, one greater than Solomon is here. The men of Nineveh will stand up in the judgment with this generation and will condemn it, for they repented at the preaching of Jonah; and behold, one greater than Jonah is here.

Lighting a Lamp – Luke 11:33-36

"No one, when he has lit a lamp, puts it in a cellar or under a basket, but on a stand, so that those who enter may see the light. The lamp of the body is the eye. When your eye is good, your whole body is full of light, but when it is evil, your body is full of darkness. Therefore be careful so that the light in you is not darkness. If therefore your whole body is full of light, having no part dark, it will be totally full of light, as when the lamp with its rays gives you light."

When in a crowd, someone will often shout something that is heard by those gathered. Luke reports an instance in which such a comment was made by a women. Her words are meant as praise, both for Jesus and his mother. "Blessed is the womb that bore you, and the breasts which nursed you!" Jesus redirects her comment, however, and responds with a different beatitude: "Blessed are those who hear the word of God and keep it!" The woman thought of Mary's blessedness from a maternal point of view; she had carried the Messiah in her womb. It would also have been a great blessing to raise him as part of her family, but there was a greater blessing. It was to hear the word of God and do it.

Jesus does not say that Mary was not blessed. Indeed she was. That she bore the Messiah and raised him was certainly a part of God's blessing on her. That was not the greatest blessing, however. The greater blessing was Mary's true and living faith. She heard the word of God and embraced it. So it is, says Jesus for everyone. We note that it is not just hearing the word of God that determines being blessed, but also doing it. The devil hears the word but does not keep it.

We make much of Mary and her faith and rightly so. She has been the subject of many sermons and devotions throughout the centuries. Jesus' words are encouragement for everyday people, however. Everyone can be blessed as Mary was if they hear God's word and obey it. Since Jesus is the Son of God, to embrace the words of Jesus is to hear and obey the word of God.

At the time of Jesus, it was not unheard of that someone might ask for and receive a sign from God. The Old Testament reported several instances of signs from God. In Judges, chapter 6, Gideon asked God for a sign to confirm his calling to lead the people into battle. God gave the sign of the dew on the fleece to strengthen Gideon's faith (Judges 6:36-40). King Hezekiah asked for a sign that he would recover from his illness (II Kings 20:8-11). God gave him a sign through the prophet Isaiah when the shadow on the sundial moved backward. The servant of Abraham, Eliezer, prayed that God would show him the right bride for Abraham's son Isaac (Genesis 24:12-14). He asked that the chosen girl would draw water for him and his camels. God granted his request by sending Rebekah to do as Eliezer prayed.

Why then did Jesus refuse to show a sign to the people and the religious leaders? The answer was that they came to him without faith. Those in the Old Testament to whom God showed signs were people of faith, and God used the sign to strengthen their faith. The religious leaders, however, were without faith. Had Jesus given them a sign, there is no indication they would have become believers. They would simply have found another reason to disbelieve. The healings and other miracles were signs enough for those willing to accept them and indications of God's blessing on the life and work of Jesus. Jesus called it "an evil generation" that seeks after a sign. This was the reason Jesus would not even speak to Herod when he was sent to him by Pilate. Herod wanted to see a sign from Jesus, but he would not have believed even if he had seen one (Luke 23:8). There would be only one sign given. It would be the sign of Jonah.

Matthew's gospel adds a statement not found in Luke. Jesus says, "For as Jonah was three days and three nights in the belly of the fish, so will the Son of Man be three days and three nights in the heart of the earth" (Matthew 12:40). The sign of Jonah would be Jesus' resurrection. As Jonah came back from his "death" in the fish, Jesus would return in triumphal resurrection after his death. Luke records another way that Jonah was a sign. He was a sign of God's presence and judgment to the people of Nineveh. In the same way, Jesus was a sign to the people that they too should repent, turn to God, and be saved.

The illustration of the queen of the South, otherwise known as the Queen of Sheba (I Kings 10:1-13), reinforces Jesus' condemnation. She traveled many miles to hear Solomon's wisdom. Jesus' criticism has two parts. She embraced Solomon with much greater enthusiasm than the Jews embraced Jesus. The condemnation of this generation was therefore deserved since someone greater than Solomon was present in the person of Jesus.

Luke then includes a statement of Jesus that sums up the need to hear and embrace God's words. The metaphor changes from hearing to seeing. If a person's eye is clear, they can see the world around them. It is this way in the spiritual realm. If we see the truth of God's word and allow it to fill us, our whole being is full of light. If we do not have spiritual eyesight to see God's truth, evil fills us with darkness. The goal is for our entire soul to be full of the light of God's truth. As the Sun's rays shine from the outside to give us light, God's word comes to us in Jesus Christ. Those whose eyes can see and whose ears can hear are truly blessed. Their lives will be full of light, and they will not need special signs. Like Mary and all the saints, they will be blessed because they hear the word of God and obey it.

Theological insights

- We give thanks to God for many blessings, for food, shelter, good friends, and ample resources. These are good but not God's greatest blessings. That the Spirit has opened our hearts to hear God's word and embrace it is the greater blessing. We should remember to give thanks for this great gift.

- In the Magnificat, Mary recognized that in the future "all generations will call me blessed" (Luke 1:48). Jesus takes the opportunity of the woman's comment to point out that all disciples are blessed when they hear God's word and obey it.

- The Queen of Sheba journeyed from her kingdom in Arabia to the south, to see if the reports of Solomon's wisdom were true. She heard Solomon's wisdom and praised God for raising up such a wise king (I Kings 10:9). Jesus said that she would testify at the judgment against the Jews because of their unbelief. Even Gentiles from Nineveh will rise up to testify against them.

Practical application

What does it take for a person to believe? We may wish that God would make himself more demonstrably known. Perhaps God should write his name in big letters across the sky. Then everyone would believe in him!

Perhaps many people would believe as a result of some dramatic demonstration on God's part. It would not mean, however, that people would love God. God's goal is to have people love him. It is not mere acknowledgment that God desires, but affection, trust, and relationship. That can only come from those who have been touched by God's Spirit and responded with humble gratitude.

We might all like a sign on occasion, and sometimes God gives one. But we have something better than a sign; it is the scriptures and the Holy Spirit. Our life of faith is nurtured, not by signs, but by an authentic ongoing relationship with God through the Spirit. This is what it means to be truly blessed, and the way to grow in the Spirit is to continue to hear God's words, embrace them, believe them, assimilate them into our hearts, and put them into practice.

Woe to the Pharisees and Lawyers
Luke 11:37-54

NOW AS HE SPOKE, a certain Pharisee asked him to dine with him. He went in and sat at the table. When the Pharisee saw it, he marveled that he had not first washed himself before dinner. The Lord said to him, "Now you Pharisees cleanse the outside of the cup and of the platter, but your inward part is full of extortion and wickedness. You foolish ones, did not he who made the outside make the inside also? But give alms of those things that are within, and behold, all things will be clean to you."

"But woe to you Pharisees! For you tithe mint and rue and every herb, but you bypass justice and God's love. You ought to have done these, and not to have left the other undone. Woe to you Pharisees! For you love the best seats in the synagogues and the greetings in the marketplaces. Woe to you, scribes and Pharisees, hypocrites! For you are like hidden graves, and the men who walk over them do not know it."

One of the lawyers answered him, "Teacher, in saying this you insult us also." He said, "Woe to you lawyers also! For you load men with burdens that are difficult to carry, and you yourselves will not even lift one finger to help carry those burdens. Woe to you! For you build the tombs of the prophets, and your fathers killed them. So you testify and consent to the works of your fathers, for they killed them, and you build their tombs. Therefore also the wisdom of God said, 'I will send to them prophets and apostles; and some of them they will kill and persecute, that the blood of all the prophets, which was shed from the foundation of the world, may be required of this generation, from the blood of Abel to the blood of Zechariah, who perished between the altar and the sanctuary.' Yes, I tell you, it will be required of this generation. Woe to you lawyers! For you took away the key of knowledge. You did not enter in yourselves, and those who were entering in, you hindered."

As he said these things to them, the scribes and the Pharisees began to press him urgently to make him speak about many things, watching him in order to catch him in something he might say.

The Bible contains a number of kinds of literature, including law, poetry, narrative, proverbs, parables, beatitudes, wisdom, gospel, and apocalypse. Within those many forms of literature, there are both promises and warnings. The promises from God are meant to encourage us. God draws us to himself through promises. The warnings, on the other hand, also serve a purpose. For those who will not be drawn to God through promises, the warnings drive them with threats. No one likes warnings, but they are useful. They keep us away from danger if we will heed them.

Luke recounts a conversation with the Pharisees and lawyers that contains a number of warnings. These come in the form of "Woes." Woes are used throughout the Old Testament. A woe expresses trouble or calamity. It pronounces judgment. It is an expression of anguish. Isaiah pronounces woes to the wicked who exploited others (Isaiah 5:8-23). Habakkuk pronounces woes on Babylon and condemns them for their oppression (Habakkuk 2:6-20). Jesus had already used a set of woes to warn the comfortable (Luke 6:24-26). The book of Revelation includes woes that pronounce God's judgment on the world (Revelation 8:13, 9:12). By using woes, Jesus condemns the practices of the Pharisees and lawyers in the most strident terms. Their lot was one of great distress because of their hearts, attitudes, and practices.

The sayings take place at a dinner party. A Pharisee invited Jesus to dinner, and he accepted. We suspect that the disciples came also. Jesus must have known that the Pharisees had rituals for the washing of hands before meals. Though it might have been good manners to defer to the host's rituals, Jesus did not. The host was apparently stunned that Jesus neglected the practice. Jesus took the opportunity for a teaching moment. We might find it rude of him not to be more respectful of the host since Jesus and the disciples were recipients of his hospitality. It would seem, however, that speaking the truth took precedence.

This critique by Jesus is typical of many of his teachings. The Jews mistakenly assumed that the requirement of God was fulfilled by outward duty, and Jesus pointed out their error. He used a cup and plate to symbolize their attitude. They washed the outside. That is, they had many outward rules and requirements, but they left the inside dirty. Specifically, Jesus says that they allowed extortion and wickedness to take root in their hearts. These were serious critiques of the nature of their religion. They worked to make the outer person clean but neglected the heart. Jesus exposed what others could not see. Their hearts were full of vile and ugly things, and it was foolish for them not to realize that God made the inside as well as the outside. Then Jesus offered a practical application. If they gave to others from the goodness of their heart, everything else, including what was on the outside would be clean. Washing the body could not make the heart clean, but cleansing the heart made the body clean too.

The Pharisees were hard of heart. They had not responded to gracious promises. Therefore Jesus declared God's warnings. They were in great danger. Woe to them! They performed the duty of tithing but neglected justice and the love of God. They should have made justice and love a priority, without neglecting to tithe.

Next Jesus criticized their ostentation. They loved status and recognition. They were proud of their standing as esteemed religious authorities. But their religion was a sham. Inside there were all sorts of evil things. Just as a person might walk across a secret grave without knowing it, all those who interacted with the Pharisees were dealing with ugly and wicked people, though they looked holy and righteous on the outside.

While the lawyers and Pharisees often saw eye to eye, there was competition between them. Luke reports that a lawyer wanted to confirm that they were excluded from Jesus' condemnation. He noted that Jesus had insulted the Pharisees. This prompted a set of woes directed at the lawyers. They too were culpable. Their first woe had to do with the law. They interpreted it carefully and imposed strict injunctions on others. While they found ways around their own laws, they would not lessen them for ordinary people.

The second woe continues Jesus' condemnation. The religious leadership had built many beautiful tombs for the remains of the prophets. It is confirmation, said Jesus, that your fathers killed them. You are their children who do as they did. They killed the prophets, and you have built their tombs. The reference to the wisdom of God is unclear. It appears that Jesus was quoting scripture, but no such scripture seems to fit. He may be quoting a source that is unknown to us, speaking from a personal revelation, or personifying himself as the wisdom of God. The point of the saying is that God had sent many prophets and apostles, whom the people had killed. A time of reckoning for their deaths was at hand. Said Jesus, their blood would be required of that generation. This was certainly the case. The destruction of Jerusalem and the great suffering it would bring upon the nation was only forty years into the future. The nation's destruction was a terrible judgment of God that Jesus said was, at least in part, because they had murdered the prophets God sent.

The final woe in this section has to do with their teaching. The teachings of the religious leaders did not help people find God. Rather, they hindered them. Since they had not entered God's kingdom, they did not want others to enter it either. Jesus indicates that their teaching role had great potential. Their words held the key to the knowledge of salvation. But the great teaching opportunity they were given had been refused, squandered, and rejected. They did not help people but harmed them.

We might imagine that these comments did not sit well with the religious leaders, especially since Jesus sat as a guest in the home of one of the Pharisees. His insults lowered their inhibitions, and their anger showed through. They began to press him urgently about many things to catch him in some mistake. Luke does not tell us the outcome, but needless to say, it was not a happy ending to the dinner party. For their good, Jesus took his opportunity to warn the Pharisees, lawyers, and scribes in the strictest terms. Everything they were doing was wrong. They would not listen, however. They lashed back in anger, desperately seeking some way to discredit Jesus.

Theological insights
- The Pharisees became experts who focused on small and trifling things but neglected the great and important matters of the law, such as justice and God's love. They kept the law in unimportant details to avoid the more difficult matters of the heart.
- Did Jesus ever speak about tithing? He makes a comment about it in this section. He criticizes the religious leaders not for tithing but for neglecting justice and God's love. He tells them they should focus on love and justice, but not leave the other, that is tithing, undone.
- Martin Luther noted that Jesus' words about giving alms are not a return to works righteousness. To give alms of those things within, said Luther, means to do good works from a heart of faith.
- There are several sins that Jesus identifies in the ways of the Pharisees and lawyers. They were full of hypocrisy, unbalanced in their religious lives, and ostentatious in their religious duties. They made difficult demands on others, were intolerant of those who differed with them, and excluded from their circle any who did not share their prejudices.

Practical application

In the words of Jesus, the Pharisees, lawyers, and scribes were hypocrites. A hypocrite is someone who shows one face to the public but is a different person inside. It is easy to be judgmental about the religious leaders, but we are all like them in some way. The apostle Paul makes the point in Romans that every person is a hypocrite. Why is this? It is because every person, apart from grace, resists God's laws in their hearts. We may perform good works for a variety of reasons. We may want the approval of others. We may be afraid of punishment, God's or the community's. To others, we may look like the best of people. Inside, however, we are different. We are full of sin and corruption. Does it make us better because we show a religious face to outsiders? No. That is the definition of a hypocrite. We are not who others think we are, and we keep up the façade at all costs.

What is the solution? It is a new heart from God. The Holy Spirit, whom God gives to those with faith, makes us a new creation and gives us a new heart. The Spirit enables us to love God, follow his commandments from the heart, and be compassionate toward others, though we always do so imperfectly. Since everyone is a hypocrite, everyone needs grace. The answer is to allow God a place in our hearts so that he might change us from within. If out of our hearts comes faith and good works toward those in need, it makes our outward actions clean in God's sight.

LUKE 12

Acknowledging Christ – Luke 12:1-12

The Leaven of the Pharisees – Luke 12:1-3

MEANWHILE, WHEN A MULTITUDE of many thousands had gathered together, so much so that they trampled on each other, he began to tell his disciples first of all, "Beware of the yeast of the Pharisees, which is hypocrisy. There is nothing covered up that will not be revealed, nor hidden that will not be known. Therefore whatever you have said in the darkness will be heard in the light. What you have spoken in the ear in the secret chambers will be proclaimed on the housetops.

Whom to Fear – Luke 12:4-7

"I tell you, my friends, do not be afraid of those who kill the body, and after that have no more that they can do. But I will warn you whom you should fear. Fear him who after he has killed, has power to cast into hell. Yes, I tell you, fear him. Are not five sparrows sold for two small coins, and not one of them is forgotten by God. But the very hairs of your head are all numbered. Therefore do not be afraid. You are of more value than many sparrows.

Acknowledging Christ Before Others – Luke 12:8-12

"I tell you, everyone who acknowledges me before men, the Son of Man will also acknowledge before the angels of God; but the one who denies me in the presence of men will be denied in the presence of God's angels. Everyone who speaks a word against the Son of Man will be forgiven, but those who blaspheme against the Holy Spirit will not be forgiven. When they bring you before the synagogues, the rulers, and the authorities, do not be anxious how or what you will answer or what you will say; for the Holy Spirit will teach you in that same hour what you should say."

One of the earliest accounts of Christian martyrdom is the account of Polycarp, the bishop of Smyrna, a town that was in what is now Turkey. He was born in the second half of the first century A.D. and was reported to have been taught by the apostle John. By the middle of the second century, he was an esteemed teacher and leader in the church.

At the age of eighty-six, he was arrested during a time of persecution and taken to the town arena. Because of his advanced age, he was encouraged to swear allegiance to Caesar and save his life. He refused saying about Christ, "Eighty-six years I have served him, and he has done me no wrong. How can I blaspheme my king who saved me?" When they threatened to burn him with fire unless he recanted, he replied, "You threaten with fire that burns for a short time and is soon extinguished. You do not know about the fire of the coming judgment and the eternal punishment that awaits the wicked. But why are you waiting? Come, do what you will."

As the story is told, the crowd demanded that he be burned alive. When he was tied to the stake, he prayed and thanked God for the privilege of being a martyr. Eyewitnesses reported that the fire, when it was lit, seemed to go around him without consuming the body. A soldier was instructed to pierce him with a sword, and when he did the blood that came out extinguished the flames. The story of Polycarp's martyrdom was spread widely and became an encouragement to Christians to be strong in the face of the persecutions they faced.

This section in Luke contains a statement by Jesus that has been important throughout the life of the church. It is the warning that those who follow Jesus must hold fast to their witness, even unto death.

The first comments by Jesus seem to be a follow-up to the previous encounter with the Pharisees and the lawyers. After Jesus' warnings to them, they pestered him with antagonistic questions. Luke reports on the crowds that continued to gather around Jesus. He describes it as being a chaotic scene at times. The crowds were so large that they trampled one another.

Jesus continued to teach the disciples, however, even amid many distractions. Though the people respected the religious devotion of the Pharisees, Jesus wanted the disciples to think more clearly about them. Their teachings were like leaven. Their doctrines grew to influence many in their culture, but it was not to good effect. Their teachings and pattern of life were hypocritical.

The statements that follow also teach. What does a hypocrite do? He or she hides his or her true self and covers it with a façade. That will ultimately be of no avail, said Jesus. Nothing that is covered up will remain hidden. It will all come to light. Even what is said in the dark and whispered in a private place will be shouted from the housetops. Though religious hypocrites hide their corruption behind a mask of piety, it will be of no avail at God's great judgment.

This is a particularly important set of sayings by Jesus. It reminds us that while we can hide our life from others, we cannot hide it from God. It is even more serious than that, however. On the Day of Judgment, all things will be uncovered, even down to whispered words we thought no one would hear. The words of Jesus give us reason for introspection. We should not live one life in the sight of others but a different life in private. We should guard our private words, our inner meditations, and the attitudes we harbor. Jesus encourages an honest life, both before God and others. As we see so often in the words of Jesus and the Bible, God knows all things. Disciples of Jesus are called to an honest, authentic, and courageous life.

Though Jesus pronounced the judgment of God against the Pharisees, the disciples understood that they were still formidable enemies. The next sayings of Jesus were encouragement, even against many odds. Jesus emphasizes his statement by starting with, "I tell you." That is, what would follow had the authority of Jesus. In addition, he called them his friends. "I tell you, my friends ..." What did Jesus want them to know? It was that there was something worse than death. People could certainly kill the body. The natural human tendency is to fear those with that power. There is another who is to be feared even more, said Jesus. Though Jesus does not mention him by name, he refers to God. God can both kill and cast into hell. He is truly the one to be feared.

Then Jesus gives the disciples more encouragement and uses a common illustration. Five sparrows can be purchased for a small amount. Though they are of little worth at the merchant's market, God knows every one who falls to the ground. Then Jesus makes a wonderful illustration. Even the hairs on a person's head are numbered and known by God. For that reason, we should not be afraid. We are of more value than many sparrows.

The comment about acknowledging Christ in front of others has been important in the life of the church. There would certainly be a temptation, in times of persecution, to deny Christ publicly and then acknowledge him when it was less dangerous. One might say, "I denied Christ but did not mean it in my heart." This statement by Jesus excludes this option. If one is a disciple, one must be so publicly no matter the cost. Jesus makes the stakes high. Those who deny him in front of others will be denied by him in the presence of the angels. These statements by Jesus have guided the martyrs, such as Polycarp, when faced with persecution and even death.

Luke includes the comment by Jesus about the unforgivable sin. It is related, not to anyone who might deny Christ under duress, but to those who resist the work of the Holy Spirit. This was the situation of the Pharisees. They did not believe because they were not open to the Holy Spirit's work in their hearts. They would never be forgiven because they would never hear the Holy Spirit's call to repent.

Jesus then instructed disciples what to do when brought before councils, governors, and authorities. They should not be anxious, spending their time writing complicated defenses. Rather, trust the Holy Spirit. In that very hour, he will give you words to say. Jesus instructs the disciples to speak from the heart. The Holy Spirit, speaking through them, will make their words effective. The speeches of the apostles before religious and secular rulers, as recorded in the book of Acts, are evidence of the truth of this promise (Acts 4:8-12, 7:2-53, 26:2-29).

Theological insights
- Judgment is a theme of this section. Christian faith is no guarantee against persecution or even death. Disciples are not to fear persecution or death, however, but rather God's righteous judgment.
- Why is the possibility of judgment so frightful? Because it holds the possibility of eternal punishment. Immediately after warning about judgment, however, Jesus reassured the disciples that they were highly valued by God.
- The argument about God's care is from the lesser to the greater. If God cares about the sparrow that falls, how much more will he care about his beloved children?
- One cannot remain on the fence concerning Jesus. As Jesus has already said, we must be for him or against him. When persecutions come, those on the fence are forced to choose.

Practical application

The second-century Christian theologian, Tertullian, said that the blood of the martyrs was the seed of the church. He had observed a curious phenomenon. The deaths of Christian martyrs did not dissuade people from becoming Christians. Rather it enlarged the church. People were attracted to something so powerful and real that people would give their lives rather than deny it.

No one likes persecution, but it has a purifying effect on the church. It winnows away those with low commitment. When persecution arises, only those with true faith remain. It is also a solution to the sociological problem of the "free rider," that is, those who use the resources of the church without adding anything to it. When persecution comes, the free riders fall away.

Some communities today realize that persecution may be their lot. Christians in Egypt, for example, recognize that martyrdom may be part of their commitment of discipleship. It has been true in that region for centuries. In some eras and places, Christians suffer only lightly. In those cases, we should not complain about slight inconveniences or the minor difficulties of Christian service. If you suffer inconvenience, difficulty, and struggle for the sake of Christ, it is not too much to ask. Remember the sacrifices of the martyrs, and serve Christ with whatever effort is required.

Riches, Anxiety, and God's Kingdom
Luke 12:13-34

The Rich Fool – Luke 12:13-21

THEN SOMEONE IN THE CROWD said to him, "Teacher, tell my brother to divide the inheritance with me." But he said to him, "Man, who made me a judge or an arbitrator over you?" He said to them, "Beware! Keep yourselves from covetousness, for a man's life does not consist of the abundance of the things which he possesses." He spoke a parable to them, saying, "The ground of a certain rich man produced abundantly. He reasoned within himself saying, 'What will I do, because I do not have room to store my crops?' He said, 'This is what I will do. I will pull down my barns, build bigger ones, and there I will store all my grain and my goods. I will tell my soul, "Soul, you have many goods laid up for many years. Take your ease, eat, drink, and be merry." ' "But God said to him, 'You fool! Tonight your soul is required of you. The things which you have prepared – whose will they be?' So is the one who lays up treasure for himself and is not rich toward God."

Do Not Be Anxious – Luke 12:22-34

He said to his disciples, "Therefore I tell you, do not be anxious for your life, what you will eat, nor yet for your body, what you will wear. Life is more than food, and the body is more than clothing. Consider the ravens: they do not sow, they do not reap, they have no warehouse or barn, and yet God feeds them. How much more valuable are you than birds! Which of you by being anxious can add an hour to his life? If then you are not able to do even the least things, why are you anxious about the rest? Consider the lilies, how they grow. They do not toil, neither do they spin; yet I tell you, even Solomon in all his glory was not arrayed like one of these. But if this is how God clothes the grass in the field, which today exists and tomorrow is thrown into the oven, how much more will he clothe you, O you of little faith?

"Do not seek what you will eat or what you will drink; and do not be anxious. For the nations of the world seek after all of these things, but your Father knows that you need them. But seek his kingdom, and all these things will be added to you. Do not be afraid, little flock, for it is your Father's good pleasure to give you the kingdom. Sell what you have, and give gifts to the needy. Make for yourselves purses that do not grow old, a treasure in the heavens that does not fail, where no thief approaches and no moth destroys. For where your treasure is, there will your heart be also.

A topic that is a surprising focus of the Bible is money, greed, and wealth. The Bible contains a surprising number of statements about those things. For example, it talks about money and wealth: "You cannot serve both God and money" (Matthew 6:24), "Honor the Lord with your substance" (Proverbs 3:9), "For the love of money is a root of all kinds of evil" (I Timothy 6:10). It discusses debt: "The rich rule over the poor, and the borrower is servant to the lender" (Proverbs 22:7), "Owe no one anything except to love one another" (Romans 13:8), "The wicked borrow and do not pay back, but the righteous give generously" (Psalm 37:21).

The Bible talks about greed and contentment: "Whoever loves money never has enough" (Ecclesiastes 5:10), "Godliness with contentment is great gain" (I Timothy 6:6), "Better is a little with the fear of the Lord than great wealth with trouble" (Proverbs 15:16). It warns about problems wealth creates: "Do not lay up for yourselves treasures on earth" (Matthew 6:19), "Woe to those who add house to house" (Isaiah 5:8), "But the cares of this age, and the deceitfulness of riches choke out the word and it becomes unfruitful" (Matthew 13:22, Luke 8:14).

A number of the parables of Jesus are either about money or use it as an illustration: the Parable of the Talents (Matthew 25:14-30), the Parable of the Shrewd Manager (Luke 16:1-13), the Parable of the Rich Man and Lazarus (Luke 16:19-31), the Parable of the Hidden Treasure (Matthew 13:44), the Parable of the Pearl of Great Price (Matthew 13:45-46), the Parable of the Workers in the Vineyard (Matthew 20:1-16), and the Parable of the Unmerciful Servant (Matthew 18:21-35).

One of the parables that talks about money and greed is the Parable of the Rich Fool. It is told in response to a question from the crowd. Someone asked Jesus to instruct his brother to divide the family inheritance with him. As a teacher, Jesus might have been expected to render a judgment on an ethical question.

There might have been several scenarios behind the question. The Old Testament law gave the firstborn son a double portion of the family inheritance, called the "right of the firstborn." While this might seem unfair to us, the firstborn was also charged with added responsibilities, such as providing for the family and carrying on the family business. Perhaps the man in the crowd thought that arrangement unjust and wanted an equal distribution. Perhaps he had a sibling who unjustly took more than allotted, and the man wanted Jesus to correct the injustice. Whatever the case, Jesus refused to do so. However, he used the moment as an opportunity to teach.

How should we think about money and wealth? Jesus began with a warning: "Beware! Keep yourselves from covetousness, for a man's life does not consist of the abundance of the things which he possesses." The statement by Jesus might be thought of as a defense of the tenth commandment, which says, "You shall not covet." Jesus states the obvious;

what makes life meaningful is not the things one possesses. Then he told a parable about a rich man whom God blessed with abundance.

The rich man had a bumper year with his crops. There is nothing wrong with that, only with his reaction. He is smug and self-satisfied. He plans to use his abundance on himself, without giving to the needy or considering how God might want him to respond. We notice that God deals with the man in the same practical way that the man thought about his abundance. The man decided to build storage facilities so he might relax and take his ease. God responds with a practical reality. His abundance will do him no good if he is not there to use it. The tragedy of the situation is that the rich man will not know God's plan for him until it is too late.

The parable highlights several important lessons. One is that we cannot take our material wealth with us. The book of Ecclesiastes emphasizes this when it notes that we may work hard to accumulate wealth but leave it to someone who will use it foolishly (Ecclesiastes 2:18, 19). In addition, being rich in material things does not guarantee that we are rich toward God. The parable makes this point. In addition, we do not know the hour of our passing. Even significant wealth does not guard us against that moment. Jesus uses the parable to remind his hearers how tragic it is to be rich in material things but not rich toward God. In the words of the parable, one is a fool to do so.

How then should we think about money and possessions? What should we do when God gives us abundance? Jesus continues to teach. In contrast to the rich man in the parable, the disciples are not to be anxious about their lives. They are not to worry about the daily necessities of food and clothing. After all, says Jesus, life is much more than those things.

He then defends his assertion. Consider how it works for the animals. The ravens do not sow or reap. They do not have warehouses in which to store their food. Yet God feeds them, and you are much more valuable to God than they are. In addition, consider that anxiety cannot add even an hour to your span of life. If, says Jesus, your anxiety cannot help with these simple things, why do you worry about the rest?

Jesus then adds a comment about the lilies of the field. They take no thought for their adornment, yet even Solomon was not clothed like one of them. If God adorns the flowers of the field who are alive one day and withered the next, how much more will he do for you, "O you of little faith."

What then is a disciple to do? He is to seek after greater things. He is to seek God's kingdom. For those who do, God, their heavenly Father will provide for them. But will God be found by those who seek him? Yes, says Jesus. He desires to give his kingdom to his children. Here then, says Jesus is an antidote to greed. Here is the way to lay up treasure in heaven. Sell what you have and give gifts to the poor. This way you will make deposits into your heavenly account. No downturn affects that account. No thief steals from it. No moths destroy it.

Jesus ends with a counterintuitive statement. We would expect him to say that our treasure will follow where we put our hearts. Instead, he reverses the order. Put your treasure in the right place and your heart will follow along with it. This is the great stewardship principle of the New Testament. Our heart follows our money. If we put our money into the things of God, our hearts will be there too. This makes faithful stewardship of our resources more than merely a way to support the life of the Christian church. It becomes a part of Christian discipleship. It is good to return a portion to God because it keeps our hearts away from the love of money, enables us to participate in the work of God, supports God's church, lays up treasure in heaven, and turns our hearts toward God.

Anxiety is part of the human situation. Since we are finite and cannot completely control our environment and situation, we worry even about simple things. Yet anxiety expresses a lack of faith in the care of God. The words of Jesus about anxiety are important in that they address the attitude and priorities of a disciple. Their priorities and perspectives are to be different than others. Had Jesus been addressing a poverty-stricken group, his words might have been different. His words, however, are not addressed to the destitute, but to those who have food and clothing but exert their effort trying to obtain more and more. In that regard, the words of Jesus are relevant to us. The disciple of Jesus is to have greater and wider concerns than the necessities of life. God, our Father in heaven, who cares for the birds and the flowers, knows we need these things and will provide for us. We are to seek after God and his kingdom first of all. If we make his kingdom our priority, other necessities will be provided amply for us. We are to trust in God's fatherly care, for we are of great value to him.

Theological insights
- At the time of Jesus, wealth was considered a sign of God's blessings. God blessed Abraham with great wealth, for example. The same is true for both Job and Solomon. In the New Testament, Lydia was a businesswoman who supported Paul and his ministry. The

book of Proverbs talks about the value of wealth (Proverbs 3:9, 10; 10:4; 14:24) but also instructs people to use riches and money prudently (Proverbs 11:28; 13:11, 12; 15:27).

- Part of the error of the rich fool was his focus on himself. We see it in his words: my crops, barns, grain, goods, and soul. His thoughts are preoccupied with himself.
- These sayings by Jesus are in line with his comments in chapter 9, verse 25. "For what does it profit a man if he gains the whole world, but loses or forfeits his self?"

Practical application

The third-century Christian theologian, Clement of Alexander, once preached a sermon titled, "Who Is The Rich Man That Shall Be Saved?" He wrestled with the question of whether a rich person could be saved and answered that he could, but he needed to hold loosely to worldly possessions. There are many dangers in being rich, noted Clement, yet God's grace is sufficient. Those who have wealth must do good with their riches. They must support both church and good causes. While wealth has dangers, it can be used in the service of God.

The danger of wealth is that we believe we do not need God. Our wealth gives us security so that we trust in ourselves rather than God. This is a false security because it only has an earthly perspective. We can, indeed, save our lives in this world but lose our souls in the next.

One antidote to greed is tithing. This Old Testament standard helps loosen the grip of money on our souls. Giving one-tenth back to God is not so much as to be burdensome, yet it is not so small as to be insignificant. Giving a tenth stings a bit, and that is as it should be. We do not want to give to God that which costs us nothing (II Samuel 24:24). The sting of tithing loosens money's grip on our minds and affections. That we give a full tithe back to God (Malachi 3:10) builds our confidence as a disciple, as all acts of obedience do.

The third-century theologian Tertullian said, "Nothing that God gives can be purchased with money." This is a good reminder. God's true riches come free of charge. We should pray for the gifts the Holy Spirit gives to the faithful. They are of true value.

The Master's Return – Luke 12:35-48

"LET YOUR WAIST BE GIRDED ABOUT and your lamps burning. Be like men watching for their master when he returns from the wedding feast, that when he comes and knocks, they may immediately open to him. Blessed are those servants whom the master will find watching when he comes. Truly I tell you that he will dress himself, have them recline, and will come and serve them. And if he comes in the second or third watch and finds them so, blessed are those servants. But know this, that if the master of the house had known in what hour the thief was coming, he would have watched and not allowed his house to be broken into. Therefore be ready also, for the Son of Man is coming in an hour that you do not expect him."

Peter said to him, "Lord, are you telling this parable to us or to everyone?" The Lord said, "Who then is the faithful and wise steward, whom his master will set over his household, to give them their portion of food at the right times? Blessed is that servant whom his master will find doing so when he comes. Truly I tell you that he will set him over all that he has. But if that servant says in his heart, 'My master delays his coming,' and begins to beat the male and female servants, and to eat and drink and to be drunken, then the master of that servant will come in a day when he is not expecting him and in an hour that he does not know. He will cut him in two and assign him a place with the faithless. That servant who knew his master's will, and did not prepare nor do what he wanted, will be beaten with many blows, but he who did not know, and did things worthy of punishment, will be beaten with few blows. To whom much is given, of him will much be required; and to whom much was entrusted, of him more will be asked.

In 1907, British Lieutenant-General Robert Baden-Powell started the scouting movement for boys. His book *Scouting for Boys* captured the attention of men and boys throughout Britain and eventually worldwide, leading to the establishment of both the Boy and Girl Scouts. He chose the motto of "Be Prepared" as a guiding principle for the movement. It encouraged young men to be ready for any challenge they might face whether it was in some everyday situation or an emergency. A Boy Scout was to be prepared to do his duty or even face danger if necessary. Over many years the movement taught young men to develop practical skills, become self-reliant, not wither under difficulties, and be useful citizens in their relations to others.

Baden-Powell, the son of a Church of England pastor and a devout Christian, may have taken his motto from the words of Jesus. If that was its origin, he accurately captured an important teaching of Jesus: We should be prepared at all times. Jesus tells several related parables that follow the theme that a disciple should seek God's kingdom rather than accumulating wealth or luxuriating in material resources. He begins by telling his disciples to keep their "waists girded about" and their "lamps burning."

The first parable is about the blessings God will bestow on those who are watchful. To gird one's waist was to pull the excess length of their long robe into their belt in preparation for running, fighting, or intense activity. To be ready for movement was how the people were to eat the Passover meal, with their loins girded and their staff in their hands (Exodus 12:11). A lamp was kept burning by providing not only sufficient oil but pure oil that was free from contaminants. The oil used in the temple was such oil (Exodus 27:20).

The example Jesus uses is of people waiting for their master to return from a wedding feast. The listeners would have assumed that the master had gone to the home of his bride to be married. He would return with his bride and expected all to be ready when he did. It would be an embarrassment to him if he were not expected. Since wedding celebrations were of uncertain length, they might return at any time. That required readiness on the part of the servants. That the servants were to be ready "immediately" meant that they should be actively watching for their master's return.

The parable ends with a beatitude that has a surprising reversal in it. Those whom he finds watching, the master will serve. Instead of serving him, he will serve them. He will gird his waist about, have them recline, and serve them. The statement seems to be an allusion to the great banquet in the kingdom of God to which both the Old and New Testaments point (Isaiah 25:6, Luke 13:9, 14:15-24, Revelation 19:9). Jesus reiterates the need for active watching when he notes that, especially if he comes late into the night, God's blessing will be for those servants who are awake.

Jesus then changes the parable to a master securing his home against a thief. If the master knew what time the thief would attempt to enter his home, he would have been awake. Jesus then warns his disciples to be ready. The

Son of Man is coming at a time when you do not expect him. Jesus often uses the term Son of Man when talking about his return, and other places in the New Testament will use the illustration of a thief at nighttime. In I Thessalonians, Paul says that the Lord will return as a "thief in the night" (I Thessalonians 5:2). II Peter says that the day of the Lord will come "like a thief" (II Peter 3:10). In Revelation 3, the Lord says that he will come "like a thief" (Revelation 3:3). In Revelation 16, Christ also issues a similar warning: "Behold, I am coming like a thief! Blessed is the one who watches and keeps his garments on so that he does not walk naked and they see his shame" (Revelation 16:15).

As there are blessings for the faithful, there are warnings for those who are not prepared. The next section, beginning in verse 41, begins with a statement by Peter. He asked if the warnings of Jesus were primarily for them or everyone. That is, were they only for close followers of Jesus or an expectation of all believers? Jesus does not answer the question directly but tells another parable in response. His words also serve as a further explanation of the previous parable.

The focus of this second parable is not a servant but a manager. It is assumed in the parable that being a manager is a position of responsibility to be desired, for the manager who does the master's will is granted even more responsibility. The backdrop of this is the great banquet that will be celebrated in God's kingdom at the fulfillment of his final plan. To be given responsibility at that banquet will be a great privilege as Joseph was put in charge of Potiphar's house because of his competence (Genesis 39:4). In the book of Acts, it was a great honor to be chosen as a deacon and be responsible for the distribution of food to the widows (Acts 6:1-6). The use of food in the parable also reminds us of the job of church leaders who feed the church with spiritual food. In this parable, it is those who are found doing the tasks they have been given who are blessed.

In contrast to the faithful manager, it is possible to take advantage of the master's absence. In the previous parable, the servant fails by not remaining watchful. In this parable, the manager fails by shirking his responsibilities. The language also changes from manager to servant. The servant treats the other servants badly, enjoys the master's pleasures, and even gives in to drunkenness. He not only does not do good but begins to do evil. A significant part of his failure is his oppressive actions toward others within his influence.

What will happen to that servant? Just as in the first parable, the master comes when not expected, and the consequences are severe. The master will "cut him in two," a punishment that is both drastic and graphic. Then he will be assigned a place with the faithless. This might be a euphemism for hell; it is the place for all those without faith. Not only will there be physical consequences, but the rich fellowship of the saints will be denied to the faithless person. He will be among those just like him, but it will not be a good thing. He will be among the murderers, thieves, and liars (Revelation 21:6, 22:15).

The final sayings of Jesus in this section are important and often overlooked. They give us information about a question that is sometimes asked, "What about people who did not know about Jesus?" The answer of Jesus, while not a full answer to the question, assures us of God's mercy and fairness. Those who knew what was expected but did not do it will be punished severely. Those, however, who did not know, though they also did wrong things, will be punished less.

The question of how God punishes people in the afterlife has been discussed throughout church history. The biblical images of God's punishment are graphic and terrifying. The problem with hell in the Bible is not that you cannot find it, but rather that you cannot get rid of it. It is too prevalent throughout scripture. The point of these sayings of Jesus is not to assure those who do not understand. The hearers of Jesus were considered those who did understand. Therefore, they should live soberly. Should they shirk their responsibilities, they will be punished severely.

Jesus concludes with a warning for those who are given much. The "much" is not defined, but we might imagine such things as spiritual gifts, leadership responsibilities, or even monetary resources. Those given much have a greater responsibility to use what they have in the service of God. We see in all the sayings of Jesus that no one gets off easy. Everyone is called to service, and there are no acceptable excuses. More will be expected of those given much. Of those trusted with more, more will be asked.

Theological insights
- Though first-century wedding practices and the relations of masters with servants may be foreign to us, the messages of the parables are clear. They call us to preparation and a commitment to the will of Christ, our Master.

- The idea of an imminent return of Christ may lose some of its urgency as time passes. The scriptures remind us, however, to remain watchful no matter the delay. If Christ does not come to us, the precariousness of life makes it that we go to him soon enough and may do so suddenly.

- There is a sense in which every person is a manager of God's resources. We are given our lives to manage. Being a good steward of what God has given us is an expectation for which we will give account.

- The idea of greater and lesser punishments in hell was the basis for Dante's descriptions of hell in his Inferno. In the poem's view, there are levels of hell, with the punishments being more severe the deeper you go. It was Dante's outworking of this and other Bible passages about hell and punishment.

Practical application

These sayings of Jesus encourage us to faithful service and active watching. Some preachers have tried to create anticipation by unveiling end-time scenarios that predict the imminent return of Christ. So far, all those who have given dates for Christ's return have been wrong. The challenge of Christian discipleship is to actively watch, wait patiently, and serve eagerly, no matter how long it takes. One only has to do so for one's lifetime, however. From the point of view of Jesus, it is not too much to ask.

Lieutenant-General Robert Baden-Powell, founder of the Boy Scouts, wrote a "final" letter to scouts in his latter years. In it, he followed up on the theme of preparation. His words are aimed toward the encouragement of good deeds and citizenship. Though they are folksy and aimed at boys, they capture something of the ethos of Jesus, particularly the parts about treating others well, staying ready, and not focusing on wealth. His words are worth repeating.

"Dear Scouts, If you have ever seen the play Peter Pan you will remember how the pirate chief was always making his dying speech because he was afraid that possibly when the time came for him to die he might not have time to get it off his chest. It is much the same with me, and so, although I am not at this moment dying, I shall be doing so one of these days and I want to send you a parting word of goodbye.

Remember, it is the last you will ever hear from me, so think it over. I have had a most happy life and I want each one of you to have as happy a life too. I believe that God put us in this jolly world to be happy and enjoy life. Happiness doesn't come from being rich, nor merely from being successful in your career, nor by self-indulgence. One step towards happiness is to make yourself healthy and strong while you are a boy so that you can be useful and so can enjoy life when you are a man.

Nature study will show you how full of beautiful and wonderful things God has made the world for you to enjoy. Be contented with what you have got and make the best of it. Look on the bright side of things instead of the gloomy one.

But the real way to get happiness is by giving out happiness to other people. Try and leave this world a little better than you found it and when your turn comes to die, you can die happy in feeling that at any rate you have not wasted your time but have done your best. 'Be Prepared' in this way, to live happy and to die happy – stick to your Scout promise always – even after you have ceased to be a boy – and God help you to do it. Your friend, Baden-Powell."[1]

Discerning the Times – Luke 12:49-59

Division Instead of Peace – Luke 12:49-53

"I CAME TO BRING FIRE on earth, and I wish it were already kindled. But I have a baptism to be baptized with, and how great is my distress until it is accomplished! Do you think that I have come to give peace in the earth? I tell you, no, but rather division. For from now on, there will be five in one house divided, three against two, and two against three. They will be divided, father against son, and son against father; mother against daughter, and daughter against her mother; mother-in-law against her daughter-in-law, and daughter-in-law against her mother-in-law."

Discerning the Times – Luke 12:54-56

He said to the crowds also, "When you see a cloud rising from the west, immediately you say, 'A shower is coming,' and so it happens. When a south wind blows, you say, 'There will be a scorching heat,' and it happens. You hypocrites! You know how to interpret the appearance of the earth and the sky, but how is it that you do not interpret this time?

Settle Your Accounts – Luke 12:57-59

"Why do you not judge for yourselves what is right? For when you are going with your adversary before the magistrate, try diligently on the way to be set free from him, lest perhaps he drag you to the judge, and the judge deliver you to the officer, and the officer throw you into prison. I tell you, you will by no means get out of there until you have paid the very last penny."

You may have heard the saying: "God may not come when you want him, but he is always right on time." This statement captures a common experience. We sometimes have to wait on God. We need God's help, but he is nowhere to be found. Finally, however, just in the nick of time, God comes through with help in our circumstances, healing grace, or an answer to prayer.

We see this in the Bible. Abraham waited twenty-five long years for God to fulfill his promise of an heir. It seemed that God had forgotten his promise, or was simply not going to fulfill it. Finally, when it seemed that all was lost, Sarah conceived and Isaac was born. Similarly, the old priest Zechariah and his wife Elizabeth had long prayed for a child. Eventually, however, she was too old, and their hope faded. When the angel Gabriel announced that Zechariah would father a child by her, he could hardly believe it. It turned out to be perfect timing, however, since their son, John, would prepare the way for Jesus.

The nation of Israel had waited a long time for the coming of the Messiah. Isaiah the prophet had spoken of him, but that was in the 8th century B.C. It must have seemed to many in Israel that God had forgotten his promise. He had not, however. Though some would not realize it, the life and ministry of Jesus were what the nation had been waiting for. In this section, Jesus marvels that people are not able to discern that the long-awaited time has arrived.

In this section, Luke has several sayings by Jesus that do not necessarily appear related. It is not surprising that Luke would recount various sayings of Jesus without putting them all in a chronological context. Jesus begins by foretelling that his person, identity, and mission would create conflicts, not always peace. One might think that the coming of the Messiah would have a unifying effect. After all, Isaiah said that he would be the "Prince of Peace" (Isaiah 9:6). It would not always be so, says Jesus. The conflicts over him will be so sharp that they will separate even the closest of relations, fathers and sons, mothers and daughters, and in-laws against one another.

This has historically been true. One family member's commitment to Christ has not always been well received by the others. It was particularly true in the early days of the church when a Christian conversion might bring a strong negative reaction from a Jewish family. It is still true today, in some Jewish communities, that there is strong hostility toward and even rejection of any Jew who becomes a Christian. Jesus will specifically say, in chapter 14, that love for him must take priority over one's commitment to father, mother, children, and even one's own life (Luke 14:26).

Here is a statement of Jesus that points to the radical nature of discipleship. Just as there is no priority greater than God, there is no commitment greater than the one to Jesus. This does not make other things unimportant but puts them into proper perspective. When Christ is at the center, other things take their right place. The commitment to put God first, others second, and yourself third is an application of this. Jesus' words indicate the radical nature of discipleship. Nothing takes priority over Jesus. There might come times when one's commitment to Jesus will bring tension and even rupture to one's closest relationships. That is a cost a disciple must be willing to pay.

In what sense did Jesus come to bring fire to the earth? Fire both purifies and destroys. As Simeon said when Mary came for her purification, her son was a "sign" that would be spoken against. The coming of Jesus created a fire on the earth, one that was necessary for the plan of God. As fire consumes the chaff, it also purifies gold. The question of Jesus' identity and mission would separate people from one another. Those without faith would be revealed. Those called by God would also come to light and shine with the brightness of the Holy Spirit.

What baptism does Jesus refer to when he says that he has a baptism with which to be baptized? He sees his death approaching ever closer. Though Jesus is a picture of calm and serenity, in his humanity, he must have felt anxiety about his upcoming suffering. He knew he had a great trial facing him. He would face evil head-on and take the brunt of its force, resulting in his crucifixion. We can understand that he felt internal distress until his mission was accomplished.

The next words of Jesus, beginning in verse 54, seem addressed to the apathy of the crowds. Jesus had given them many stern words of judgment, yet they must have seemed unconcerned. He notes that they are wise in worldly ways. They know that clouds that come from the west have blown in from the Mediterranean Sea and will carry water. A wind from the south will bring heat from the desert. They could not discern spiritual signs, however, because they were hypocrites. Their religion was mostly for show, and true faith did not live in their hearts. With all the healings and miracles Jesus did, he must have marveled that faith did not awaken in them. That he was the promised Messiah should have been obvious to any with ears to hear and hearts open to God.

Jesus then gives another warning, beginning in verse 57. Just as a wise person will settle with his accuser on the way to court, so you should not delay in making peace with God. Even what might seem the great commitment required by Jesus is not too much, because those who have not settled their account with God will be judged harshly. The punishment of God will be severe, and it will not be easy to pay off that great debt. Though the words of Jesus refer to human relations and striving to settle debts quickly, they are ultimately a reference to our great need to be reconciled with God.

Theological insights
- John affirmed that the Messiah would baptize with the Holy Spirit and fire (John 3:16). Jesus would bring the fire of God's love for those who received him and the fire of his judgment for those who did not.
- The prophets had promised that great things would accompany the coming of the Messiah, but his identity and the nature of his work were hidden in the Old Testament. Those who sought to discern it by reason only could not do so. It was only perceived by faith.
- The church through the centuries has sought to discern the "signs of the times" in order to relate the gospel to the surrounding world, hold fast to the truth against theological drift, and know what ought to be done in its moment in history.

Practical application

In what sense is the nature and identity of the Messiah hidden in the Old Testament? It is hidden in that only glimpses of his identity are revealed. Since he was to come from the line of David, people assumed that he would be a warrior who would vanquish the nation's enemies and reign as their king. But the words of scripture gave confusing clues about him.

Moses said that God would raise up another prophet like him (Deuteronomy 18:15-19) to whom the people would listen. But in what way would he be like Moses? Isaiah, the prophet, described a "shoot from the stump of Jesse" who would bring wisdom and peace. Under his rule, the earth would be filled with the knowledge of God (Isaiah 11:1-10). Daniel had a vision of someone "like a son of man" who would be given an everlasting kingdom (Daniel 7:13-14). Jeremiah spoke about a new covenant in which God's law would be written on people's hearts (Jeremiah 31:31-34). Ezekiel promised "one shepherd" who would care for God's people (Ezekiel 34:23-24). Zechariah said that the nation would look upon the one they had "pierced" (Zechariah 12:10).

Isaiah's words about a Suffering Servant were strange and unclear (Isaiah 52:13-53:12), and most people did not connect them with the Messiah. How could God's promised Messiah possibly suffer in the ways the prophet described? Isaiah also spoke of him with divine language (Isaiah 9:6), yet how could any human also be "Mighty God" and "Everlasting Father?"

The answer would be revealed in the appearance of Jesus Christ, who was God come among us in flesh and blood. It would be his death and resurrection that would finally reveal the great mystery of God's plan. He came to set the people free not through military prowess but his saving death on the cross. He came to complete his mission through his suffering and sacrificial death. The surprise and wonder of it all would be part of God's great gift to the world and the demonstration of his astonishing love.

LUKE 13

Bearing Fruit – Luke 13:1-9

Repent or Perish

NOW THERE WERE SOME PRESENT at that time who told him about the Galileans whose blood Pilate had mixed with their sacrifices. Jesus answered them, "Do you think that these Galileans were worse sinners than all the other Galileans, because they suffered this way? I tell you, no, but unless you repent, you will all likewise perish. Or those eighteen on whom the tower in Siloam fell and killed them – do you think that they were worse sinners than all the others who live in Jerusalem? I tell you, no, but, unless you repent, you will all likewise perish."

The Barren Fig Tree

And he told this parable: "A certain man had a fig tree planted in his vineyard, and he came seeking fruit on it and found none. He said to the vine dresser, 'Behold, these three years I have come looking for fruit on this fig tree, and found none. Cut it down! Why does it waste the soil?' He answered, 'Sir, leave it alone one more year, until I dig around it and fertilize it. If it bears fruit, fine; but if not, after that, you can cut it down.' "

These comments by Jesus begin with a reference to Pontius Pilate. Christians know the name Pontius Pilate because he presided over the trial of Jesus and ordered his crucifixion. Who was he? He was the governor of the southern region of Israel from the years 26 A.D. until 36 A.D. When, in the year 6 A.D., Caesar Augustus removed one of the sons of Herod the Great, Archelaus, from governing the region, he appointed a Roman governor in his place. Pontius Pilate was the fifth such governor and kept his headquarters in the city that Herod the Great had built by the Mediterranean

Sea, Caesarea Maritima. For special occasions, such as the Passover, Pilate went to Jerusalem. It was on one such occasion when he was there that the trial of Jesus took place. Since Pilate was in town, he had to be consulted by the priests for an execution to take place.

The relationship between Pontius Pilate and the Jews was turbulent. The Jews were difficult to govern, and their religious practices often put them at odds with the culture and values of the Roman world. In general, it was a volatile political and social climate that was difficult for anyone to manage. Jewish historian Josephus records several incidents of conflict between Pilate and the Jews. On one occasion, Pilate brought Roman military standards bearing the image of Caesar into Jerusalem. This caused widespread protests until Pilate relented and removed the images. On another occasion, Pilate used money from the temple treasury to build an aqueduct. This was money that would have been considered "Corban" (Mark 7:11) and only available for holy uses. This sparked riots which Pilate quelled by sending soldiers dressed as civilians into the crowd to murder protesters. Pilate's actions could be brutal and unsympathetic, but he was certainly dealing with a difficult people. His willingness to deliver Jesus to be crucified at the request of the priests may be an indication of the uneasy but necessary working relationship he had with the religious class.

The incident that Luke reports is not mentioned in any non-biblical sources and is not mentioned in other gospel accounts. It seems to indicate some instance in which Pilate had pilgrims killed in or near the temple during one of the festivals, perhaps the Passover. That would have "mixed their blood with their sacrifices" as Luke records.

The comment by someone about Pilate's violence may have been in the context of Jesus traveling toward Jerusalem. Jesus had begun to travel toward Jerusalem for the final time (Luke 9:51). Someone sympathetic to Jesus may have been warning him about the dangers that were associated with being in Jerusalem at the Passover, because of the willingness of Pilate to resort to violent measures.

Jesus did not respond to the potential threat that going to Jerusalem might involve. He certainly understood that he would, indeed, be killed during his time there. Instead, he used the comment as a teaching moment to encourage repentance. The Jews might have assumed that the Galileans were killed because of their sinfulness. It was a common belief that people's troubles were retribution for their sins. The disciples of Jesus, for example, asked him on one occasion whether a certain man's parents had sinned to cause him to be born blind (John 9:2). Jesus focuses his comments on the universal need for repentance. In addition to the Galileans whom Pilate had murdered, a tower in Siloam had fallen and killed eighteen people. This incident must have been common knowledge. Was it because of their sins? No, says Jesus. Again he points out the need for repentance by everyone. "Unless you repent, you will all likewise perish."

When suffering takes place, we search for meaning. Did I cause my own suffering? Is this God's judgment in some way? We sometimes, however, find no satisfactory answers. Jesus does not give an explanation for the incidents. Rather, he points to a more urgent matter. There is a judgment before which everyone will stand. Be ready for that judgment, and all will be well. Life is tenuous. We do not know when we will stand before God. For that reason, there is great urgency to be ready.

The Parable of the Barren Fig Tree continues the theme. A sign of sincere repentance is bearing fruit. Here again, the matter is urgent. The time to bear the fruit of right living is now. This was particularly true for the nation of Israel and the city of Jerusalem toward which Jesus was journeying. God had often sought from them the fruit of faith only to find idolatry and unbelief (Isaiah 5:1-7, Micah 7:1-7). In the parable, we see that the landowner's patience is running thin. He is ready to uproot the fig tree and plant something that will bear fruit. The listener is invited to ask, "Is God's patience wearing thin? Am I in danger of God giving up on me?"

The gardener wishes to give the plant one more chance. He will dig around it, fertilize it, and see what happens. Then, says the gardener, if it bears fruit, fine. If not, you can cut it down. The three years that he had sought fruit on the tree may be an allusion to the three years of Jesus' ministry. The Messiah of the Jewish people had been among them for three years. Would they receive him and bear the fruit of faith?

This is a poignant parable, especially as Jesus travels toward Jerusalem. The nation of Israel is on the verge of losing its place in the plan of God. Their Messiah has come to them but will be crucified in Jerusalem. What will God do? Will he destroy the nation and send his blessing elsewhere? The words of Jesus are haunting when we understand the historical record, and here we see the prophetic ministry of Jesus. In 70 A.D. the nation of Israel will be overrun and Jerusalem destroyed. Christianity will start in Jerusalem among the Jews but spread to the wider world. Many in Israel will reject it, but the Gentile world will embrace it. In the end, the nation of Israel will not bear the fruit of faith in Christ. History will record the judgment of

God against it. It will also record the ongoing spread of the gospel throughout the Gentile world. In the face of such a future, this parable is a plea to the nation of Israel to repent, while there is still time.

Theological insights
- Everyone wants to find meaning in suffering. Christian theology asserts that God is such a watchful Father that everything that he allows to happen to us will ultimately work for his plan and our good (Romans 8:28).
- God's judgment is different from human judgment. We believe that if we do not suffer, we are better than others. The words of Jesus call us to the regular practice of repentance, knowing that we too have many faults in need of correction.
- If, on occasion, we observe God's chastisement of others, we should not be proud but, rather, repent knowing that God's patience toward us allows us time to do so as well.
- Life is uncertain. Accidents happen. We should be ready to stand before God's judgment at any time.
- Jesus is the great gardener of God's vineyard. He nurtures and sometimes disciplines us with patience so we may bear fruit.
- God calls people to serve as gardeners in his kingdom, nurturing others toward faith and fruitfulness. Everyone has someone whose faith they can nurture.

Practical application
The Parable of the Barren Fig Tree was spoken to the Jews but is written for our sakes. It reminds us of the importance of bearing fruit. To bear fruit is to use our God-given gifts, deal honestly with others, love the truth, and remain faithful in worship. It means giving attention to prayer, living with integrity, doing our best, learning the faith, and spreading the gospel. It includes listening with compassion, sharing our faith, forgiving freely, giving generously, serving eagerly, and caring for the poor. In short, bearing fruit is living a life that reflects Christ. In John 15, Jesus teaches that the key to bearing more fruit in the future is to bear fruit now. It is the fruitful branch that the Father prunes, so it may become even more fruitful. As we live faithfully and bear fruit in the present, God refines our character, deepens our gifts, and opens new doors for greater impact in the future.

Healing on the Sabbath – Luke 13:10-21

A Woman with an Infirmity

HE WAS TEACHING IN ONE of the synagogues on the Sabbath day. Behold, there was a woman who had a spirit of infirmity for eighteen years. She was bent over and could not straighten herself up. When Jesus saw her, he called her and said to her, "Woman, you are freed from your infirmity." He laid his hands on her, and immediately she stood up straight and glorified God.

The ruler of the synagogue, being indignant because Jesus had healed on the Sabbath, said to the multitude, "There are six days in which one ought to work. Therefore come on those days and be healed, and not on the Sabbath day!"

Therefore the Lord answered him, "You hypocrites! Doesn't each one of you free his ox or his donkey from the stall on the Sabbath and lead it away to water? Then ought not this woman, being a daughter of Abraham whom Satan has bound eighteen long years, be set free from this bondage on the Sabbath day?" As he said these things, all his adversaries were shamed, and the entire crowd rejoiced for all the glorious things that were being done by him.

The Mustard Seed and the Yeast

He said, therefore, "What is kingdom of God like, and to what shall I compare it? It is like a grain of mustard seed that a man took and planted in his garden. And it grew and became a large tree, and the birds of the air made nests in its branches."

Again he said, "To what shall I compare the kingdom of God? It is like yeast that a woman took and hid in three measures of flour until it was all leavened."

Some people are "rule followers." Perhaps you know someone like this. Perhaps you are one yourself. Rules have many benefits. They help ensure fairness, order, and safety. They help things run efficiently. People who are rule followers find it particularly irritating when someone parks outside the lines, does not use their turn signal, breaks in line, ignores an

RSVP request, or wears white after Labor Day. This account in Luke shows how, while rules have their place, they can sometimes get in the way of compassion and common sense.

The story of the woman with the infirmity begins with Jesus teaching in the synagogue on the Sabbath day. It should be noted that Jesus was constantly engaged in his teaching ministry. This was a central aspect of his ministry to both his disciples and the people. On a typical Sabbath, Jesus would be found in a synagogue teaching the people. His healing ministry accompanied his teaching ministry, and he gave attention to both.

The incident took place in the synagogue on the Sabbath day. Jesus and the disciples, like many among the Jewish people, attended Sabbath worship. There is something special about the gathering of God's people. When the people of God gather for worship, prayer, scripture, and sermon, it is often a time when God's presence is particularly felt. As this is true for people today, it was true in the first century and one of the reasons people attended their local synagogue faithfully. How especially true it must have been when Jesus taught in the synagogue.

There was a woman present who had, as Luke says, "a spirit of infirmity." The Greek word used means " infirmity, weakness, sickness." It is unclear whether Luke intends to say that her illness was demonic or whether he simply means that she was ill. That she was bent over would indicate to our minds some sort of spinal disfiguration. The number used in the previous story in which eighteen people were killed by the tower of Siloam, seems to have no connection with the eighteen-year length of this woman's illness. That she had been disfigured for so long would have been a source of significant difficulties for the woman as well as social embarrassment.

Though it was the Sabbath, Jesus did not hesitate about whether to heal her. Luke says that when Jesus noticed her, he called to her and declared that she was freed from her infirmity. He then laid his hands on her, a sign of personal care, and she immediately stood up straight. Luke reports that she glorified God. We can imagine that she felt a tremendous sense of relief, joy, and gratitude. She did not hold back in her praise to God.

The point of tension in the account comes when the leader of the synagogue spoke to the crowd. Where the Sabbath was concerned, those in the religious establishment were adamant rule followers, and the proper use of the Sabbath was a growing point of contention between the religious leaders and Jesus. Luke says that synagogue leader was indignant. He did not address Jesus but the crowd. He was evidently seeking to turn them against him. "There are six days in which work is to be done. Let everyone come and be healed on those days, not the Sabbath."

We have previously said that the keeping of the Sabbath was one of the primary identifying marks, along with circumcision, of the Jewish religious identity. We might sympathize with their confusion about what was appropriate and not appropriate on the Sabbath. The religious establishment of the day had gone to an extreme, however, in its Sabbath observance and lost sight of common sense.

Jesus responds to the challenge and with some indignation himself. "You religious leaders are hypocrites," he says. Then, as he will do on occasion, he argues from the lesser to the greater. "Which of you does not care for your animals on the Sabbath, leading them to their food and water? If you show such care for your animals, should not this person be shown the same consideration?" Jesus' logic is impeccable and compelling.

To explain why the woman's healing was urgent, Jesus notes that she was a daughter of Abraham whom Satan had bound for eighteen years. The use of the term "daughter of Abraham" confers on her the dignity of a worthy member of the people of God. That she was bound by Satan gives all the more reason that she should be released immediately. This incident becomes a complete triumph for Jesus over the religious leaders. They are put to shame and the crowd rejoices. Jesus is honored and the crowd recognizes the wonderful things he is doing. Because of Jesus, the entire crowd, with the exception of the religious leaders, gives thanks and praise to God.

The words of Jesus that the woman was "bound by Satan" raise the question of the nature of her illness. His words do not necessarily indicate demon possession. It may simply be Jesus' way of saying that Satan is the instrument of the various ills that have come into the fallen world. With the sin of Adam and Eve, disease entered the world – sickness becoming the forerunner and the foreshadowing of our inevitable death. The New Testament does not see every illness as a direct action of Satan (John 9:1-3), but rather as part of the human experience in a fallen world. The healing ministry of Jesus was God's breaking of the power of Satan and of the results of the Fall.

Once again, Jesus demonstrates that he is "Lord of the Sabbath" (Luke 6:5), with the authority to determine its appropriate use. God obviously "works" on the Sabbath. He hears prayers and manages the world, even on the Sabbath. Jesus also exercised his ministry on the Sabbath. Jesus signals that, if God does good on the Sabbath, we too are allowed to do so. The Sabbath is a rest from evil actions, as should every day be, but not a rest from doing good. Here is an account from the life of Jesus that teaches us the importance of concern about the suffering of others.

Jesus tells two parables that emphasize lessons that can be gleaned from the healing of the woman with the infirmity. They are parables of the kingdom of God and describe what the kingdom is like. The nature of God's kingdom is multifaceted. One parable is not sufficient to describe its complex nature, but each parable shows one facet of it.

The first parable is the Parable of the Mustard Seed. The mustard seeds to which Jesus refers are very small. According to one count, it requires 750 mustard seeds to make a single gram of weight. Yet the seeds grow well beyond their small size and become a bush that can reach ten to twelve feet tall. This is a parable about beginnings and endings. The kingdom of God may begin very small. Small events, like the healing of a sick woman, may seem insignificant in the grand scheme of things, but we cannot determine the end from the beginning. In the end, great things may happen. The picture of the birds nesting in the branches of the tree is a picture of rest, security, and peace. The kingdom of God provides safety, comfort, and nurture for the people of God. What better picture of the nature of the church and the outcome of its work could Jesus have given us?

Jesus continues to reveal many reversals in the kingdom of God. A poor woman finds grace and is healed but the leader of the synagogue opposes God's work. Just as a small amount of yeast causes an entire loaf to rise, so the kingdom of God has great influence. Small beginnings should not be despised. Who knows but that the emergence of God's kingdom will, at one point, change the entire world?

Theological insights
- Jesus gave attention and priority to his teaching and healing ministries. The church today should also give priority to these.
- The fifth century theologian, Augustine, said that as the woman's illness caused her to stoop over, so sin causes us to bow down and be unable to look heavenward. The healing of Christ enables us to look heavenward and embrace the good things of God.
- The passage reminds us that people take priority over rules.

- Praise to God is always the appropriate response to his healing and redeeming power.
- The religious leader wanted to make the issue the observance of the Sabbath. Jesus made the issue the importance and dignity of the woman.
- We should not disparage small beginnings. Where God is concerned small things grow well beyond their measure.

Practical application

The inclusion of the account of the healing of the infirmed woman is just one of many ways Luke's gospel affirms the importance of women. In a male-dominated era, Luke affirms the importance of women and shows how Jesus treated them with kindness and respect. Some instances in the Gospel of Luke are:

- Luke details the roles of women in a number of the birth narrative stories (Mary's role in Luke 1, Elizabeth's role in Luke 1, Anna the prophetess in Luke 2).
- A number of healings related to women are recorded – Peter's mother-in-law in Luke 4, the widow's son in Luke 7, Jairus's daughter in Luke 8, the woman with the issue of blood in Luke 8, and the woman with the infirmity in Luke 13.
- Luke lists the names of women who followed Jesus and provided for him out of their means (Luke 8:1-3) – Mary Magdalene, Joanna, and Suzanna).
- Jesus allowed Mary to sit at his feet and listen to his teaching in Luke 10, something normal associated with men.
- Various parables and teachings feature women (the Parable of the Lost Coin in Luke 15:8-10 and the Parable of the Persistent Widow in Luke 18:1-8)
- Women were witnesses to the death and resurrection of Jesus (A number of women watched the crucifixion while the disciples fled, in Luke 23; observed the burial of Jesus, in Luke 23; and were the first witnesses of the resurrection, in Luke 24.)

Though certain roles may be different for men and women, then and now, Jesus treated both men and women with dignity and worth. As Jesus will later call Zacchaeus a "son of Abraham" (Luke 19:9), he bestows on the woman the same dignity, calling her a "daughter of Abraham." This story is a reminder that the church today should treat all people with dignity. Both men and women are equal in the eyes of God and an important part of his work in the world today.

The Narrow Door – Luke 13:22-35

Will Few Be Saved?

HE WENT ON HIS WAY through towns and villages, teaching, and traveling on toward Jerusalem. Someone said to him, "Lord, will only a few be saved?" And he said to them, "Strive to enter by the narrow door, for many, I tell you, will seek to enter in and will not be able. When once the master of the house has risen up and shut the door, and you begin to stand outside and to knock at the door, saying, 'Lord, open to us!' then he will answer and tell you, 'I do not know where you come from.' Then you will begin to say, 'We ate and drank in your presence, and you taught in our streets.' And he will say, 'I tell you, I do not know where you come from. Depart from me, all you workers of unrighteousness.' There will be weeping and gnashing of teeth when you see Abraham, Isaac, Jacob, and all the prophets in the kingdom of God, and yourselves thrown out. And they will come from the east, west, north, and south, and will recline at the table in the kingdom of God. And behold, there are some who are last who will be first, and there are some who are first who will be last."

Jesus Mourns Over Jerusalem

At that same hour, some Pharisees came, saying to him, "Leave here and go away, for Herod wants to kill you." He said to them, "Go and tell that fox, 'Behold, I cast out demons and perform cures today and tomorrow, and the third day I complete my mission.' Nevertheless, I must go on my way today and tomorrow and the next day, for it cannot be that a prophet would perish outside of Jerusalem."

"Jerusalem, Jerusalem, you who kill the prophets and stone those who are sent to you! How often I have wanted to gather your children together, like a hen gathers her brood under her wings, and you were not willing! Behold, your house is left to you desolate. I tell you, you will not see me until you say, 'Blessed is he who comes in the name of the Lord!' "

One of the fascinating archeological sites in the Middle East is the Jordanian city of Petra. This ancient city, no longer inhabited, is known for two iconic features. One is the treasury building that greets visitors upon their entrance into the city. The other is the narrow, natural path one has to walk to enter the city. The winding gorge is a natural water channel formed long ago. In places, it narrows to only six feet wide. It is three-quarters of a mile long and over 250 feet high at points. The narrow path made for an almost impregnable entrance that protected the ancient city and enabled it to flourish from the 4th century B.C. until the second century after Christ.

Is the way of Christianity narrow? Jesus responds with a partial answer to that question in this section. There is a narrow door by which one must enter into Christianity. Jesus encourages people to strive to enter by that door.

This passage continues what is sometimes called the travel section of Luke's gospel. Beginning in chapter 9, verse 51, Jesus sets his face toward Jerusalem on what he knows will be his final journey there. This travelogue will continue through chapter 19 when Jesus arrives at the city and enters triumphantly on Palm Sunday. Luke notes that, on his journey, he went through the various towns and villages, teaching as he went toward the city.

This discussion is, in some ways, a follow-up to the previous parable in which a tiny mustard seed grows into a large bush in which the birds nest and find rest. It would be natural to ask, "How large will the kingdom of God be?" "How many people will find rest in it?" It may also be that the question of how many people are saved was a common topic of discussion among religious scholars and students. As he traveled along, someone asked Jesus the question: "Lord, will only a few be saved?"

Jesus does not answer the question directly but shifts the focus from how many to whom. What is important is to consider what is required to be saved and, in particular, whether you are among that number or not. What one should do is strive to enter by the narrow door. Many, says Jesus, will seek to enter in but not be able.

The problem becomes, in the words of Jesus, that the narrow door becomes a closed door. At some point, the Master rises up and shuts the door. Then you will recognize, says Jesus, that you have been shut out. You will cry out to be allowed entrance, but the response from within will be stern. "I do not know where you come from." Those outside will complain that they deserve entrance because of their familiarity with him. We "ate and drank" in your presence. We heard your teachings. Again, the response of the Master is stern. "I do not know where you come from." He tells them to depart and calls them workers of unrighteousness. There will be weeping and gnashing of teeth.

To what is Jesus referring? His comments are certainly aimed at those Jews who did not believe in him. Their defense is that they ate and drank with him. This might be a reference to the Passover festival and the eating and drinking that was part of it. People will complain that they observed all the required religious duties. They attended all the required ceremonies. Yet, according to the words of Jesus, the mere performance of religious duty did not protect their lives from being essentially unrighteous. They did not do the one thing required which was to enter by the proper door. That the Master does not even know them signals their complete lack of true faith.

The degree of regret felt by those on the outside is made worse by seeing those who do enter. Those on the outside will see Abraham, Isaac, and Jacob on the inside. These were the great patriarchs of the Jewish faith whose faith was regularly applauded. In addition, all the prophets will be there among the gathered crowd. To make things worse, people will come from every direction, east, west, north, and south. They will sit at the table in the kingdom of God. From our vantage point, this statement seems a clear reference to the inclusion of the Gentiles in the saving plan of God.

The image of those inside reclining at table points to an idea that runs throughout scripture about a great eschatological feast that celebrates the coming of God's kingdom at the end of time. This feast represents the culmination of God's great plan when sin and death are destroyed, when all things are restored, and when God's people are united with him in eternal fellowship and love. Scripture references to this feast are found in such places as Isaiah 25, where it says: "On this mountain, the Lord of hosts will make all peoples a feast of rich food, a feast of choice wines, of rich food full of marrow, of well-refined choice wines" (Isaiah 25:6). The Parable of the Wedding Feast talks about the kingdom of heaven being like a wedding feast a king prepared for his son (Matthew 22:1-14). Revelation says,

"Blessed are those who are invited to the wedding supper of the Lamb" (Revelation 19:9). Jesus himself will later say to the disciples, "I confer on you a kingdom, even as my Father has conferred on me, that you may eat and drink at my table in my kingdom" (Luke 22:29, 30).

The sayings of Jesus in this section are a stern warning and seem to be particularly directed at the Jewish people. His ministry was almost over at that point. He was traveling toward Jerusalem where he would give his life and then rise again. Their window of opportunity was wide open, but it would not be forever. Now was the time to enter by the narrow door. What was the narrow door? It was not a code of conduct or another set of religious principles or even a new way of thinking about their faith. It was Jesus himself. He is the door. All who place their faith in him find entrance into God's salvation. Those who seek to go in by another way find themselves shut out.

At the end, Jesus affirms one of the reversals of the kingdom of God. Some who are last will be first, and some who are first will be last. This may be in reference to the Gentiles who were, in the eyes of the Jews, among the heathen who were outside of God's grace. The Jews thought of them as last, but they would find their way successfully through the door. From the east, west, north, and south, the Gentile world would embrace the gospel. This is what the apostle Paul said in his final statement in the book of Acts. "Let it be known to you, therefore, that the salvation of God is being sent to the Gentiles, and they will receive it" (Acts 28:28). Those to whom all the promises of God had been given would, tragically, find themselves on the outside. As it turns out, the Master of the house is Christ himself. All who wish entrance must come to him in faith.

The final part of this chapter records the anguish of Jesus over the fate of the Jews, as symbolized by the capital city of Jerusalem. His comment is precipitated by a warning about the evil intentions of Herod. One of the striking things about the three and one-half year ministry of Jesus is that he avoided conflict with the local political leaders, one of whom was Herod the Great's son, Herod Antipas. He ruled the region of Galilee as tetrarch and was concerned about whatever took place in it. We have already learned that Herod was curious about Jesus and looked for an opportunity to see him (Luke 9:7-9). But Jesus had no predictable schedule and was constantly moving from village to village. It was certainly also the plan of God that their paths not cross until an encounter with Herod during Jesus' trial (Luke 23:7-12). It would not be surprising that Herod would wish Jesus harm, as someone warns Jesus. The ruler did not like anyone disrupting the social order in his area, which Jesus was certainly doing, creating such excitement among the crowds.

Jesus' words about Herod are dismissive. He knows that his death will not be at Herod's hands but at Rome's. His response shows that he holds no fear of him. His use of the term "fox" about him is certainly descriptive. Herod was shrewd, manipulative, and self-interested. Jesus' lack of fear is that he knows his death will take place in Jerusalem. As it was the center of the people's religious life, it was also the heart of its corruption.

The lament of Jesus over Jerusalem follows naturally from his comments about the narrow door. His words are spoken as the pre-existent Christ who has followed the nation's journey since its beginnings. What has been characteristic of the capital city? It has been their rejection of God as illustrated by their murder of the prophets. From the heart of their religious life has come, not righteousness and justice, but murder and corruption. Yet God's heart has always been to gather them up, as a hen does her brood, and shelter them. They would not respond, however. What then would be their fate? The words of Jesus are chilling. Their house is left to them desolate. Whatever they seem to have is taken away from them (Luke 8:18). If they reject God's own Son, there will be little left them of God's grace. That wretchedness will remain until they are willing to listen to the preachers God sends. They had rejected the prophets, but God will continue to send preachers. Only when they are finally willing to listen to those God sends will the nation turn its heart to God again.

Theological reflections
- Jesus did not answer the question of whether few or many are saved. Knowing the answer to the question would satisfy our curiosity but not lead us to salvation.
- That the door into the kingdom is narrow seems to indicate that the number of those saved is small. Yet Jesus also says that they will come from the east, west, north, and south to sit at table in the kingdom of heaven.
- There is great mystery in the workings of God in the world, particularly in God's election of people.
- Christianity is a narrow way in that it goes through Jesus Christ. It opens people to a broad way of love, truth, joy, and hope.

- Jesus highlights the importance of the role of preachers and people's reception of them. God sends preachers to proclaim the good news. If people will listen to them, they will hear the gospel and can be saved.
- The town of Petra, with its narrow entrance, was never conquered. It was eventually abandoned because of shifting trade routes and earthquakes that damaged its infrastructure. In spite of numerous challenges, Christianity continues to grow and flourish. The way to God is Jesus Christ. The door is narrow, but the love of God is wide and expansive, and people continue to flow into it.

Practical application

How does a Christian explain and defend the belief that salvation is only found in Jesus Christ? It is not a doctrine created by Christians to protect Christianity but a belief that arises from within it. The Bible itself calls Christ the only way of salvation (John 14:6). He is the narrow door through which people must enter if they wish to be saved.

Someone might object by saying, "Haven't there been many religious leaders who showed the way to God?" The response of Christianity is that God's only Son, the second person of the Trinity, only came to earth once. He came in the person of Jesus Christ. While others may have had useful religious insights, no one revealed the true character, will, and plan of God except his Son. Only Christ could reveal the Father because only Christ came from him. God designated the law as the guide to faith in Old Testament times, but since the coming of Jesus, he has designated that all who would come to him must do so through his Son.

The way of Christ is open to all, but not everyone is willing to come in. Why would someone not be willing to enter through the door of Jesus? There may be many reasons. Many people want to be spiritual but do not like the restrictions and boundaries of Christianity. Some people want a level of proof that faith does not provide. They may believe, wrongly, that science has disproven the existence of God. Some people who claim intellectual doubts are actually resistant for moral reasons. They know they will be required to change their lifestyles if they commit to being a Christian. Some may have little spiritual interest and think such things are for others and not for them.

The apostle Paul wrestled with the Jewish people's rejection of Christ in Romans 9, 10, and 11. In the end, he argued that God has allowed their rejection until the full number of the Gentiles has come to faith. Then there will be a recognition of Jesus as the Messiah and a widespread turning of Israel back to God. We all await that day and pray for its coming. We pray for a heart, among Jews and all people, to embrace the gospel from the lips of the preachers God sends.

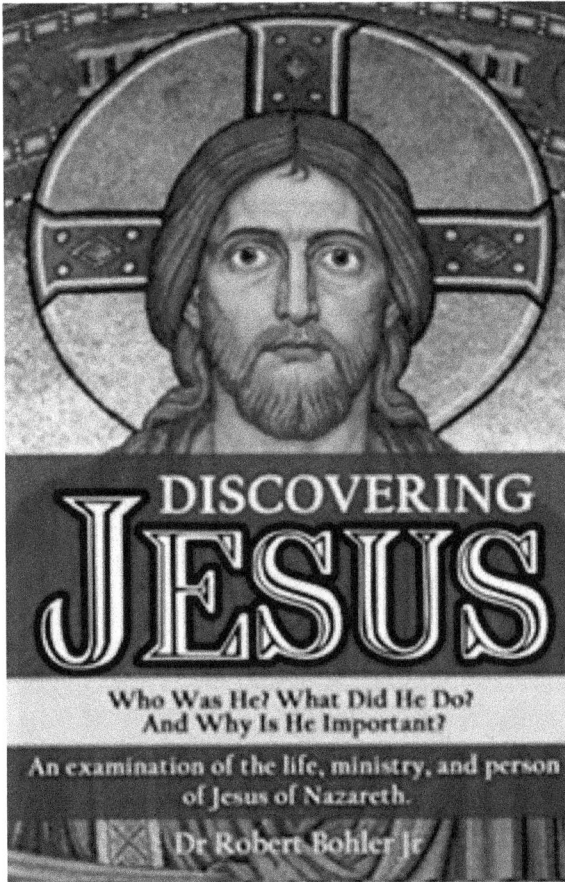

Who was Jesus of Nazareth? To many he is a hazy historical figure who seems irrelevant. Yet over 2 billion people in the world today believe no one has ever existed like Jesus Christ. In *Discovering Jesus* we examine the life, ministry, death, and resurrection of Jesus Christ. We seek to uncover what has made him the most important religious figure in the world. You will find this examination of the life of Jesus interesting and intriguing.

Available on Amazon.

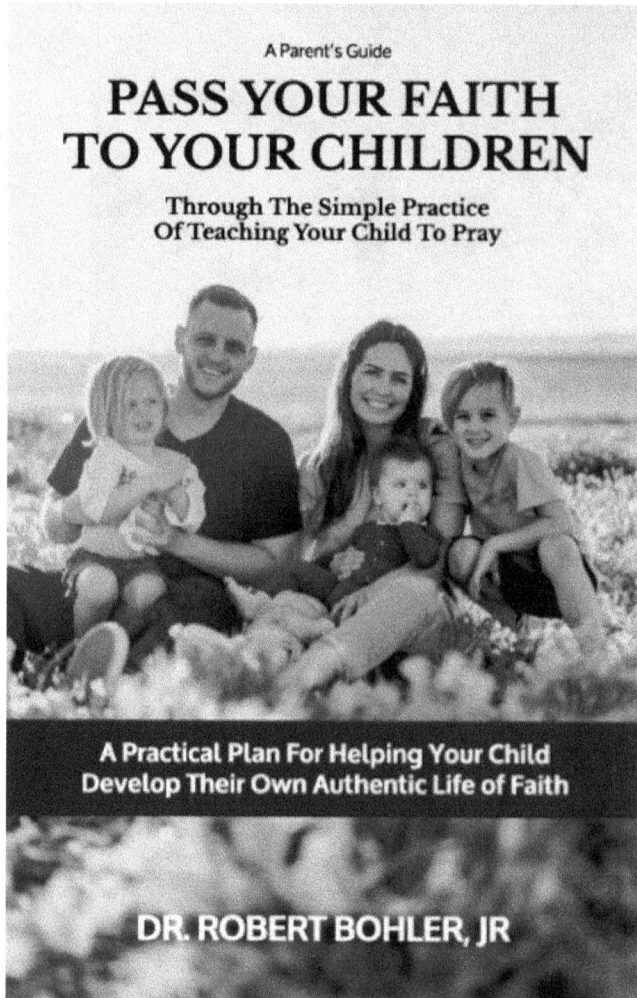

A Parent's Guide

PASS YOUR FAITH TO YOUR CHILDREN

Through The Simple Practice Of Teaching Your Child To Pray

A Practical Plan For Helping Your Child Develop Their Own Authentic Life of Faith

DR. ROBERT BOHLER, JR

What is the most important job you have as a Christian parent? It is to pass your faith along to your children. But how can you do so effectively? In this book, Dr. Robert Bohler, Jr. helps parents develop a deep and authentic faith in their children through the simple practice of teaching them to pray. This is something every parent can do, with a little instruction, AND IT IS THE MOST IMPORTANT JOB A PARENT HAS!

Available on Amazon.

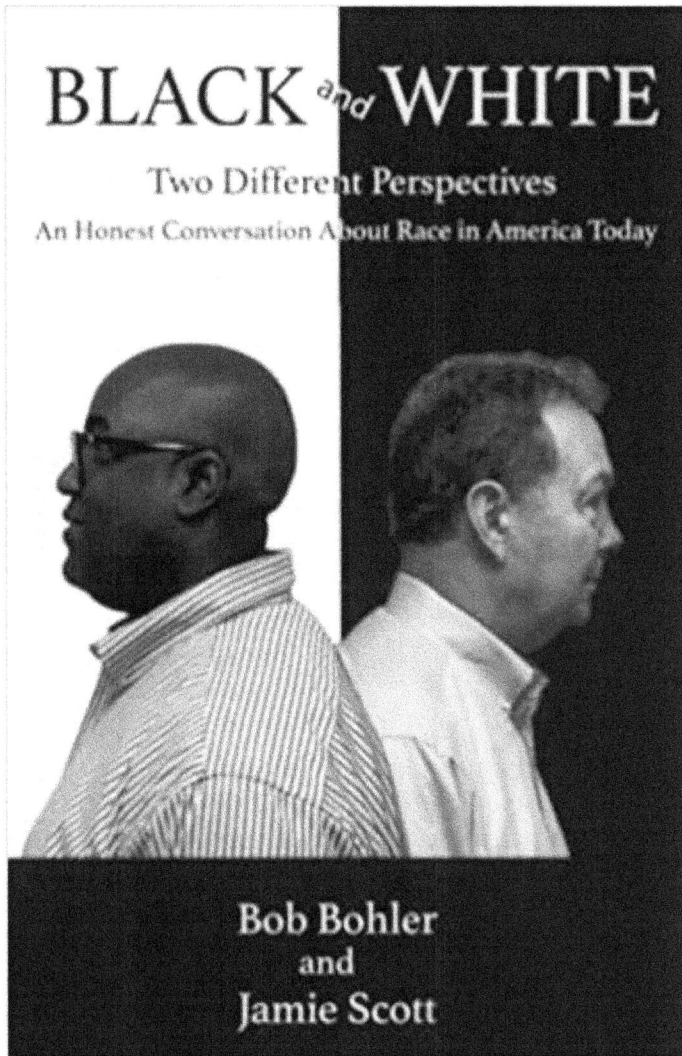

BLACK and WHITE

Two Different Perspectives

An Honest Conversation About Race In America Today

Bob Bohler
and
Jamie Scott

Robert (Bob) Bohler and Jamie Scott share their stories then use them to engage in conversations about race and culture. Bob grew up in middle-class America. His college education led him into a career, first in engineering, then as a Christian pastor. Jamie grew up in the inner city projects, on the "mean streets" of Athens, Georgia where he got into crime and drugs at an early age. He spent 20 of his first 37 years in prison until a Christian conversion changed his life. Their different stories make a great starting point for a discussion of the racial and cultural differences that divide America today. Study guide included.

Available on Amazon

Have you wanted to understand the Christian faith better? In *Learn the Vocabulary of the Christian Faith,* by Robert Bohler, you will get a comprehensive overview of the Christian faith by looking at important terms used in Christianity. These terms, such as: atonement, justification, Trinity, sanctification, Holy Spirit, incarnation, kingdom of God, resurrection, and many more, help define Christian belief. The book is written to be accessible to beginners but to have sufficient depth so that lifelong disciples will learn from it. Here is a way to get a comprehensive grasp on Christian belief in a way that will enhance your understanding of it and your love for it.

Available on Amazon.

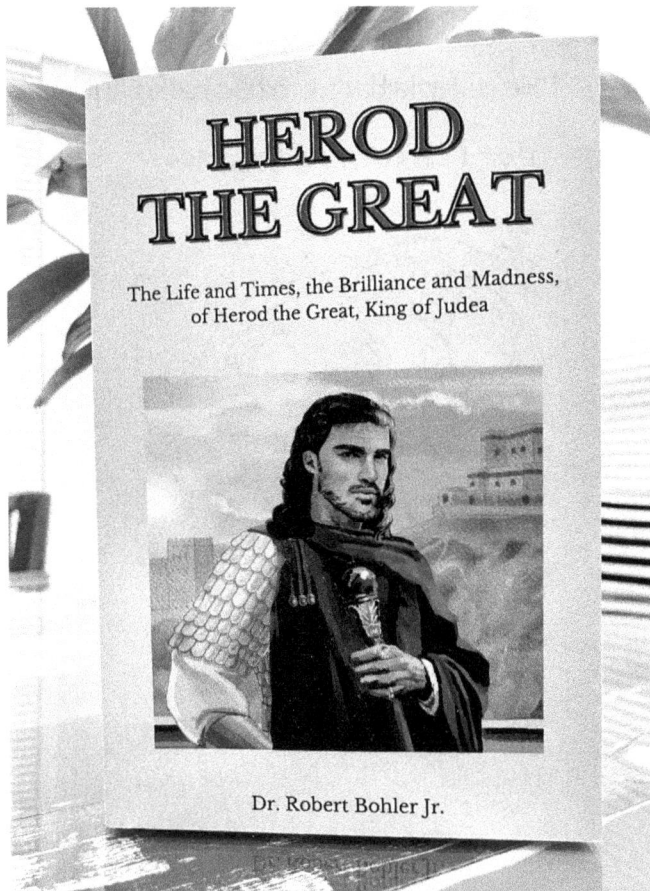

HEROD THE GREAT

The Life and Times, the Brilliance and Madness, of Herod the Great, King of Judea

Dr. Robert Bohler Jr.

There is no better way to understand the times leading up to the birth of Christ than to understand the life of Herod the Great. He ruled Judea from 37-4 B.C. and lived in one of the most interesting eras in history, knowing Julius Caesar, Mark Antony, Cleopatra, and Augustus. He was brilliant but also wicked. His life is a fascinating study of human nature, full of stories of intrigue, duplicity, and clever leadership. His life is a soap opera without parallel about which you will enjoy reading.

Available on Amazon.

The Christian Catechism

For Families And Disciples

A Teaching Tool For Church And Family

Dr. Robert Bohler, Jr.

The Christian Catechism For Families And Disciples is a teaching tool to be used in church and home. This catechism overviews the Christian faith using memorable questions and answers that provide a simple way to teach and learn foundational Christian doctrines, vocabulary, and beliefs. It is especially designed to help parents pass along the content of the Christian faith to their children. It is also available with accompanying commentary to facilitate the use and understanding of the catechism.

Available on Amazon

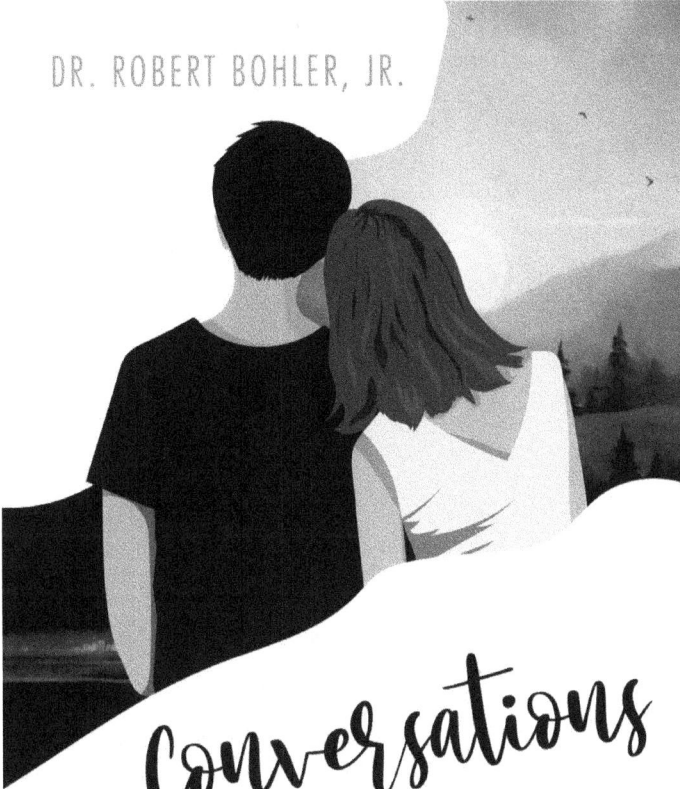

DR. ROBERT BOHLER, JR.

Conversations with Josh

ABOUT DATING, SEX, AND MARRIAGE

Conversations with Josh is an engaging conversation for teens about love, sex, dating, and marriage. This book provides teens with reliable guidance, from a Christian perspective, as they begin to date and think about how to navigate those precarious waters. Teens will find this helpful because it deals with difficult questions. Parents will find at an avenue for conversation with their teen.

Available on Amazon

[1] "BP's Last Message." *The Scouting Pages*, 20 June 2019, thescoutingpages.org.uk/bps-last-message/.